World Megatrends

Towards the renewal of humanity

Adjiedj Bakas

infinite ideas

*"One generation plants the trees;
another gets the shade."*

Chinese proverb

For my mother Soemintra Bakas-Sital:
thanks for your love, wisdom,
coaching and understanding.

First published in 2009 by
Infinite Ideas Limited
36 St Giles
Oxford, OX1 3LD
United Kingdom
www.infideas.com

A CIP catalogue record for this book is available from the British Library

ISBN 978–1–906821–07–4

Research by Trend Office Bakas
Cover by Baseline Arts Ltd, Oxford
Design: Wentelwereld Grafische Vormgeving, Westkapelle, The Netherlands
Printed and bound in Malta

Contents

Part III. Agenda for the next 5 years:
Prepare yourself for the Megatrends

Columns:

preface

An era is coming to an end, as all of us can sense. The current Economic Depression, the fifth in the past 200 years, marks the end of an old era, and the start of a new one. Like the four past Depressions too marked the transition of one era to another. Yet what will the new era look like? "The present is big with the future," according to Rudyard Kipling. Naturally. The future is now. We are already witnessing the first contours of the most important trends that will radically change the world in the coming decades. There are already prototypes of several major technological developments that will come onto the market within ten years. For humanity, this will definitely be a century of transition. West and East will share power in this century, after centuries of Western domination in the world. A G20 of twenty major economies, including the ones of former poor nations as Brazil, China and India will rule the world economy. In the last halve of the 20th century we experienced great progress as humanity. For example until the early 1970s China was as poor as Somalia, yet at the beginning of the 21st century the country's economy ranks upon the top 10 in the world. In the past 30 years in both China and India a middle class of about 400 million people emerged out of the under classes, a major achievement indeed.

Technology changed the way we work, live and entertain ourselves. Energy, which we used to take for granted, became a major issue, as did climate change. Money makes the world go around, yet the current Economic Depression illustrates how vulnerable the world's financial system is. Food is becoming a major issue, since the world population grows faster then ever. And demographics change. Ageing is influencing most countries in the West, Japan and China. And the fact that there are currently 80 million redundant boys in the fighting age between 15 and 35 years old in the Islamic world is a major destabilizing factor in today's and tomorrow's world. Migration and demographic warfare create power shifts in the world as we saw in Georgia and Kosovo. More power shifts are due, thanks to demographics. And despite or thanks to all technology, spirituality is becoming more important. Currently Silicon Valley is ranked the most religious and spiritual place on earth. Yet what will happen to religion if we find live

on other planets in space? What if God has done the same he did on Earth on other planets as well? Will individually designed spirituality replace the world's major religions? How will we define happiness in the future? What is the future of love? Many questions will ponder us during the next couple of years. Therefore politics, economy, technology, demographics, spirituality and futurology form a cocktail that decision makers in the 21st century cannot live without.

Trendwatching is exceptionally interdisciplinary and multidisciplinary. You can only recognize trends if you combine knowhow from various disciplines and professions. As a trendwatcher, I pay particular attention to how countries, organizations, people and the world change, and how resultant needs are thus changed, or how technological inventions change people's lives and lifestyles.

This book describes, in an international framework, the twelve Megatrends which will radically change life in our world in the coming decades. Some people might find this book provocative. Others might find it inspiring. Contrary to many people I find this the most positive and inspiring time to live in. I believe that the future may be bright, and that we can make life on earth better than ever.

Several people inspired me and contributed ideas and research material to this book as Wim de Ridder and Rob Creemers. Books of futurologists as James Martin inspired me as well. Minne Buwalda and Mark Schipper edited the final version of the manuscript. Liesbeth Timmermans contributed tremendously to the historical research. My literary agent Adrian Weston sold the book rights. My publishers at Infinite Ideas do a great job. Others contributed in other ways: Leo and Maurice van der Kant (Assemblee Speakers Agency), Ricardo Fakiera, Liesbeth van Dijk, Avi Goodall, Karel Hille, Jan Hartendorp, Peter Fingar, Marjet van Zuijlen, Frits Huffnagel, Vinco David, Hans Nieukerke, Willem van Meer, Annette Nijs, Jan van der Kaaij, Karin Snijders, Luuk Wessels, Rob Schwarz, Albert van den Brink and the team of Speakers Academy. Andrew Esson (Baseline Arts) designed the cover and Thiërry Tetenburg (Wentelwereld) the rest of the book.

This book is based on various research programs, books of several inspiring authors, lectures and other publications, discussions and interviews with about 250 people from several continents, brain-storming sessions, personal observations and interpretations, and (field) studies and future scenario's of Shell, the CIA, IMD in Lausanne and many other sources.

Many thanks to everybody for their time, energy, knowledge, involvement and inspiration. Without them, this book would never have appeared.

Adjiedj Bakas
Amsterdam, Tel Aviv, Paramaribo, Mumbai, Summer 2009

introduction

Beyond Yaria. A much needed unified world to deal with the megatrends

Many people fear the future, yet we are on the brink of an inspiring new age. True, the future won't be fair to everybody, just as the past wasn't. But in this so-called 'people's century', we will be able to organize our own happiness in a much better way than we used to. In the near future we will work in different ways; we might live to 120 years old; healthcare will change tremendously giving us more control over our wellness; and robots will be common elements in our lives – robots and men will play soccer together. Nature will be treated with more respect. Mass intelligence will enable us to assimilate more knowledge than ever. Physical and virtual worlds will blend; social networks enable us to connect to whoever we want.

In the new Age of Aquarius, which is supposed to start soon, if it hasn't already, we will develop an ability to be spiritual without being a member of a specific religious denomination. The 'Personal God' then becomes dominant and the major religions will lose major market share to Him or Her.

Gaia, the system which operates the Earth, will become of utmost importance as nature will become more disrupted in the next couple of years. However the growth of the world population must slow down to a more sustainable 2 billion.

The oil age will come to an end, sooner than many stakeholders currently assume, and the new energy economy will emerge. Nanotechnology, genetics and biotech will renew the economy and technology will enable to perform more work with less people. Agriculture will be renewed and shortages of fresh water will inspire people to farm in new ways.

The world develops in several gears at the same time. In the 'first world' of currently rich countries, such as the UK and US, people speed ahead. In the 'second world' of emerging markets, such as China and India, people speed fast forward towards the lifestyles of the 'first world'. In the 'third world', countries like Oman and Costa Rica, people move forward, but very slowly. In the 'fourth world', which includes Pakistan and Gaza, nation-states implode, population growth soars and violence grows. The losers of the fourth world move in increasing numbers towards countries in the first world, thus disrupting these societies.

Population policies become necessary, the role of governments change, security concepts change. Technology revolutions, the end of privacy, the future of nature, trying to colonize space, new media and new heroism: it's all part of the cocktail of an exciting future.

This book takes twelve megatrends from different realms and looks at the whole picture of the future, illustrating it with inspiring examples from all over the world. The book reaches beyond today's problems and is highly accessible. Containing little jargon and transcending hype, it is provocative and ambitious in its scope.

The current crises in terms of the world's economy, energy, natural environment, fresh water and food are symbolic of the end of one era and the start of a new one. It is an opportunity to reinvent ourselves and the world. We can make use of technology, knowledge, social networks and other new sources to create even more fulfilling lives and lifestyles while also preserving nature, unlike we have been doing in the past.

All of this will only be feasible if the leaders of today's and tomorrow's world unite and overcome the differences among them. This has happened before, for example during the famous conference at Yalta at the end of World War II, when Churchill, Roosevelt and Stalin met each other, overcame their differences and laid the foundations of a new world order. This world order has functioned, despite its shortcomings (like the Cold War), for almost three-quarters of a century now. The eldest grandsons of these three leaders of yesterday's world, met each other in the city of Maastricht and discussed the new world order 'beyond Yalta'. The essentials of what they said are included in the pages below and complete the introduction to this new book: learning from the past, entering a new future.

Adjiedj Bakas

Beyond Yalta

At the start of February 1945, the heads of government of the United States, the United Kingdom and the former Soviet Union met at what was codenamed the Argonaut Conference, now commonly known as the Yalta Conference or the Crimea Conference. President Franklin D. Roosevelt, my grandfather, Prime Minister Winston Churchill, and the Secretary General of the Communist Party's Central Committee, Josef Stalin, sat down together and reached an agreement on the new post-World War II world order. When asked how proud I think the three wartime leaders would be today about the agreement that they reached at Yalta, I wouldn't say it was much of a matter for pride. What was agreed was merely a reflection of the reality of the armies on the ground.

By the time of the Yalta Conference, Mr. Stalin already possessed half of Europe. And the reality was that neither Mr. Roosevelt nor my grandfather could do very much about it, even if they had wanted to. (Mr. Roosevelt seems to have been more concerned with breaking up the colonial powers than with the fact that a new empire was about to rise in the heart of Europe.) There is a famous saying that possession is nine-tenths of the law, and this was certainly true at Yalta. The agreement the three statesmen reached was, therefore, hardly the desired blueprint for the new Europe, but a sketch of what had become the military reality at the end of the Second World War. Europe's destiny was decided at gunpoint. And for the Central and Eastern European countries, Yalta meant the beginning of fifty years of communist oppression.

However, by focusing solely on this bitter legacy of the agreement, it is easy to overlook the positive value of the Yalta Conference. Although all had their own personal agendas, for the first time in history three world leaders sat down together to discuss what the world should look like in the future. And although the outcome may not have been all that successful, to some extent my grandfather and President Roosevelt, as the leaders of the democratic nations, did stand together against the totalitarian ambitions of Josef Stalin. Furthermore, at Yalta also lie the origins of the United Nations as an international platform to solve conflicts through cooperation and in a peaceful manner. These are principles that not only need to be remembered, but that should also serve as guidelines in the twenty-first century.

The modern world is faced by tremendous difficulties. Terrorism, poverty, climate change, economic crisis and energy dependency are all problems that should be addressed by the international community as a whole. It is time for today's world leaders to sit down again and to set their differences aside and draw the outlines of a common future.

I warmly remember a lady I met in Poland, whom as a child had lived in the ghetto of Warsaw. She described how, in their darkest hour, she and her family heard my grandfather

speaking in a BBC broadcast on the radio. Although she couldn't understand English, she said she realized that if she and her family were to survive the war, it depended on that one strong and unseen voice coming from a radio. Let now the international community be such a voice and formulate what it has to say.

Winston Churchill Jr. is a journalist and the eldest grandson of British leader Winston Churchill (1874–1965).

No more Yaltas?

'No more Yaltas!' This is just one of the many statements in which former president George W. Bush referred to the 1945 Yalta Conference. At Yalta, the British Prime Minister Winston Churchill and the Soviet leader Josef Stalin together with my grandfather Franklin D. Roosevelt tried to draw the outlines of a post-war Europe. In the opinion of George W. Bush, however, small nations somehow tend to 'become expandable' every time the powerful ones sit down together to negotiate their smaller brothers' freedom. Needless to say that Bush didn't write all of his speeches himself, but speechwriters usually are intelligent people and they know what they are talking about. With these words they expressed the sentiments of a large group of people in the United States and we can find the same views in the writings of many journalists and political commentators.

But was Yalta really that bad? The historian Arthur Schlessinger summarized it rather well when he wrote that the post-war division of Europe didn't result from words on paper, but from a diplomacy of armies. The mere fact that by early 1945 the Soviet army had already conquered half of Europe put Stalin in a very powerful position, not only at the negotiating table but also afterwards. As Chip Boland, my grandfather's interpreter at Yalta, put it: 'The Red Army gave Stalin the power to carry out his wishes, regardless of his promises at Yalta. Stalin held all the cards and he played them well,' with the result that, except for Stalin, nobody really got what they wanted at Yalta.

However, the conference also saw the beginning of a new international organization called the United Nations, in which the Soviet Union was also involved, regardless of how divided the world ended up after the Second World War. And the true value of Yalta is that – although one of them was powerful enough to go his own way – the three leaders at least did sit down and to some extent negotiated.

In the past decade we have witnessed an America acting worldwide in a very unilateral way. Whether it's international trade relations, environmental concerns or the war in Iraq, America hasn't invested much – to put it mildly – in its relations with Europe, Russia and the rest of the world. I think that was a major error and it makes me extremely sad. It reflects a diminution of the kind of values that I consider to be truly American, the kind of values that I grew up with living in the White House (both as a child and a teenager) with my grandparents Franklin and Eleanor Roosevelt, two formidable characters who strived for an America that acted with responsibility in an international environment.

Now that a new administration has taken over we can expect to see an improvement in foreign relations. But at the same time there is a tendency – and not only in the United

States but in many other countries – to focus more on domestic issues and to close the eyes and the borders for the outside world. In this time of economic crisis, it is obviously tempting for individual countries to fall back on their own positions and to take measures that protect their own economies and societies but that do not necessarily benefit the world as a whole. Under these circumstances, it is time for the world leaders to sit down and to contemplate the future they want. In other words, it is time to return to Yalta.

☐

Curtis Roosevelt is a journalist and the eldest grandson of US leader Franklin Delano Roosevelt (1882–1945).

Yalta, a disaster?

I am always surprised when people claim that the Yalta Conference was a 'disaster', a criticism that is mainly heard in the West. According to the critics, Winston Churchill and Franklin D. Roosevelt left the conference empty handed, while Josef Stalin came out as the winner. To them I can only say one thing: can't you read? Read the documental evidence and explain to me how you can still call the conference a disaster. Of course, my grandfather – whose name I still carry today with great pride – had a strong hand of cards with many trumps and he played them cleverly. But it was Britain and the United States that had dealt him this hand, by repeatedly postponing the invasion of Western Europe and by leaving Russia to fight the German army on its own.

At the time of the Yalta Conference, the Red Army had liberated half of occupied Germany and was on the verge of entering Berlin. At that time the English and American troops were still hundreds of kilometres away. For the defeat of Hitler, Stalin had sacrificed the lives of twenty million Russian soldiers, a sacrifice that would have earned credit for politicians far less competent than my grandfather. But this doesn't mean that at Yalta he simply pushed through his own plans. The question of what needed to become of Poland was a sensitive one for all three leaders and together they decided on a solution. The credits for setting up the United Nations go completely to president Roosevelt. The trio also decided to prosecute the war criminals and a blueprint for the Nuremberg trials was drawn up. And Stalin promised Churchill and Roosevelt to start a front in the Far East and to help bring Japan to its knees. These are results that without doubt were to benefit the United States and Britain just as much as the Soviet Union.

Winston Churchill once said: 'We have no allies, only interests.' Churchill's statement was true at Yalta and is still true today. The United States and the Western European countries need new sources of energy because their own are running short whereas gas and oil are still readily available in Russia and in the Middle East. And phrases like 'the human rights issue', 'democracy' or 'the war on terror' are being used to justify invading other countries, like we have seen in Iraq. These same slogans are used to put pressure on Russia, not because the Western countries really care about these issues – nor is there something wrong in Russia that would justify invading it – but simply because they are after Russia's natural resources. The Western nations are pursuing their own interests and they are willing to go to war for them.

Sixty-four years ago at Yalta, Stalin, Roosevelt and Churchill had their different interests as well and they all tried to pursue them as much as possible. But instead of threatening each other with rhetoric, they sat down together. And in doing so they managed to strike a balance between these interests in a peaceful manner. I don't see how – in this day and age – anybody can look on Yalta as a failure, let alone how anybody dares to call it a disaster. □

Jevgeni Dzjoegashvili is the eldest grandson of Soviet leader Stalin (1878–1953).

These contributions are based on a talk-show in which the grandsons participated. It was held in Maastricht, the Netherlands, on 1 October 2005, and was organized by the Assemblee International Speakers Agency (www.assemblee.nl).

part 1

Megatrends of the Past

There was a time when time as we know it didn't exist. Time must, after all, be related to a period, and you can only define it if you have a sense of time, a sense that you only have if you know day and night, a division in days, hours, minutes and seconds. And that only became possible when the sun, the earth and the other planets in our solar system came into being. This began to happen with the Big Bang 13.7 billion years ago. Up until then we had a 'primordial soup', actually an enormous cloud of immensely hot gas and dust. There were many of these primordial soups in various places in the universe. Between them, there were black holes that occasionally swallowed some of the soups and reduced them to almost nothing. The universe still has primordial soups and black holes. Luckily, the closest black hole to us is a long way away, so we don't have to be afraid of it swallowing our world. We will only get close to a black hole in the distant future, which is not a problem for us, but might be for our distant descendants. The primordial soup is also cast as the Mother Goddess and old cultures refer to her as Cybele.

Back to our primordial soup. When it burst apart in the Big Bang (for reasons still not understood), the building blocks of our current solar system were formed: the sun and the earth plus the various planets (Jupiter, Saturn, Mars, Pluto, Uranus, Neptune, Venus and Mercury) and their moons. As the entire assembly of planets developed their own circular dance around the sun, our measures of time came into being.

During the course of the Big Bang, some posit that a dry wind came up, almost wiping out any potential for life on earth. In the Bible it is described thus: 'Darkness was upon the face of the Earth'.

In 2008, the Big Bang was simulated under laboratory conditions in Switzerland. This caused great fear amongst some people: would the experiment not also create black holes that would swallow the earth and humanity? Thankfully, that didn't happen and we will learn a lot of interesting things about how the earth was formed from this experiment in the coming years. But, imagine that we then discover a second earth somewhere in space with life on it. Humans, humanoids or totally other beings? Would God then have been lying? Would the story of Creation no longer be valid because He pulled off the same trick elsewhere? What future will the classic religions still have then?

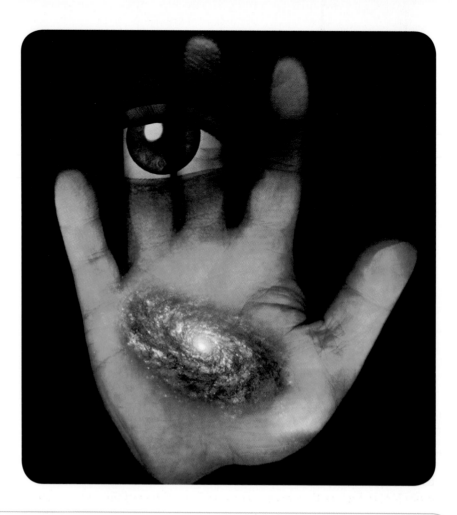

Is life all just a dream?

British astronomer Martin Rees says: 'Over a few decades, computers have evolved from being able to simulate only very simple patterns to being able to create virtual worlds with a lot of detail. If that trend were to continue, then we can imagine computers that will be able to simulate worlds, perhaps as complicated as the one we think we're living in. This raises the philosophical question: could we ourselves be in such a simulation and could what we think is the universe be some sort of vault of heaven rather than the real thing? In a sense, we could ourselves be the creations within that simulation.' So, what is really real?

The eternal struggle between the sun and Saturn

From the beginning, the sun stood for the 'good' in life and Saturn for the 'evil'. The struggle between the two heavenly bodies, between good and evil, has been the backdrop to the entire history of humankind, and will continue to dominate the future. In various parts of the world, and in various cultures, this struggle was symbolized. The sun has always been a positive god symbol for mankind, right from the moment we appeared on earth. At the same time, Saturn was always the symbol of death. Saturn makes everything on earth finite; he is the god of destruction or death, often depicted as Father Time. Because of Saturn, everything eventually dies. If we can defeat him, then we as humans are finally the winners of the fight between good and evil.

Another influence that is always felt in our lives is the 'Fall of Man', as told in the Bible. The snake in this famous story symbolizes the transition from paradise to a unrulier period for mankind on earth. According to the esoteric teachings, this refers to a real change in the cosmos: the separation of sun and earth. At the time a totally new element is believed to have come about in mankind: procreation with sex. Unavoidably because of this our emotions became more chequered: hunger and desire, dissatisfaction and frustration, worry and fear. In the classic tradition, Lucifer could be the manifestation thereof.

Fire, water and the first life

In the beginning, our planet was fiery ball of rock and dust. It still has a molten core but, as the earth cooled, many different solid layers formed around it, full of raw materials. The outer shell became the wettest, because of the oceans, and an atmosphere developed. The poles keep the earth in a certain balance and the earth has large concentrations of ice there. These ice caps melt from time to time and this has happened over numerous periods throughout history. It is happening again now. There's nothing new under the sun.

Of all the water on earth, only 1% is fresh; the rest is salty. At one time, the earth's surface was in the main a very large ocean of salt water. That is where life first came into being in the form of microbes – microscopically small organisms that were each made up of a single cell (and therefore called single-celled organisms). These organisms floated around and gradually developed into water flora and fish-like creatures.

However, the earth began to further congeal and dry up, and volcanoes started developing in the earth's crust. The first continent, which we now know as Pangaea, was formed as a result of various earthquakes, volcanic eruptions and other natural forces. The microbes that until then had lived in the ocean were washed onto the shores, and gradually developed the capabilities of amphibians.

The forces of nature broke up the mother continent and the parts started to drift apart. Thus the current-day continents were formed: the Americas, Eurasia, Africa, Antarctica and Australia. Later, further substantial pieces broke off, like Sri Lanka and Madagascar. They also started to drift. The continents now appear relatively stable in terms of their form, size and location. One can no longer imagine that they could break up again, start drifting, or change shape in other ways. Neither can one imagine that new continents could be formed by the forces of nature, or that old ones could be entirely or partially devoured by the sea again, though people have always fantasized about it. However, there are currently fault lines in the earth's crust between the continental plates, like in San Francisco and Ethiopia, where there is indeed a danger of land splitting off again.

The amphibious creatures on these land masses were transported around the globe as the continents drifted. Because they could live on land and in water, they gradually developed more and more character-istics of full-time land-dwellers. Some of them eventually evolved into ape-like creatures, the forefathers of man and apes, called *pre-homi-noids*. The first traces of pre-hominoids come from what is today Africa and date from the period known as the Pleistocene period. These pre-hominoids had, just like most plants, the organs of both sexes: each of them was both man and woman and they could fertilize themselves and multiply. Thus the story of Adam, who reproduced Eve from his rib, came about. However, Adam was not a man, but a hermaphrodite and there-fore bred Eve from himself. The Bible story is therefore to some extent correct. Charles Darwin, who mapped out evolution did not refute this story either, he was too religious for that. Only later did most animals and people have separate sexes: hermaphrodites were a thing of the past. A small number of people are still born as hermaphrodites; however we have had separate sexes for more than a thousand years. Keeps things simple. The first people were vegetarians: Man only started eating meat later. The first people couldn't speak. Communication was with gestures and throaty noises: "grunt, grunt".

Stone Age

The Pleistocene began about 1.6 million years ago and ended about 10,000 years before Christ. The Pleistocene period includes the Stone Age, so-called because our ancestors were then making tools and weapons from stone: blades, clubs and axes, for example. Although they initially only made tools, these primitive peoples went on to also make works of art from bone, antlers, ivory and stone (rock paintings and images). During the course of the Stone Age, it became customary in various parts of the world to bury the dead and include in the grave gifts like spices, drink, tools and jewellery.

After a period of transition from vegetarianism, people became meat eaters in most regions. They fed themselves by hunting, using pits and traps. The mastery of the use of fire around 400,000 BC made it possible to prepare food differently and its edibility and digestibility improved. This represented an enormous improvement for humans, who had short intestines, a weak lower jaw, blunt teeth and only one stomach. People began to develop spirituality (e.g. worshipping the fertility goddess Magna Mater) and they believed in magic and witchcraft to aid their hunting. The magician played an important role in many groups. Fur

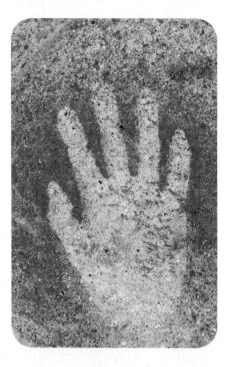

and other hides provided them with clothing and shelter.

Over time, people learned to communicate verbally. The first speech obviously would have been extremely simple but their vocabularies grew and languages evolved as the Stone Age progressed. These early people didn't have any writing skills but they left some records in the form of cave paintings, some of which date back 20,000 years. Formal written records and the development of alphabets came much later.

The Stone Age consisted of three periods. The Old Stone Age (which began around 1 million years ago), the Middle Stone Age (100,000 to 10,000 BC) and the New Stone Age (which ended as the Bronze Age began roughly 8,000 years ago).

Middle Stone Age

It was in the Middle Stone Age when humankind began to develop considerably. They lived in groups of hunter-gatherers and fishers but the size of the groups was limited by the scarcity of food. These groups were based mainly on the coast and on the banks of rivers and lakes. Hunting and fishing continued to be the primary source of food but people were gradually learning to domesticate animals such as cattle, goats and dogs.

The climate improved, which meant that more trees and forests appeared. During this period people learned to build boats and sleds and the first trading started. Towards the end of the Middle Stone Age, some groups started tilling the soil and creating pottery. Abstract motifs dominated the art of the time.

New Stone Age

In the New Stone Age, the trade between the various groups increased and nascent cultures emerged. Connections between the groups were initially made by water in canoes and boats constructed from wood and hides, then on land along tree-trunk roads and peat dykes with sleds and carts. The wheel was invented during this period in Eurasia, though not in America, where people continued to develop without the wheel until the arrival of the Europeans. The carts were pulled by cattle, reindeers and later by horses. In this period people started to believe in reincarnation. Ancestral worship started, alongside fertility rights and belief in one or other Sun God (which was interpreted differently according to culture or region), witchcraft and demons.

The economy changed: hunting became less important as cattle ranching and farming became more of a priority. The ground couldn't sustain extensive farming, so the groups of people moved time and again when the soil was depleted. People were hence still essentially nomadic. And though some people now believe the fairy tale that primitive man lived in such harmony with nature, it is nonsense.

After the Stone Age

Following on from the developments of the Stone Age, farming and ranching increasingly merged. Grain grew in the wild and other crops were cultivated: wheat, millet and barley in Africa and Europe, rice in Asia and potatoes and corn in Central and South America. People also learned to breed sheep, horses, goats and pigs, which meant that there was a constant supply of food and the groups and families grew. People started living in villages and later in towns, of which Jericho (*c.*8,000 to 6,000 BC) and Çatal Hüyük (*c.*7,500 to 6,200 BC) were the largest. Remarkably enough, this process occurred almost simultaneously at different places around the world. Why? Not known. There are many guesses, like that people started to do so after collective dreams or hallucinations, as postulated by Jonathan Black in his book *The Secret History of the World*. This has not been proven.

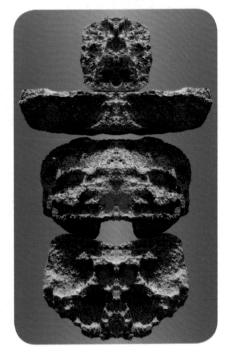

Art had initially consisted of jewellery made from shells and stones and bones, but in this later period precious metals and gems began to be used. The period was also characterized by stamp seals with handsome reliefs. Copper was first used at that time, at first hammered, later cast. The first temples were also being built and the first clay tablets written. The 'picture writing' of the time gave way later to word and phonic signs.

Mysterious period of transition

The Shang Dynasty, from around 1,800 to 1,200 BC, was a period of transition that is shrouded in mystery, yet formed the basis for what became China. The bronze work from the Shang period is known, but the inscriptions on it, in a now-lost precursor to written Chinese, have still not been deciphered. There are many myths about that period. According to some, monsters lived on the earth then. In China they were called the Miaotse. They also appear in the Afghan myths. The Buddhas that have now been destroyed by the Taliban in Bamyan were supposedly not statues of Buddha but life-size statues of giants that lived at the time. Giants also appear in Greek as well as African mythologies of the time and the statues on Easter Island are meant to be proof of that. Humankind was preparing itself for an enormous acceleration in its development in those times. In the Greek myths, the gods mixed with people; in the later Christian myths the angels mixed with people. And similar stories also appear in other cultures: New Age followers, for instance, state that at the time extraterrestrials mixed with people. Whatever may have happened, no proof has (yet) been found.

Also among the significant myths of this time are the great flood, as described in the Bible, and the disappearance of Atlantis. In ancient accounts of the flood (c.3,000 BC), mention is made of a boat builder who constructed an ark to bring some people and animals free of sin to safety. In Judaism and Christian teachings, he is called Noah; in Indian tradition, Manu; and in the Sumerian stories (from present-day Iraq), Utnapisjtim. According to Plato, Atlantis, the once powerful island civilization in the Atlantic, disappeared during an earlier flood (c.9,000 BC). Some now suggest these floods were probably caused by the melting of the polar ice caps during earlier periods of global warming.

Flood

About 3,000 years before Christ, the 'Flood' occurred. This flood, probably a series of tidal waves in various parts of the world, shortly after each other, appears in many myths. These myths all mention a man who built a boat in which he brought some of the people and animals to safety. In Judaism and Christianity, he is called Noah; in the Indian tradition, Manu; and in the Sumerian stories (in the current Iraq), Utnapisjtim. According to Plato, Atlantis, the mythical lost island in the Atlantic Ocean that was once so rich and powerful, disappeared during an earlier flood (around 9,000 BC). These floods were probably caused by the melting of the polar ice caps, by a warming up of the earth in those times. Soon after crocodiles were swimming in the warm water at the North Pole. Their frozen remains were recently found by geologists who were excavating there.

Gilgamesh epic

The first literary story in the world was probably written down around the period of the flood in what today is Iraq. This Gilgamesh epic covers topics like death, friendship and suffering – topics that are still relevant today.

Gilgamesh lived about 3,000 years before Christ and was the builder of the famous walls of Uruk, the largest city in Sumeria. As the son of a god and a man, he was the strongest man on earth, but because of it he was also lonely. The gods created an equal for him: Enkidu. When they meet, they soon become friends. However, soon after Enkidu dies, to the great grief of Gilgamesh. His fear of death sets him off on his quest for immortality. He even made it to the threshold of the spiritual world, but failed at the last moment. ☐

Solving problems collectively

What we currently call 'historic time' started around the period of the flood. Around this time, a change in climate had a decisive effect on the transition to a new era. High temperatures and drought created the contours of the current deserts that impose their stamp on the earth as a belt from west to east. On the various continents, it can be seen that people established their homes and farms on the fertile banks of the rivers and lakes. This took place in east Africa along the Nile, on the Hoang-Ho in China, in India along the Indus, in South America around Lake Titicaca and in the Middle East along the Euphrates and the Tigris.

Living together on these rivers required a different way of life: people were required to find solutions for communal problems and management and defence became indispensable. At the same time, economic activity became focused on producing and distributing food and trade flourished further. Not everyone was still busy with the primary production of food: the division of labour started slowly and occupations began to emerge. The development of trades had its roots in the discovery of bronze with which early metalworkers manufactured not only tools but also weapons, statues, kitchen utensils and jewellery.

In this period, impressive stone buildings were also erected, the Egyptian pyramids being the best example. We also see that the picture writing develops into language, like the hieroglyphics of the Central American Olmecans and the African Meroans and Egyptians, and the cuneiform in Sumeria. The territories of these societies continued to grow and empires were formed. Language, culture and religion bring to life communal ideas and views.

Deepening of religious understanding

Curiously, around 500 years before Christ, a new religious resurgence surfaced on different continents as people looked for a deeper understanding and interpretation of their lives. The answers to these essential questions about life influenced the thinking about humanity and existence for centuries.

According to the Indian tradition, Buddha, the first man to ever reach Nirvana, lived on earth at the time. Nirvana, also called nibbana, literally means extinguished or washed out. People who attain this state have transcended human suffering by having liberated themselves from their desires, aversion and confusion. In China, a more philosophical route was followed, thanks to Confucius. His teachings are still current in China and the surrounding countries. They are based on six core values: humanity (*ren*), childlike obedience (*xiao*), justice (*yi*), decorum (*li*), faithfulness (*chun*) and reciprocity (*shu*). Taoism, which has its basis in the books *Tao Te Ching* (Book of the Way and the Power) and *Zhuangzi*, arose in the same region. The Persian prophet Zarathushtra evidently also lived around 500 BC. Zoroastrianism, the official religion of the Persian Empire, has three principles: good words, good deeds and good thoughts. As will be often expounded in later times, according to this school, mankind is always involved in a fight between good and evil. The two gods Ahura Mazda (the god of good) and Ahriman (the god of evil) symbolize this fight. There are still people who adhere to Zoroastrianism.

Greek Cradle

It was not only religion that had a resurgence around 500 BC. Principles about structuring society also came into being and they have influenced societies for centuries ever since, particularly in Europe and the Americas. In Athens, democracy was invented: a perception of political power in which the majority of the people are in control. This form of constitution has not always been common. In the course of the nineteenth and twentieth century, it was rediscovered and modernized; belief in democracy was stronger than ever. Examine the arguments that form the basis of the wars waged by Western powers; these are, after all, often justified in the US and UK as 'bringing democracy'.

Of an entirely different magnitude are the cultural enrichments that the Greeks bestowed on the world. They invented the theatre: the tragedies, comedies and satires that were performed were a public education in religion and morality. Greek gods like Zeus, Apollo, Hades, Demeter and Aphrodite feature regularly in them. They could already count on thousands of spectators. The plays by Sophocles, among which are *Antigone* and *Oedipus*, and Euripides' *Medea* form part of the standard works, even today.

Also in the arts, the Greeks, whose 'golden age' was between 500 and 400 BC, created new trends. Statues departed from their uniform position with their left leg forwards, arms straight along their bodies and an empty smile. The statues created by the Greeks are more human, with anatomically accurate bodies and an impassive calm gaze. It is then not surprising that the Greeks considered man to be the centre of the universe. That can be clearly seen in temples on which 'know yourself' is chiseled, a command that incidentally was embraced by the Freemasons and cannot be easily overlooked in their lodges.

Another qualifying contribution from the Greek tradition is attention to both mind and body. The Olympic Games, which were already organized in the eighth century BC, are *the* example of the focus on the physical. The views of prominent philosophers like Socrates, Plato and Aristotle even today influence the way in which we view ourselves and our environment.

Divine emperors

While the Roman Empire was growing in Europe, the Chinese had also created their empire first in about 220 BC. Emperor Qin Shi Huangdi decided in that period to build a vast wall as a defence against the Mongolians. By doing so, he created the basis for a relatively isolated position for China, while the various subsequent dynasties mainly ensured stability. The Han dynasty, with Confucianism as its state doctrine, forms the foundation for the coming centuries. This continuity is clear to see in Chinese music, which is characterized by a common tonic and corresponding harmonics. The tonic was already established by imperial decree in the third century BC. In spite of its isolated position, China remains the (cultural) middle point of the east Asian world. It influences Japan with its writing, music, medicine and expressive arts; otherwise, the island has a mainly isolated position. The power is in the hands of the emperor, called a tenno, who, it was believed, was a descendant of the sun goddess Amaterasu.

In North America, the Indians continued to move around as nomads, while in South and Central America, large empires were established. Here the divine emperors were also the rulers. They built cities with terraced pyramids, on the top of which were temples or observatories for observing the stars and heavens. Just as on other continents, the cosmos played a central role in the lives (religious and quotidian) of the people, with the solar calendar as the best-known example. However, less is known of these empires than of their counterparts on the other side of the Atlantic, simply because the later European conquerors wreaked havoc and the indigenous peoples' writings have only partially been deciphered. A comparable story applies to the African and Australian history. However, part of the issue there is also that historical stories were more often passed on orally than in writing.

Roman Empire

The first large world empire that dominated the now splintered Europe was the Roman Empire. From Rome, the Romans extended their empire bit by bit. In the second century, it reached its largest size and included all countries of the Mediterranean Sea, part of the Middle East, Europe up to the Rhine and a large part of Great Britain. Although the Roman domination was not simple militarily, it established a long and stable period that brought mainly prosperity and welfare. Roman villas, with central heating and heated baths, were some of the most luxurious in history.

The Romans were an example to later generations, mainly in the areas of administration and military skill. In the fields of art and religion, they reverted to the ideas of earlier civilizations like those of the Greeks and Etruscans. The Romans also refined the Arabic construction of domes and arches and attached great importance to the concept of

'space'. Roman law still forms the basis for many legal systems. Additionally, and not unimportantly, are the common language (Latin) and the refined logistics (of which the aqueducts are the most visible) that the Romans spread throughout Europe. Later, both prove to be useful in spreading Christianity.

Introduction of Christendom

Jesus Christ and his preaching have had worldwide influence for generations. On a practical note, we actually owe our current calendar system to him. There is scientific proof that shows that Jesus Christ actually existed. He claimed that he was the representative of his father, God, on earth and had a number of followers. After his death, Jesus' teachings were spread thanks mainly to his apostles. For a long time Christianity was seen as 'merely' a branch of Judaism. Then the Roman emperor Constantine in the fourth century converted to Christianity after a vision, and thus paved the way to its lasting influence. Slowly but surely, the traditional, polytheistic Roman religion made way for Christianity as the only religion. This not only happened in Europe, but also in large parts of North Africa. This transition marks a trend to a world where the truth more often coincides with the idea of a single god – as happened certainly once the Christian belief spread further around the world and, later, also as the monotheistic Islamic faith came into being and continued to grow.

Another event that was initiated by Emperor Constantine was the division of the Roman Empire into West and East. In the fourth century he moved the capital, Rome, to the present day Istanbul, under the name Constantinople. This marks the beginning of the end of the West Roman Empire, that soon became unmanageable and could no longer ward off attacks from surrounding tribes.

In Europe, a veritable migration starts and the united Roman Empire is replaced by a multitude of states. The division of this mighty Empire confirms and reinforces the existing differences between East and West, differences that can be explained – according to the famous Greek doctor

Hippocrates in the fourth century BC – by the climate. Because of the changing seasons in Europe being more extreme than in Asia, the Europeans apparently had a wilder and more war-like character. On the other hand, the climate changes ensured that the European mind was stimulated and that they did not become too passive. Europeans were freedom lovers. The Asians were more peaceful and more interested in art than in war. However, they submitted more easily to tyrants and despots.

Arabian prosperity

With Europe entering a turbulent period after the fall of the Roman Empire, a new fervor came into being in the Middle East. Aside from the population growth and intensifying trade, this was mainly due to the prophet Muhammad. He was born in 570 in Mecca and in his fortieth year he has the first visions of God, who appointed him as the last prophet until the end of time. Muhammad preached belief in one God and the Last Day of Judgement and soon experienced opposition in Mecca. He felt forced to flee to Jathreb – later known as Medina – where he established the first Muslim community. Again this time it is God who instructs him how this society must be structured. That makes the religious and administrative institutions inseparable in the Islamic tradition.

Upon Muhammad's death in 632, almost the whole of Arabia was Muslim. His succession caused so much discussion that rival groups, who are still rivals today, formed (the Sunnis and the Shiites). The Islamic belief was further spread in the course of the seventh century after a wave of conquests. Under the leadership of Omar, the Persian Empire, the eastern part of the Roman Empire and Egypt were subjugated and, in the early years of the eighth century, the Iberian Peninsula was conquered. Second only to China, this was the biggest empire on earth. The Muslims integrated the old Greek, Chinese, Jewish and Indian knowledge. Addi-

tionally, trade provided silk, porcelain, paper and the compass from China, and the number system and spices from India. Less well known is that trade with African states flourished. Various African kings had become Islamic and made pilgrimages to Mecca. The Africans provided gold and salt, but also slaves (Arab leaders preferred castrated black men for the protection of their harems). The Arabian empire bloomed until the invasion of the Mongols at the beginning of the thirteenth century.

It was not only the Middle East that experienced a golden age. At about the same time, the great South American Tiahuanaco civilization peaked. However, there was then a period of climate change around 1100, which resulted in heavy rainfall, and it proved to be the catalyst that brought about the end of this impressive civilization.

Monotheism, but not really

The three current global religions that originated from the Middle East – Judaism, Christianity and Islam – all preach a radical monotheism, the belief in one God. Yet all three have roots in traditions and religions before them that all were polytheistic. They all believed in more than one god and believed that a connection with the cosmos was obvious. Astronomy and astrology, therefore, also played an important part in those religions. For instance, important Christian holidays are on astrological dates: Easter being the first Sunday following the full moon that falls on or follows the vernal equinox, and Christmas is on the first day after the winter solstice, when the rising sun begins to move visibly back, reversing its direction along the horizon.

Sexual abstinence and power

Though sexual abstinence plays a role in various traditions, the Christian vision, as expressed by Augustine, represented a fundamental change. Augustine, in the fifth century, was the first to actually write down the religious rules of Christianity. His works also have a philosophical component and later inspired others like Thomas Aquinas and Calvin. He stated that Adam and Eve's disobedience put an end to the ideal balance between human will and human passion. God therefore decided to punish man with a powerful sexual desire that would never entirely be tamed by man's will. Every sexual act became thereby a melancholic reminder of the fall of man, making it no longer desirable. Even in wedlock, sex was not a very virtuous activity, and should have only one goal: reproduction. A consequence of Augustine's vision was that sexual abstinence was considered a great virtue; the more one abstained the more one was devoted to God.

There are also elements in other religious faiths that strongly embrace the suppression of sexual lust. However, sex is often seen as something positive. The realistic erotic scenes of the Hindu Khajuraho complex (built between 950 and 1050) in the north east of India would be unthinkable in Christian churches.

Augustine created fertile grounds for men and women who established celibate societies in monasteries. The monasteries and other Christian institutions soon had an important place in society and their input was appreciated both in social and administrative fields. The church, with the Pope at its head, became a significant factor of power in Europe. This trend ran parallel to the expanding Islamic faith, in which religion and power are tied even closer.

Coups, with various degrees of success

Around the turn of the of the first millennium, we see military power used worldwide to create change. In Japan, the power of the emperor is limited for the benefit of the military leader, the Shogun. He runs the country via powerful families in a feudal system while the emperor continues to play a religious role.

In Central America, a similar taking over of power happened. Just as with the Shoguns in Japan, the Aztecs were initially appreciated because of their military capacity. They manage to create an ever-expanding empire through marriages and conquests.

The Christian Europeans, spurred on by Pope Urbanus II, felt obliged to recapture the holy places in Arabia from the Muslims. An imposing group of enthusiasts mobilized for these crusades, of which the first started in 1095. Under the banner 'God wants it', they went down fighting; the desired result of these military expeditions was never achieved.

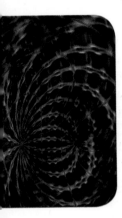

Gunpowder for weapons and energy

Gunpowder is a chemical mix of sulphur, charcoal and saltpetre. It is not exactly clear when this flammable mixture was discovered but it is certain that the Chinese deserve the credit. It is said that they discovered gunpowder in the tenth century and it arrived in Europe in the thirteenth century, where the first military applications of gunpowder were developed. With these weapons, projectiles could now be fired from a larger distance, so that warfare became more anonymous and the bastions once considered safe became more vulnerable.

Gunpowder was also used in the eighteenth and nineteenth centuries for generating energy and it also contributed to the development of steam engines and steam trains. Nowadays it is used, among other things, to activate airbags in cars. ☐

Aggressive (dis)order

One of the largest empires that ever existed was created at the beginning of the thirteenth century by Genghis Khan. This great Mongol warrior managed to unite rival Mongolian nomads in what is today part of Russia. He was helped by the bad economic tide and climate changes.

The Mongolian fighters went to work aggressively, thereby rapidly expanding their empire. A part of China was conquered, during which about 35 million Chinese died. Towns and villages in Middle Asia were razed to the ground and the venerable Arabian culture was forced to its knees. Genghis Khan also invaded Europe but was stopped at the Danube.

On a more positive note, his domination ensured stability in Middle Asia, making the trade route between Europe and China more accessible and safer. This was golden opportunity for traders and explorers, Marco Polo being the best known of these. In this same period, South America was ravaged by clan wars and anarchy.

More prosperous and more independent

At the beginning of the second millennium, the European population expanded as better farming techniques provided increasing yields and better quality agricultural products. In cities like Bruges, Ghent, Venice and Genoa, and also the Hanseatic towns, the economy flourished. The urban population swelled and showed greater independence than was the norm in the existing feudal system. The feudal system was based on nobility leasing land to the peasant farmers who supplied food in return. The prosperous cities, however, were no longer dependent on the ruling class; in fact, it was soon the other way around. Thus, slowly but surely, the trend came into being that the inhabitants of the cities became a new power factor alongside the existing religious and noble institutions.

This obviously had consequences at the political level. In England, this was clearly visible with the signing of the Magna Carta in 1215. This is seen as the beginning of constitutional development, in which the ruling elite must increasingly share power with the citizenry. Similar developments occurred in France and Spain. We can subsequently see the contours of the modern-day European countries emerging.

Black Death

In the fourteenth and fifthteenth centuries, crises prevailed in Europe: the Ottoman Turks were impatiently threatening the borders and the Hundred Years War was being fought between France and England. Natural circumstances, however, were more worrying. There was insufficient food for the steadily increasing population and a colder climate had also resulted in harsher winters at the beginning of the fourteenth century. Famine ensued, and it is known that 10% of the population in the Flemish cities died at that time. But the real suffering had yet to come.

In 1348, the plague broke out for the first time. This disease had entered Europe via the trade routes and brought death on a massive scale: herever it took hold, half the population was killed. It has been estimated that during these outbreaks of the Black Death, one-third of all Europeans died, about 25 million in total. This represented an enormous blood-letting for Europe. Naturally a scapegoat had to be found and it was quickly found in the Jews, who until then had lived quietly in small communities in the villages and cities. A wave of anti-Semitism passed over Europe.

Seize the day

After the centuries of crises, we see Europe recover again around 1500 – clearly the reason why historians call this the end of the Middle Ages. Italy appears to have been where the seeds of this productive growth germinated. Merchants in prosperous trading states like Florence, Genoa and Venice increased their power at the expense of the ruling elite. At the same time, the influence of the church was waning. The new rich created a new enthusiasm and optimism: earthly affairs became interesting and man played a pivotal role; the qualities of the learned and artists were once again appreciated. The compelling Christian and social ties of the Middle Ages began to loosen and the traditions and teachings of the Greeks and Romans were studied avidly. Through this, the Europeans came into contact with the developed Arabs, who were still present on the Iberian Peninsula.

The literal Italian translation of 'rebirth' is the name given to this period: the Renaissance. As a movement that had mainly the European upper class in its grip, it cleared away the dark ethos of Middle Ages, 'memento mori' (be prepared for death), and made way for the lighter 'carpe diem' (seize the day).

A new love of classical antiquity can be seen in the arts, where Botticelli puts 'the birth of Venus' to canvas and Michelangelo immortalizes 'the Creation of Adam' in the Sistine Chapel. At any rate, art experienced a true revival in this period. Insight into the laws of perspective and an increased knowledge of geometry is reflected in more symmetry and order. The sounds of the first opera could also be heard in Italy in about 1600.

Letterpress printing

A life without newspapers and books seems unimaginable to most of us today. They had their origins more than 500 years ago with the invention of letterpress printing. Writing had already existed for centuries in various cultures and there were also simple techniques to reproduce small numbers of copies. The printing press, though, allowed mass duplication and the written word took off.

The mechanical printing process was probably invented in China around 1000 but it was not until the 1450s when the German Johannes Gutenberg developed it in Europe. It was an immense success. One of the reasons that it was so successful in Europe, but not in China, is that the Latin alphabet contains 'only' twenty-six characters.

That letterpress printing had such an influence on the course of history was not so much because of the technological advance it represented, but more the effect that its output had. Thanks to the printing technology, knowledge and information could be disseminated on a huge scale. The press facilitated the expression of opinions and the exchange of ideas. □

Voyages of discovery

The Chinese had already discovered the American continent and Australia by 1421. However, when the fleet returned, disaster struck in China and as a result nothing was done with these discoveries. The fleet and the charts of the new regions that Commander Zheng had discovered were destroyed. One chart survived, though, and it arrived in Europe via the Silk Road. Columbus then got his hands on it.

The new enthusiasm in building the late Middle Ages stimulated the Europeans' desire to trade and their urge to explore. They believed that there were other, more lucrative, ways to get their hands on the luxury products of the Silk Road, namely by sea. Maritime expeditions were sent from Portugal in the direction of the African coast. When in 1487 the furthermost point of the Cape of Good Hope was reached, the way to South and Southeast Asia was open. Naturally, the opportunity to trade with Africans was not passed over. The Spanish also departed with a fleet and arrived in America in 1492, where they found a New World inhabited by Native Indians. Felipe Fernández-Armesto describes in *How the World was Discovered* why this journey was such a break with the trends: 'The creation of this world across the ocean is a remarkable twist in the development of western civilization. When other civilizations extended their territories, they did so step by step in adjacent territory and across small sea straits ... Even the early and extraordinary history of the Indian Ocean follows this pattern ...'

Whereas the Chinese, Vikings, Polynesians and Arabs had already discovered overseas territory, the Europeans took the discoveries one step further by making trade flourish and maintaining close contact with their home countries. This European expansion therefore began to create the first global economy.

While the first voyages of discovery were focused on trade and getting to know the New World, conquests and colonization soon started. Much later, in the eighteenth century, the British started a prison colony in Australia as a solution for their overcrowded prisons. In America, the riches of the Aztecs and Incas were plundered and destroyed; many of the indigenous peoples lost their lives to the war-mongering Europeans and the unknown sicknesses that they brought with them. The Europeans established trade settlements and plantations all around the world and from these locations the inhabitants of the 'old continent' came into contact with an abundance of new products, like corn, potatoes, spices and rice, not to mention exotic luxury goods.

The Europeans, however, did not trade only in products; they also traded people. From Africa, more than 6 million slaves were transported to the plantations in North and South America – a pitch-black page in history, the problematic evidence of which we still see today. It is not without reason that the American people's choice of Barack Obama, the nation's first black president, is seen as a remarkable event. Fernández-Armesto is of the opinion that the significance of the voyages of discovery cannot be underestimated: 'There is hardly an aspect of world history from that moment on that cannot be explained in the context of these discoveries in the years around 1490, or the power of the fantasy of the West-European seafarers.' And: 'The world had clearly entered into a new phase in its history in which the westerners played an important role for the first time by taking production oriented initiatives.'

Three great Muslim empires

After the invasion of the Mongols, three large Islamic empires come into being in a relatively short time: the Ottoman (in Turkey), the Safawi (in Iran) and the Mogul (in India). All reached their zenith in the sixteenth century.

The Ottoman Empire was established at the end of the thirteenth century by Osman, or Ottoman. In 1366, this civilization chose Edirne, on the border between Turkey, Greece and Bulgaria, as its capital. The Ottomans continued to acquire territory in the Balkans and, at the height of their influence, the Ottoman Empire stretched as far as the Danube at Vienna and they could also be found on the Arabian Peninsula and in North Africa. Their most important feat militarily is, perhaps, that they conquered Constantinople in 1453 and in so doing heralded the decisive end to the Byzantine (previously East Roman) Empire. The sixteenth century saw their art and architecture flourishing in a golden age of poetic art.

Muslims had already been in India since the eighth century. At the end of the twelfth century, there was a sultanate in Delhi, but from 1398 there were once again divisions. There was more unity and stability at the beginning of the sixteenth century under the leadership of Babur of Kabul. Characteristic of the Mogul dynasty that then arose was the tolerance towards non-Muslims. Here too we see a refinement of music, literature and architecture. One of their most well known buildings is today still a symbol of India: the Taj Mahal.

The history of the Safawidi Empire is mostly characterized by religious discussions. It was here that the Shiite Islam became a state religion. It was certainly different to the tolerant attitude of the Moguls and Ottomans; even Muslims with different religious beliefs were not welcome at the Salafids.

Christian Quarrels

While the European nations overseas expanded their territories, it remained restless on the Continent. There wasn't, however, continuous fighting all those years as we have become more accustomed to in the twentieth century. One of the most important reasons for the unrest was the schism in the Christian church. Though in Africa there had already been a schism in the fifth century from the orthodoxy in the church, this schism hit the church, with its power base in the centre of Europe, in the heart. There was opposition to the mighty riches of the churches and the luxurious life style of the clergy, the pope in particular. When Luther proclaimed his criticism in public in 1516, he found many supporters in all of Europe, resulting in a definite schism in the Catholic Church. The Reformation, as the movement is called, caused a dichotomy in Europe between the sober Protestants on the one hand and the Burgundian Catholics on the other. This dichotomy had given rise to disputes between the countries' religious communities for centuries.

New perception of mankind
In the seventeenth and eighteenth centuries, a basis was laid for modern-day society. Once again, politically and economically powerful Europe was the breeding ground for this revolution, which started in the sciences. Physics and astronomy had been embraced by scientists like Copernicus, Huygens, Galileo and Newton. Although the Chinese already knew that the world was round and orbits the sun, in Europe the scientific evidence of the fact began to be publicized. Other contemporary discoveries were gravity, the circulation of blood, hydrogen and the first battery. Additionally, the Frenchman Denis Papin discovered that energy can be generated using steam. A revolution was unfolding: it was the first time that exploitable energy could be seen to be supplied not by manpower or by nature (in the form of wind or water). Karen Armstrong refers to this development in her book *The Battle for God*. To paraphrase: 'All the discoveries were characterized by a pragmatic, scientific spirit that slowly undermined the old conservative, mythical ethos and made ever more people receptive to new ideas about God, religion, the state, the individual and society.'

Jointly, these new ideas are called the Enlightenment. A belief developed in the unlimited possibilities of human reasoning. Stupidity, superstition and intolerance were put out with the trash. Philosophers like Kant, Spinoza, Voltaire, Rousseau and Montesquieu created models of new societies in which the principles of freedom, equality and brotherhood were central: these had to replace the class-based society, the dominant position of the church and the absolutist rulers. Question marks were placed on slavery, which was forbidden by law in various European countries at the beginning of the nineteenth century.

In 2009, Western people still live to a large extent according to these principles. They do not appear to have lost their strength. In present-day debates on Islam, it is often heard that the Muslims have not been through a period of 'Enlightenment'. The Enlightenment not only had consequences at a political level, religious perceptions also changed. To take Armstrong's assessment again: 'Thus, in a time in which science and unfettered rationality made brilliant advances, life became increasingly pointless for a growing number of people who, for the first time in the history of mankind, had to do without mythology.'

States unite

The trend of enlightened thinking quickly reverberated around society. When the British colonies in North America detached themselves from the colonizer in 1776, they used these principles for the organization of their state. The Declaration of Independence is permeated with the same conviction that can also be found in Barack Obama's rhetoric: 'All men are created equal'. It was a noble concept, were it not completely self-evident at the time that women and black slaves were not referred to. God is noticeably absent in these political foundations of the new state. 'From then on, religion in the United State would be a voluntary and private affair. This was a revolutionary step, that is called one of the biggest achievements of the age of reason,' writes Armstrong.

The separation of the powers into administrative, legislative and judicial power, as described by the philosopher Baron de Montesquieu, was applied in the new country. The rational architecture of the Enlightenment, based on classic antiquity, was also adopted by the Americans. The best-known result can be seen almost every day on the TV news: the White House.

In Europe, the new thinking was also concretized, thanks to the French Revolution in 1789. The monarchy was replaced by a republic, the parliament rules the French people and the feudal system is dispensed with. These concretized ideals were further spread across Europe via Napoleon at the beginning of the nineteenth century. The various countries became nation states, increasingly deriving their right to exist from the sense of being a nation that their inhabitants generated. The Christian religion met with increasing criticism in Europe. Marx talked of religion as 'opium for the people' and Darwin put people on an equal footing with animals with his theory of evolution, undermining the special creation by God. What's more, in 1882 Nietzsche announced: 'God is dead'.

In South America, at the beginning of the nineteenth century, we can also see the spread of the ideals of the French revolution. The freedom fighter Simón Bolívar picked up these ideas in Europe and when he returned to South America he saw to it, together with Antonio de Sucre, among others, that the colonizing powers disappeared. In 1819, following the example of North America, he proclaimed the Republic of Greater Columbia, to which parts of present day Venezuela, Colombia, Panama and Ecuador belong. This federation was, however, destined to be short lived; in 1827 it fell apart.

Industrial Revolution

In the sixteenth, seventeenth and eighteenth centuries, the world had four large centres of power: Europe (though it was a collection of rival states), the Ottoman Empire, Mogul India and China. With hindsight, however, we must conclude that Europe had the most influence on the course of world history since the eighteenth and nineteenth century. One of the reasons for this is perhaps the colonization of North and South America, initially, and in the course of the nineteenth century also of large parts of Africa and Asia. Another element was the increasing economic interest that was germinating in Europe. It was there, after all, that mercantilism started, the first world economy was created and a world market came into being. Another economic development that mustn't be underestimated is the Industrial Revolution. Historians Van der Wee and Aerts describe this as follows: 'By far the most important aspect of the Industrial Revolution in England and in the subsequent industrialization of the European continent, was that commercial capitalism after about seven centuries of development made way for the industrial capitalism of the present day. From then on it was no longer trading, but industry that determined economic growth. Technological development became more important than organizational development.'

I will immediately address this technological progress. We have seen that science leaped forward in the seventeenth and eighteenth centuries and the knowledge acquired then was later applied in practice. Consider the steam engine, developed by James Watt at the end of the eighteenth century, which represented the giant step from manual to mechanized labour.

The sequel to the mechanical innovations was transport: the steamship and the steam train. At the end of the nineteenth century these machines were having such a profound effect on mobility and goods traffic that there was talk of a transport revolution.

At the end of the nineteenth century industrialization entered a new phase as the assembly line, steel, oil and electricity formed the basis for further mechanization. The difference between this period and 100 years previously is that the companies in this phase of development fertilized the latest innovations themselves by financing research. The development of industry and companies led to more complexity and it became essential to engage specialists for specific parts of the organization: hence the birth of the manager.

Electricity and oil discovered

We can no longer imagine a world without oil or electricity. Both sources of energy are practically as old as the world itself but only became important in our lives over the past hundred and fifty years.

Electricity is an ever-present force in the universe, which has been active for more than 13 billion years. On earth, lightning is its most tangible form. At the end of the eighteenth century, it was the Italian Alessandro Volta who took the first step towards understanding this power. He noted that if he placed a copper disk on one side of his tongue and a zinc disk on the other side, and pressed the edges of the two against each other, then he felt a tingling sensation in his tongue. Volta discovered that this worked with all metals as long as they were separated by a small amount of salty water. He experimented further and was able to lead this power through a wire. Because it flowed so quickly, like water down a fast-flowing river, it was given the name 'electrical current'.

In the first half of the nineteenth century, oil was found a number of times when drilling for water or salt. This prompted the American industrialist George Bissel to drill specifically for oil and he established the first American petroleum company. Initially, the oil was distilled to create kerosene, which was ideally suited as lamp oil. Later, the residue became important: gasoline. ☐

Population grows and groans

An indispensable element of the Industrial Revolution was the population growth. Between 1750 and 1950, the European population grew by about 400 million – something unprecedented in history. People also lived longer as a result of better sanitation (e.g. with the arrival of sewers) and medical advances. In the eighteenth century, for example, a vaccination for smallpox was discovered; these epidemics subsequently caused far fewer deaths. At the same time it became apparent that there was sufficient food for the growing number of people, partly due to the introduction in Europe of the potato and other products from the colonies. For the first time in history the population and food supplies did not keep each other in check, but stimulated each other's growth.

Millions of Europeans soon found work in the new industries. The ideals of freedom, equality and brotherhood expressed in the French Revolution no longer appeared to be fully tenable and this large group of the population, the proletariat, was plainly exploited, as so aptly described by Charles Dickens. Karl Marx was one of the first to address this issue. At the end of the nineteenth century, social legislation was slowly introduced, under pressure from the socialist parties, which moderated the consequences of liberal thinking. Women also demanded equal rights and, in the First Feminist Wave, they entered the battle for the right to vote, a goal that was achieved for many at the beginning of the twentieth century.

Communicating at a distance

Using runners (like the Greek soldier Phidippides who ran from Marathon to Athens), birds, horses and stage coaches, people had already been communicating with one another across large distances for some time. However, the technological advances in the nineteenth century added a new dimension to communication. The cable telegraph and, later, the telephone made long-distance contact between people far quicker and more convenient.

This communication revolution further developed in the twentieth century thanks to innovations like radio and TV. And in this era, the word 'revolution' is truly applicable. The information revolution is said to have started in 1971 with the introduction of 'the computer on a chip' by Intel. The result was that the existing computers could be made cheaper and smaller. The first personal computer, or PC, left the IBM factory in 1981. Slowly but surely, information technology and telecommunications began to boom.

I can already no longer imagine a world without computers, just as I cannot imagine a life in which I cannot share my experiences, follow the news or stay abreast of current affairs, quick as a flash. This revolution has shrunk the world; so has the emergence of a 'common language', English. We must, however, realize that in 2002 less than 1% of the African population had access to a computer and that Finland in 2001 had more internet users than the whole of Latin America.

Tensions exposed

In the nineteenth century, the basis was laid for the present-day American society. The population grew, mainly with immigrants from England, Ireland and Germany, who were attracted by the enormous availability of farmland and job opportunities. The cultural–mental constellation of the country appealed to the imagination; the 'American Dream' became a concept that, right up until today, inspires potential immigrants.

The Civil War between 1860 and 1865 exposed the tensions in this 'promised land' and put an end to 600,000 American lives. One of the points of dissension was slavery, which was seen by the southern states as an economic necessity and by the northern states as degrading. The north

won the domestic war, the United States remained a unity and slavery was abolished. However, the roots of segregation still ran deep, so that blacks in American society were consistently subordinated to the whites. In 1964, a legal end was made to this, although the lines of discrimination still run criss-cross through society. Interestingly enough, the struggle for power between the Democratic and the Republican Parties also originated in the period of the Civil War.

Imperialism

The European powers reached their peak between 1870 and 1914. After the Europeans lost their power in North and South America between the end of the eighteenth century and the beginning of the nineteenth century, they spent much of the 1800s mainly caught up in internal political, social and economic developments. In the same period, the patchwork of states in Germany became politically one nation; the same occurred in Italy.

However, a new expansionism emerged in about 1870; it focused on Asia and Africa. Until then, the Europeans had in the main only established trading posts in coastal regions. The need for extra raw materials for their industries and populations, and the desire to find additional markets, tempted the European countries into a new colonialism. This development was given a different name, however: modern imperialism.

The difference with the former colonialism was threefold. First of all, this expansion was characterized by an unmistakable pursuit of power. European countries like Great Britain, France and Germany did not want to be outmanoeuvred by one another and wanted to prevent rival countries taking possession of strategic areas; it was a race. A second difference is explained by Michel Beaud in *A History of Capitalism*: 'If the world economy is a system of production ratios and corresponding exchange rates, that include the whole world, then imperialism is the worldwide spread of capitalistic production and exchange rates, a spread that culminated at the beginning of the twentieth century under the control of the British, German, French and American capitalism and the bourgeoisie of these countries.' Thirdly, some believed that it was Europe's mission to let the blind see, by spreading the principles of the white, enlightened, Christian society. The trend of the supposed superiority of the white race, which was also prevalent in the United States, is a fact.

Africa divvied up, Asia appropriated

The reasons why African nations are currently economically lagging behind the rest of the world and their continuing political turmoil originate from pre-colonial times. However, the nineteenth century impe-

rialism didn't help them to break out of the negative spiral. The European powers wanted to expand their power and, after centuries of only having occupied the coastal regions, they marched into the interiors. Thanks to the technologically advanced European weaponry and an effective defence against malaria, the battle with the Africans was quickly won. Between 1884 and 1885, during the Colonization Conference in Berlin, Africa was divided up among the European nations. The continent was divided like a cake between France, England, Portugal, Italy and Germany, which explains the many straight lines currently visible on the African map. This division didn't take the borders of existing civilizations and mutual political groupings into account at all. The only thing of importance to the Europeans was power and economic gain.

The trend of wielding unbridled power under the guise of moral superiority continued in Asia. The British presence in India was strengthened in order to maintain its own position. Neighbouring countries like Burma were added to the British Empire and the Malay Peninsula was conquered from the Dutch. The Netherlands consolidated its power in Indonesia. France applied its power in Southeast Asia. In addition, the Russians expanded their sphere of influence by bringing Turkmenistan and Afghanistan under their control. Though China has never been conquered, it was forced at the end of the nineteenth century to trade with the Europeans: Hong Kong had to be yielded to the British and other harbours were opened. Japan didn't feel threatened by the new imperialism; rather, the Japanese were inspired. At the end of the nineteenth century they created, following the example of the West, a modern industrial nation with a constitution, parliament, railways, electricity, fashion, press and modern education. Emperor Mutsuhito, who had re-taken power from the Shoguns, was the great force behind this modernization operation. Eventually, Japan felt so powerful that it also started to show imperialistic tendencies.

The end of emperors and tsars

The social tensions, inherent in the industrial society, continued into the beginning of the twentieth century. In European countries, these were channeled via the legislature, while in the colonies in Africa and Asia, opponents were suppressed. In China and Russia, little was done during the nineteenth century with the enlightened political ideas and social unrest. The results became clear at the beginning of the twentieth century: in both countries, dynasties were built and toppled through the centuries. In China, the Qing dynasty was successfully dismantled by Sun Yat-Sen. In 1912, he formed the Republic of China, of which he was president for only a few months. In spite of this, he was seen as the Father of the Fatherlands and many statues of him continue to exist.

In Russia, the first revolutionary success in 1905, after losing the war against Japan, was not immediately fatal to the Tsar. Through reformations, which included establishing a parliament, the Duma, he was able to temporarily satisfy the revolutionaries. Tsar Nicholas II was, however, driven out in 1917 and, after a bloody civil war, the communists grabbed power under the leadership of Lenin. For the first time in history, a society was structured according to the Marxist model: a country without capitalism and with an equal sharing of money and goods.

From optimism to cynicism

At the beginning of the twentieth century, Europe found itself gaining momentum, as described by Rik Coolsaet, professor of international relations: '... sometimes the world is more in transition than usual, namely when the waves flow together concurrently and start a true acceleration on the "river of time". We talk of a turning point, a juncture. At such moments man is bewildered, because there are no simple explanations.' According to him, this means that earlier developments come together in this phase and a lot changes. Cheerful optimism concerning the possibilities for man, politics and technology was also prevalent. There was a great belief in the ability of both the people and the country. In this mood, countries continued to show their might. This militaristic atmosphere created a weapons race and modern imperialism gave this power struggle a bitter taste. Two great alliances were formed: on the one hand, there was the Triple Alliance between Italy, Germany and Austria-Hungary; on the other hand there was the Triple Entente between France, Russia and England.

In 1914, in Sarajevo, the fuse to the powder keg was lit; the weapons stockpiles were deployed and the forged alliances quickly mobilized – The Great War, as it was then called, began. Initially, the optimistic atmosphere prevailed; the general expectations were that the war would be over in a matter of months. Nothing could be farther from true: the First World War would last until 1918 and more than 20 million people would lose their lives.

This war, which was mainly staged in Europe, became a world war because the Ottoman Empire, Russia and the United States intervened. Suddenly, various allies worldwide took up arms against each other.

The First World War paid the prevailing optimism a hefty blow. What was left to believe in after having experienced this mass slaughter? The once so fantastic technology now was shown to provide the instruments for mass murder. The trust in the old moral values and in traditional politics was also sorely affected. In Italy and Germany, the fascists and national socialists got a foot in the door.

Deep recession and communist success

After its brief yet successful involvement in the First World War, the United States resumed its isolationist position. The economy flourished and new consumables like the car, radio and movies provided the backdrop for the Roaring '20s. In 1929, this changed quite suddenly and radically: the market was saturated, buying power was too low and the stock market in New York collapsed. Even the famous economist Irvin Fisher didn't fully realize the consequences. In 1929, he said: 'The share prices may fall, but a disaster is out of the question', and in 1930: 'The outlook is excellent, at least in the short term.'

That stock market crash, which is regularly referred to in 2009, not only had a negative effect in America, but in the whole world. In America, the banks and companies went bankrupt, national income fell drastically and millions of people lost their jobs. The prospects in the 1930s looked alarming. In Germany, which was also heavily affected by the crisis, Adolf Hitler came to power in the elections in 1933. He quickly structured the society according to his own national socialist criteria.

In Russia at the end of the 1920s, where Lenin in the meantime had cleared the field for Stalin, a new economic route had just been taken. Stalin implemented a series of five-year plans. By building up heavy industry from scratch, press-ganging labourers, forcing farmers into cooperatives and murdering opponents, some progress was booked for the next ten years, but Russia remained substantially poorer than the West.

Art inspired

Art has always inspired people to make new art. The Egyptians, the Romans and, later, the Renaissance movement got their inspirations from previous societies. Nowadays, with the possibilities of modern communication, there is a near-optimal access to art worldwide; art from all times.

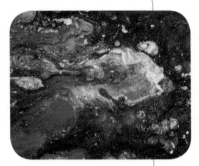

Art has always had a big impact on society, both in free and enforced ways. Examples in the twentieth century of art that intended to force people to embrace a society can be found in communist and facist states. Both used art to give their rule a human and justifiable touch. Opposed to this is art that is, and was, used to protest against a system of rule that is not endorsed by the people.

In general, one could say art has become more free with the ageing of our history, which is in line with the democratization that has taken place in most of the world. Art is used to express what is happening in society. Look, for example, at the abstract paintings starting from mid-nineteenth century. As photography was invented, new forms of painting had to be invented. Abstract painting gave the artists a renewed attention from the public. Art today is immensely diverse and it is not likely to stop evolving. This is a result of the complex and technologically advanced society we have.

Second World War

The Second World War from 1939 to 1945 would overshadow even the horrors of the First Great War. More than 50 million people lost their lives, of which 6 million were Jews, most of whom died in the concentration camps that Hitler had specially built for the purpose of exterminating them. The systematic genocide that the German dictator set in motion had not been seen before on this industrial scale.

German sociologist Gunnar Heinsohn carefully researched the setting of World War II and how it could have taken place. He is known for his theory of the 'youth bulge'. He argues that an excess in the young adult male population predictably leads to social unrest, war and terrorism. This is because, to a large extent, the third and fourth sons can find no prestigious positions in their existing societies, which leads them to rationalize an impetus to compete through religious or political ideology. Heinsohn claims that most historical periods of social unrest lacking external triggers (such as rapid climatic changes or other catastrophic changes in the evironment) and most genocides can be readily explained as a result of a built up youth bulge. A most tragic example in history was twentieth century facism: European colonialism, conflicts such as that in Darfur, the Palestinian uprisings and terrorism are other examples.

The war started in Europe, where Hitler's Germany relatively easily overpowered one country after the other. With the support of the Italian dictator Mussolini and the non-aggression pact with Stalin, Hitler was tactically strong. He was, however, unable to conquer Great Britain.

The war spread onto the world stage when Japan, as an ally of Hitler and Mussolini, attacked the American naval base at Pearl Harbor on Hawaii in 1941. That humiliating act drew the United States into the war. Japan occupied large parts of Southeast Asia and established their notorious concentration camps.

The course of the war tipped when, in 1942, Hitler made a failed attempt to conquer the Soviet Union and subsequently faced extra resistance from Stalin's troops. In Southern Europe the British and American troops established several beachheads, and in Southeast Asia and the Pacific, Japan was slowly pushed back by the British and Commonwealth troops and the Americans. In 1944, the Americans and the British launched the liberation of Western Europe from the beaches of Normandy, while from the east the Soviet armies dealt constant blows to the German occupation.

The American atom bombs dropped on the cities of Hiroshima and Nagasaki signalled the definite end of the war. The destructive power of the atom bomb gave every potential war in the future a whole new dimension.

Struggle for world domination
The United States and the Soviet Union both emerged from the Second World War as victors. Though their cooperation was one of the factors of success, shortly after 1945 a power struggle had already started, one that would hold the world in its grip for more than forty years. Because this power struggle mainly resulted in tense stand-offs that never erupted into conflict, this period was called the Cold War.

Typically, the whole world was the stage for these competing states. They divided the world, as it were, with their own society as a shining example of how life should be. The Soviet Union went the furthest in expanding its sphere of influence and subjected countries in Eastern Europe to their communist regime. The communist ideology was also embraced by many in Asia, causing a split in Korea and Vietnam. Under the leadership of Mao Zedong, China also embraced a communistic form of government.

The American influence was mainly tangible in Western Europe, where political and cultural trends were quickly imitated. Militarily, they also came to terms, which in 1949 led to the establishment of the North Atlantic Treaty Organization (NATO). After the war, the United States had a close involvement with the Japanese, which led to the Emperor losing his divinity and sovereignty being handed over to the people.

The power struggle between America and the Soviet Union led to various races. There was the arms race, in which the development of ever-more powerful weapons of destruction was of the order of the day. Technological resources gave this conflict an ingenious character, with the secret services taking the leading roles. This is clearly reflected in the James Bond films. Remarkably enough, the earth became too small a playing field for the Russians and the Americans; both apparently wanted to safeguard their position in the universe. In 1961, the Russian Yuri Gagarin was the first man in space; in 1969 the American Neil Armstrong was the first man to walk on the moon. In sport too, the two superpowers competed for gold – at the Olympic Games they were always well matched.

The basis for a new world order

After the Second World War, the world was reordered. The war undermined the power of the European countries in their colonies. With increasing frequency, nationalistic and independence movements arose, forcing the colonizers to depart. One by one, the former colonies obtained their own governments but this was, however, not without a struggle. Thanks to Mahatma Gandhi, a mostly peaceful route was taken in India and the country was divided up into Hindu India and Islamic Pakistan in order to channel the tensions between the population groups. A year later, China became a communist state when Mao Zedong emerged as winner from an internal power struggle.

During this period there was also a large influx of Europeans into the United States looking for a better future. Europe was a mess and seemingly did not provide a bright future at that time. The United States actually promoted the influx, which continued until the mid-1950s, when most West European countries had created enough wealth to tempt their citizens to stay in Europe. In the 1960s, Nothern Europe experienced his own influx of people from Southern Europe, and later from Turkey and Morocco when their economies needed more workers than they had available.

The West European countries increasingly formed a joint power base after the Second World War. By institutionalizing economic cooperation (in 1951 in the European Coal and Steel Community, and in 1957 in the European Economic Community), the sting was removed from the previously sensitive relationship between France and Germany. The post-war urge to rebuild, together with the Marshall Plan aid from the United States, brought Europe unprecedented social welfare. Illustrative of this is the growth of the

French economy, which grew annually by 8% between 1955 and 1960. In Japan, a comparable economic miracle took place.

Most of the Western European countries chose the same direction for their system of government: that of the welfare state. The existing social legislation was expanded extensively with laws that arranged social security, including family allowances and provisions for old age. Coolsaet articulates the nature of this state in sharp terms: 'After 1945 the state became a welfare state, a sort of insurance company that ensures economic growth and at the same time protects the population against the risks of the free market. The state protected its inhabitants against the instabilities of fate, disease, accidents, handicaps, from the cradle to the grave.'

Along with the growing influence of the United State in the world economy, a new form of business was emerging: the multinational. Before World War II, there were already some multinationals but after the war their number and impact increased dramatically. Corporate giants like General Electric, Texaco, Philips became the new powers next to national governments. They operated in multiple countries and had sales figures which, in some cases, were bigger than the gross domestic products of individual countries.

Government for the world

After the First World War, it had already been tried to establish a body run for and by all the countries of the world. In 1918, it was called the League of Nations. However, it wasn't destined to last very long and it turned out to have very little power, particularly because large countries like America didn't join. In 1945, this was tried again: the United Nations was established. This was, at least, a more successful body than the League of Nations but the power of the UN fluctuates. Looking back on the past fifteen years. After the successful performance of the UN forces during the First Gulf War (1990–1) they became, in the words of Coolsaet, 'generally accepted as the heart of international peace and safety.' Only a few years later, during the ethnic conflicts in Yugoslavia and Rwanda, the UN lost its credibility. In 2003, this reached its lowest point when America invaded Iraq without a mandate from the UN Security Council. Other institutions of the UN, like UNICEF, the World Health Organization or the World Bank (which actually isn't part of the UN), are less affected by these fluctuations. In 2000, the Millennium Objectives were formulated, based on six basic principles: freedom, equality, solidarity, tolerance, respect for nature and shared responsibility (an echo of the American Declaration of Independence and the French Revolution).

Deregulation and religious revival

Many issues that are still relevant today can be traced back to the 1970s, when the economic revival following the Second World War received a body blow: growth slowed down, unemployment rose, inflation grew and buying power dropped. Additionally, the oil crises in 1973 and 1979 had a destructive effect. Coolsaet describes how the existing economic policy instruments didn't have any effect and the governments decided to try a different tack: 'The state obstructed free competition and innovation – and the free development of the individual. Government expenditure had to be cut urgently as it was obstructing the growth of the economy. State enterprises had to once again be privatized and myriad regulations had to be relaxed. The world started a love affair with liberalization and deregulation.' The citizens who were also looking for something to hold on to felt betrayed. Coolsaet writes: 'The state had removed its protective cloak. The forces that the citizens found themselves confronted by were way above their heads. That was one of the causes of the much discussed "gap between citizens and politics"', which also explains the increased support for more radical political parties.

Another trend that was visible in the 1970s was the explosive growth of religions worldwide. A clear trend therein was the popularity of fundamentalist groups like the evangelical Protestants in America, radical Hindus in India, the Sikhs and Jewish fundamentalists. The most obvious example of this religious fervour was undoubtedly the the taking of power by Ayatollah Khomeini in secular Iran. Many people in 1979 were surprised by this revolution; they had expected that religion had all but died and was only of any importance to a few 'fools'. Armstrong makes clear where this revival comes from: 'Modern society had achieved a lot, both ethically and materially. They had reason to believe in its righteous character. Democracy, freedom and tolerance had a liberating effect, at least in Europe and the United States. But the fundamentalists couldn't see that, not because they were being difficult, but because they had experienced modern times as an attack that threatened their most cherished values and appeared to threaten their very existence. Towards the end of the 1970s the Jewish, Christian and Islamic fundamentalists were ready to parry the attack.' They were even successful, as Armstrong describes: 'The fundamentalists had taken faith out of the shadows and shown that in a modern society there was an enormous number of supporters that it appealed to.' During the final two decades of the twentieth century, religion would chalk up more striking results.

Also in the 1970s, in China, an essential change occurred in society. Under the leadership of Deng Xiaoping, the economy was reformed into a capitalistic model while the communist principles in politics remained intact. This proved to be an excellent move for China: between 1979 and 1994, annual economic growth of around 10% was recorded.

Communism dismantled

The Marxist ideal of a classless society fell to an all-time low in 1991 as the Soviet Union falls apart. In 1985, Mikhail Gorbachev, president of the Soviet Union, started this development. The existing situation forced him to restructure the economy (perestroika) and to allow more transparency (glasnost). This led, among other things, to the communist countries in Eastern Europe detaching themselves from the Soviet Union, after which democratically chosen governments came into power. The fall of the Berlin wall in 1989 symbolized the end of the era in which Europe was divided into East and West. In 1991, Gorbachev's position in his own country proved untenable. Yeltsin succeeded him and dismantled the Soviet Union. The result was fifteen sovereign republics, of which Russia is still the largest.

The feeling of liberation was short lived. The certainties of previous decades disappeared and the new era was, above all, hard: the economy started up slowly and there was a lot of poverty. A small group, at least in Russia, was able profit from the economic vacuum and enriched itself rapidly. One regularly hears that people, especially the older members of society, long to return to the old times of the Soviet Union with its communist values.

The fall of the Soviet Union, which occurred with remarkably little bloodshed, also had repercussions for the balance of world power. The political and economic disarray in Russia meant that America emerged from the Cold War as the only superpower. Coolsaet describes how an uncertain period then began: 'In the nineties it was indeed not imme-diately clear what the driving force, the motor and the rules of play in world politics would become. ... The nineties were therefore also transi-tion years, a transition from a known world order to an unknown, with uncertainty as a result.'

Globalization

Coolsaet describes the idea that arose after the Cold War: 'In the eyes of many it appeared that globalization heralded a radically new chapter in world politics. This term not only applied to the economic and financial dimensions of this phenomenon, but also to the insight that many issues contained a global dimension that surpassed the capacity of individual countries. The realization that far-off events could also be of great influence in ones own country stimulated a new form of cosmopolitanism, the awareness of human solidarity on a global scale.' The world had actually become friendlier because of it: the number of wars has diminished, human rights are being better respected and the number of democracies has grown. Still, though, we saw a number of violent border conflicts in the 1990s: for example, between India and Pakistan, Ethiopia and Eritrea and between Israel and the Palestinians. The most radical are the civil wars in Rwanda, Yugoslavia, Sierra Leone and Somalia, where once again it is apparent that extremism, nationalism and ethnic cleansing are of the order of the day.

It also slowly penetrates that globalization has a drawback; namely, the growing divide between rich and poor. The world is actually a lot more affluent, yet the difference between 'rich' and 'poor' has only become bigger. In 2003 it was calculated that the richest 1% earned in total just as much as 57% of the poorest. Additionally, the economy of Southeast Asia received a hefty blow at the end of the 1990s and the West suffered the dot-com crisis. Thus, the belief in the predicted blessings of the liberal and capitalistic system has been dented a few times. This is fodder for anti-globalists, like Naomi Klein, who call ever more loudly for a new world order. The terrorist attacks of September 11, 2001, and the current economic crisis will undoubtedly prove to be a rich feeding ground for them.

part 2

Megatrends of the Future

Introduction

The lessons learned and the world's next super model: scenarios for tomorrow

Looking at the world and humanity in years gone by, as described in Part I, the megatrends of the past become clear. They might influence or even re-create some of the megatrends of the future as well. History always repeats itself, although in different ways. One of the lessons learned is that climate change is nothing new. Climate always changes in cycles, just as it is changing again now. Another thing we learn is that there is a correlation between wars and a surplus of under-employed males in the 'fighting age' between fifteen and thirty-five years old. (There is more about this theory later in the book.) Another lesson learned is that, although humans have always tried to govern nature, Mother Nature is mightier than human beings, and she always strikes back. We also learn that periods of population growth are always followed by periods of population decline, as should happen again now. A further conclusion is that the world economy also develops in cycles, like the seasons in a year. We cannot prevent economic winters (recessions) nor severe economic winters (depressions), such as the one we are currently experiencing. The economic depression that started in 2008 has many similarities with the one of 1870; more than with the one of 1929, although many believe the latter. Depressions and major crises in the financial institutions always happen on the brink of a new era, an era of new technology. We also learn that spirituality is more important than it seems, and that many economic waves are the same as astrological waves.

So, knowing the megatrends and waves of change of the past, we'll move into the second part of this book, which deals with the twelve megatrends that will change our future. For the future of the world and the next super model for the world's economy and society there are four scenarios to be designed.

What will the new super model for the world economy look like?

It is no longer enough to pronounce American neoliberal capitalism dead. What will take its place during the course of the twenty-first century? Is there such a thing as a crisis-proof economic model? Will there be a new economic order and would it still be global? What will be the ideal relationship between the market and government? Can the capitalist paradigm (as a matter of course, the free market creates balance and prosperity for everyone) be thrown into the wastepaper basket and what would the new paradigm then be? Which region of our multipolar world has the most future-proof model? In the world of 2009, you can no longer put these fundamental questions solely to Westerners.

Prominent experts in various fields from all over the world are mulling over new ideas and seeking a clear vision of the future. New economic models are now emerging from those deliberations. Kishore Mahbubani proclaims his belief in the Asia model while Wouter Bos champions the superior values of the European model and the Brazilian economist Marcelo Neri commends the success story of his country. Macroeconomist Willem Buiter of the London School of Economics sees the emergence of the Russian or Singaporean model. The young geopolitical analyst Parag Khanna (New America Foundation) is putting his money on Europe whereas Amy Chua, globalization expert at Yale University, doesn't yet want to write off the US and proves to be critical about the alternative models.

Scenario 1: Singapore

In this model, democracy is replaced by the entrance of enlightened despots onto the political stage. The world's leading powers would transform themselves in similar way to Singapore, which until the 1960s was still a poor, marshy country but is now one of the world's richest countries. The economic model is capitalistic, but the state plays an important role in this through, amongst other things, state investment companies. This model is not very ideological, being chiefly pragmatic. It is less religious, more spiritual. Norms

World Megatrends - The Future of a World in Transition

and values are important, and they are also conventional. Diversity is a normal fact of life, but firm action is taken against extremists. Law and order prevail, with the death penalty as the ultimate punishment. Science and technology are given a free hand.

In this scenario, globalization perseveres and we make the best of the climate change. The one-child policy is brought in throughout the world. Anger management is a cornerstone of the model so the underprivileged class and unemployed do not revolt against the established order. Those at the top link together human and artificial intelligence. Luck is defined particularly in pragmatic terms.

Scenario 2: Back to the Middle Ages

In this scenario, the current world order falls apart, as it did in 1870, when globalization was at a peak, as it is again now. Medieval times return. The Euro as a single currency implodes, just as its Medieval equivalent, the Taler, did. Power blocs are dissolved as the EU fragments, just as the Austro-Hungarian monarchy imploded shortly after the start of the twentieth century. The new world is more violent, extremists rise and the combination of economic meltdown, food shortages and climate crisis brings out the worst of humanity. We experience a major setback in science and chaos is the common value. In this new world, order elites lose their status and weak democracies co-exist beside dictatorships.

Final remarks

I personally hope that the first scenario becomes the new reality. However, when contemplating the likelihood of such scenarios you also have to take wild cards into account. These can radically change the future, in the same way that a joker can change a game of cards. From the situation in 2009, I expect that it will take a year or two for the banks throughout the world to fundamentally reform. The banks are the global economic motor: money makes the world go around. During that period, everywhere in the world, the

power of the state will grow. There will be mass unemployment and social unrest will develop. Because of that, there will be a market for extremism. Globalization will take a considerable step backwards, albeit temporarily. Subsequently, globalization will once again get under way because there are many problems that cannot be resolved by a loose collection of nationalistic groups.

I believe that globalization offers many advantages, even if only in terms of peace. As a rule, economies that are interdependent do not wage war with each other. In world history, we have known the longest periods of peace in periods of reciprocal economic dependence of trading partners and different economies. However, globalization always has its disadvantages, and these also have to be addressed now. Many people feel out of place in a world that has become too homogeneous. Many fear that just a single culture will survive throughout the world, in which there is no longer room for their local individual characteristics. Glocalization is therefore the motto.

The big issues, such as climate change and managing the earth's energy and raw materials, require international cooperation. To bring about a sense of urgency in individual people, investments should be made in storytelling. Leaders are more able to touch people with stories than with a dry summary of facts, figures, statistics and tables. The future is now!

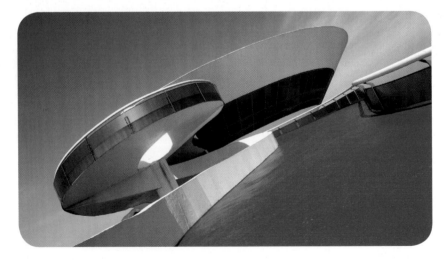

Megatrend 1

Towards twelve pillars of power

BBC Portable News Service
News headlines: Your personalized news for 5 January 2023, 8.30 a.m.
Yesterday, Empress Cixi II of China offered the prestigious membership of the CATA, the Chinese Atlantic Treaty Organization, to the European Union during a state dinner at Buckingham Palace. She did this in the presence of King William V and European Union president David Beckham. She also announced that the introduction of gay marriage in China has significantly reduced the problems caused by the surplus of men. Since children can now be cloned, Chinese gay couples can also meet the one-child policy of China. Chinese gay couples are, however, obliged to have and raise daughters, thus compensating for the shortage of women in China. The Empress thanked President Beckham, who had suggested this course of action, which had proved successful in various European regions, during his first state visit to China in 2017.

The European Union today set the price of a human life at €80,000. If a citizen spends more than this amount on healthcare annually, euthanasia becomes obligatory. People will receive notification by mail that they have been removed from the digital population register; the letter will include a golden euthanasia pill that must be taken within twenty-four hours of receipt.

In London, the twentieth Women's Park was officially opened. This is a new milestone in the segregated facilities for men and women, such as trams, hospitals and parks, which have been introduced in a number of European regions since 2013. This new park is in line with the directive of the European Sharia Commission, under the leadership of Ken Livingstone.

The Awake Pill is celebrating its tenth anniversary. Thanks to this pill, Europeans now only need two hours of sleep a day. In 2007, we still slept on average eight hours a day, and in 1900 that was ten hours a day. Management of boredom has become an important priority in Europe since the introduction of this innovation.

Yesterday, three new nuclear power stations were opened simultaneously in Slovakia, Belgian-Flanders and Germany. The architecturally stunning stations will supply energy for the fleet of hydrogen cars in these European regions. This will bring these regions to the level of California, where all cars from this year onwards will have to run on hydrogen and biogas.

The finals of Scoot-mobile dancing and Zimmer-frame football are being held in Paris today. The events are being broadcast live and can be followed on mobile telephones by the children, grandchildren and great-grandchildren of the participants, of whom the youngest is 89 and the oldest 112.

From today, it is official: the World Government has announced that there are more robots living in the EU than people and, for the first time, there are also fewer pigs than people in the EU. In 2008, doctors showed that pig organs work perfectly in the human body, and an increasing number of infected human organs have been replaced by organs from pigs or artificially created organs. This resulted in a mass slaughter of pigs. Europeans now live longer and healthier lives and health costs have been reduced by 50%.

The famines in Africa, Indonesia, Iran and Pakistan have so far this year cost the lives of more than 300 million people, and current prognoses suggest that an additional 400 million people will die in these regions by the end of the year, the World Government announced today. This is a consequence of over-population. The World Government has forbidden any emergency help to these regions, because otherwise the agreements on world population reduction made at Climate Convention Gore X in January 2022 will not be achieved. At this convention, under the leadership of Al Gore, agreement was reached to reduce the world population from 6 billion people in 2007 to just 4 billion in 2050, rather than the figure of 9 billion people previously forecast by the United Nations for 2050. The population explosion, it was concluded, was the major reason for the greenhouse effect. The meteorite Belle II, which hit the earth in 2012, caused a population reduction of one billion people. The world is thus on the right path, reported the World Government with satisfaction.

Personalized messages and advice

Our news service is synchronized to your financial, spare time and business diaries, and thus we can offer you the following advice for today:

- You do not need to wear warm clothing for your 13:15 business lunch; you should, however, take an umbrella. Your lunch is with a person from India. He is from the city where a large university campus was built last week; you are advised to mention this to him. You can obtain more information about him via his avatar.

- Select code 9595 during your 16:00 hairdresser appointment. This code is for the trendiest hairstyle around at the moment, very suitable for men now that they no longer turn bald and for men in your age category (50+); it can also withstand the heat of summer. Even when temperatures rise in the afternoon to 40 degrees Celsius, the air-conditioning in your hat will work perfectly and your hair will blow seductively in the wind.
- Your investments have been automatically adjusted in line with developments in the US, China and Europe. ☐

Twelve pillars of power

In the new economic world order, twelve pillars of power will design our future as humankind. This chapter will introduce them. In this new economic world order, the financial industry will attain a new position and fulfil new roles.

The world economic, political and military power relationships were, for a long time, clear. After the end of the Second World War, two countries – the United States and the Soviet Union – were the only economic and military superpowers. The 'cold war' raged between the two of them, and other countries chose one side or the other. Also after the Second World War, Japan developed into the second richest country in the world, although this was not translated into political, diplomatic or military power. However, the fall of the Berlin Wall in 1989 and the disintegration of the Soviet Union in 1991 radically changed this picture of the world.

At the start of the twenty-first century, the United States still tops the league of the world order, but is seeing its power reduced in some ways. Other countries are growing stronger. Worldwide, a new economic order is emerging that will overturn the current balance of power. This is partly caused by the rekindling of Chinese ambition. China was a superpower earlier in its history (e.g., during the Han, Tang and Ming dynasties), but time and again lost that position. By 1421, China had discovered America and Australia, as argued by Gavin Menzies in his book *1421*. The Chinese carefully mapped out these continents (Columbus had those maps so he knew exactly what he would 'discover') but they never pushed ahead with colonization. The world today would be a different place if they had. Napoleon once said, 'China is a sleeping giant'. That giant is now waking up. Mark Steyn, in his book *America Alone*, states that by the end of this century, America will be the only free Western power and Europe will no longer exist as we know it today because decades of prosperity and peace have made the continent lazy and weak, ripe for the picking by new powers.

The following twelve groups will form the pillars of the new economic world order.

i   Seven economic blocs
ii   Six superpowers
iii   World governmental institutions
iv   Multinationals
v   Tigers
vi   Mixed power and dormant regions
vii   Lost regions
viii   Peaceful networks and diasporas
ix   Angry tribes and networks
x   Technological industry
xi   Religious and moral groups
xii   Financial institutions

i. Economic blocs
The foundations of the European Union were laid in 1951 (under a different name). As a voluntary union of nation states (currently 27 of them), it was economically successful in the beginning of the twenty-first century. With almost 500 million citizens, the EU generated an estimated 30% share of the world's nominal gross domestic product (US$16.6 trillion in 2007).

The EU developed a single market through a standardized system of laws, which apply in all member states, guaranteeing the freedom of movement of people, goods, services and capital. It maintained a common trade policy, agricultural and fisheries policies, and a regional development policy. Fifteen member states have adopted a common currency, the euro. The EU has developed a shaky role in foreign policy: the members agree to disagree about many foreign policy issues. It has also developed a pan-national role in justice and home affairs, including the abolition of passport control between many member states. The EU operation is a hybrid of intergovernmentalism and supranationalism. In certain areas, it depends on agreement

between the member states. However, it also has supranational bodies, able to make decisions without the agreement of members. Important institutions and bodies of the EU include the European Commission, the European Parliament, the Council of the European Union, the European Council, the European Court of Justice and the European Central Bank. EU citizens elect the European Parliament every five years.

Despite its flaws, the EU model is currently being copied in many areas in the world. A bloc not only gives economic advantages, but also has the advantage of making former rivals economically interdependent; hence, it's no longer in their interest to wage wars against each other. In the EU, for example, France and England, who don't really like each other, waged wars against each other for centuries, yet are now interdependent in an economic way. They have now been at peace with each other for the longest stretch of time in history. Uniting rivals such as Pakistan and India and China and Japan in one Asian union might prove to be the most lasting investment in peace in Asia. And peace is good for business.

In North-America, NAFTA was created in 1994. It is a trade bloc formed between the US, Canada and Mexico. In South America, three trade blocs currently exist: Caricom in the Caribbean, and Mercosur and Unasur on the South-American continent. It is expected that these three will merge into one South-American trade bloc in the future. In Russia and the Caucasus a new bloc is to be expected: let's call it the Kremlin+. In the Middle East two blocs might be expected: first, a moderate one, including Turkey, the Emirates and Israel, probably named the Ottoman Union; second, a more Islamist one, let's call it the Osama Union, uniting the fundamentalist forces in the Middle East and North Africa. In Europe, naturally the European Union will stay, yet this bloc will become more economic and less cultural or political (as it's currently trying in vain to be). In Asia, trade blocs like the Association of

Southeast Asian Nations (ASEAN), South Asian Association for Regional Cooperation (SAARC), Asia–Pacific Economic Cooperation (APEC) and others exist. It is expected that in the future these will merge into a single Asian trade bloc, an ASEAN+. In recent years, growing Chinese clout combined with a sympathetic diplomatic posture has helped reorientate the power structure of Southeast Asia towards China. China has become number one or number two trading partner of virtually every country in the region. Seeking strength in numbers, Southeast Asian governments not only strive to tap into China's new wealth, but also to embed Beijing in a thicket of organizations and dialogues in the name of 'community-building' and closer integration. Japan, South Korea and, to a lesser extent, India, Australia and New Zealand also participate in this exercise. In her book *Asia's New Regionalism*, Ellen Frost argues that we are witnessing the resurgence of a 'pre-colonial Maritime Asia' – the sweep of coastal communities, port cities and towns, and waterways connecting Northeast and Southeast Asia, India and Australia. Maritime Asia is the locus of Asian wealth and power. It is where 60% to 70% of ASEAN people live, where the biggest cities are and where globalization-driven investment is concentrated. To take better advantage of this asset, ASEAN governments should explicitly build Maritime Asia into their vision of integration and work with local officials, business representatives and civil society groups to remove the barriers impeding its natural flow, which include border taxes, tariffs, quotas, corruption, crime, antiquated transport links, duplicative security checks and restrictions on labour mobility. For example, ASEAN governments should extend and develop a legal framework for the ASEAN bloc's 'single window' programme, which aims at limiting the cargo clearance of container ships at a major port to one thirty-minute stop and validating it for the entire region.

ii. Superpowers

Superpowers are the second pillar of power in the twenty-first century. In the new age, those countries, according to the business bank Goldman Sachs, will be the United States, Japan, and the so-called BRIC countries – Brazil, Russia, India and China. We shall thus have a world with six superpowers. Incidentally, Russia will be the smallest superpower, economically speaking. The Russian economy runs parallel to oil and gas, which makes the economy extremely one-sided, and the countries Russia exports to in time want to get rid of their depedency on the autocratic Russians. What's more, Russia is facing a serious decline in its population. Even so, the oil and gas reserves in Russia are so large that it will be able to earn a lot from them for some considerable time, not least thanks to the pipelines to the EU, China, Japan and India.

In 2007 a Russian submarine planted a flag on the bottom of the Arctic Ocean. According to the Russians a large portion of the North Pole forms a natural extension of their country, a point of view that other countries, including the United States, do not share. The North Pole is not only known for its melting ice caps, but also for the potentially large amounts of raw materials it holds, including oil and gas.

Russia is also struggling with problems on its borders. After the Soviet Union broke up, Russia lost its control of the outlying regions so that it can

to tackle the problems in the world. The United Nations is not able to prevent further growth of the already too large world population. The UN Security Council does not represent new powers such as the BRIC countries. UN peacekeeping troops and NATO forces are fighting wars that can never be won, as in Iraq and Afghanistan, thanks to the surplus of fighting-age boys over there. Boys from a one-son family are sent to fight against boys from a eight-sons family. They have so many spare troops, these wars can never be won.

Financial institutions such as the World Bank and the IMF are not able to govern adequately the complex world economy and its new financial player. Henry A. Kissinger stated: 'The International Monetary Fund as presently constituted is an anachronism. It has been a bystander in the financial crises of the twenty-first century, which have been produced by practices within the private sectors. The IMF has sought to adapt, but too slowly; it needs to be reformed.'

Nout Wellink, president-director of the Dutch Bank, agrees with Kissinger: 'Globalization in the financial world has a direct impact on the institutional setup of the international financial system. Previously, countries that got into financial problems automatically turned to the IMF, where they could borrow money under all sorts of terms and conditions. These days they no longer need the IMF, but can turn to a variety of other sources [like hedge funds and sovereign wealth funds, ed.] that usually do not impose all sorts of difficult conditions. The relevance and role of organizations like the IMF or the World Bank is clearly diminishing, because "the market" is taking it over. A trend that I think will continue for some time yet.'

Wellink does not expect a type of financial world government to arise, but rather sees a self-regulatory market as the ultimate authority: 'What one would like is to develop some sort of self-regulatory systems, systems that also have good buffers, as there will certainly be crises from time to time. The ever-present irrational behavior of people – like spending everything and more in times of plenty – must be able to be dealt with and corrected by the system, by the market itself.' All the same, an international financial/economic consultative body will remain necessary.

According to our analysis at Trend Office Bakas, it is most probable that the seven economic blocs will create an institution in which they will negotiate trade and world financial and economic issues, as well as issues of morality and politics, how to divide natural resources (e.g. at the North Pole) and how to organize space travel. Since this institution will only consist of seven parties, it will most probably find it easier to reach compromises than in the current UN, where more than 140 parties need to reach an agreement, a lost cause from the start.

We also expect, and strongly advocate, the creation of a World Crisis Fund, which can be used in times of emergency. We do not expect there to be a world army that might be used to fight large-scale wars in the future. Major wars will be out of fashion; wars on a much smaller scale will erupt more frequently (e.g. in the form of attacks by terror networks). Smaller local armies, often privatized, will fight these wars. Neither nation states nor global institutions will no longer be able to fight wars on this scale or be able to give the people the security needed in the new time and age. We can see the pirates off East Africa coast as a present-day example of such conflicts.

iv. Multinationals

Multinationals are more powerful than many countries. Exxon Mobil, for example, had profits in 2007 that were greater than the GDP of Bahrain and Yemen combined. In today's world, more than a hundred companies report annual sales in excess of $50 billion, whereas only about sixty countries report an annual GDP of more than $50 billion. Of course, sales and GDP cannot be taken as equivalents, but these figures give an insight into the economic power wielded by some companies.

Multinationals may have their origins in one country, but a multinational is never nationalistic. For a multinational, national issues are less important than international issues. Multinationals have become superpowers that considerably influence decisions about life and work, economy and society in the countries in which they operate. The board of a multinational is often more powerful than a government.

v. Tigers

Tigers are areas in the world with a strong economic foundation and efficient talent management. They are ambitious, well governed, full of confidence and wealthy, but in size simply too small to play the role of superpower. The key question to ask is in which direction they will move. Sometimes tigers are independent smaller countries; sometimes they are regions within countries. Tiger countries include Switzerland, Singapore, Chile, Taiwan, Vietnam, South Korea, and Canada. Some tiger regions within countries are Bavaria in Germany, South China, Punjab and Maharashtra in India and South Brazil.

vi. Mixed power and dormant regions

Some regions, countries and cities in the world will be divided between strong and weak parts. A lot of big cities, for example, have rich parts where highly skilled people live and work. They are expected to become even richer in the future; they anticipate that their skills will gain them ever more money to invest and to spend. They obtain a liberal lifestyle, love globalization and technology and for them multiculturality is in most cases a form of natural enrichment. On the other hand, this same city harbours a large group of people who are losers in the process of globalization. These 'angry tribes' are becoming poorer, have no relevant skills for the new world order, and do not possess the spirit, ambition or intelligence to obtain anything at all. Technology makes them jobless and the ghetto-ization of the neighbourhoods in which they live is creating tension. In several regions of the world, we see these mixed power regions emerge. Keeping these powers in balance and managing the anger of the losers will become one of the major issues in these parts.

Several such regions and countries are currently dormant. Some have reached considerable heights in economic or cultural fields, but have now gone into decline. They are reasonably stable, with a population that is predominantly grey. They are not innovative, do not excel in any single field, perform averagely, live from investments made in better times, and are really areas and nations that have gone into retirement. Their populations have few ambitions to become world-beaters and their institutions have withered. Life is quite pleasant in these regions thanks to the peace and the stable political climate. Everyone has had their five minutes of fame in history.

In the 1920s Argentina and Uruguay were among the eight richest countries in the world; now they are a long way from that position. In 1900, Britain was the sole superpower in the world; now it's not a super-power at all. Losing a leading position can happen abruptly but most often it happens gradually. If you earn, say, 5 euros less every month than the month before, you don't feel the loss so urgently that you see any crucial need for change. This scenario led to the decline of Argentina in the early 1900s and it might lead to the decline of some of the mixed power regions in the twenty-first century.

vii. Lost regions

As mentioned above, there are winners and losers in globalization. History has never been fair and the future won't be fair either. Some regions and some peoples will be the losers of the future. Lost regions have little or nothing. The largest part of the population there lives in poverty, afflicted by permanent lack of water, (civil) war, corrupt government, extreme population growth, human rights contraventions and so on. These are countries such as Chad, Pakistan, Afghanistan, Congo, Somalia and Sudan. On the whole, they have few prospects. The people of these regions are permanently angry with themselves as well as with the rest of the world, and it isn't possible to relieve their anger. What these regions have in common is the prevailing mood of injury. In fact, there is a mixture of perceived superiority and an inferiority complex.

When these countries act out their anger, it is sometimes supported by the population, sometimes not, and sometimes only with partial backing. Since they are all dictatorships, it is difficult to estimate exactly how great the support is because objective sampling isn't possible. Nationalistic arguments are often used to justify the anger. Although economically less important, or otherwise irrelevant, their anger can be frightening to the rest of the world, and the lost regions can blackmail other pillars of power tremendously. The current rise of Islamism in Europe is possible thanks to their ability to scare indigenous Europeans successfully.

President Obama will look at Pakistan as a potential nightmare. Most media attention focuses on neigbouring Afghanistan but Pakistan is potentially a bigger problem because of its nuclear arsenal. In certain regions of Pakistan, radical Islamist groups are gaining ever more political power, which poses a threat to stability within Pakistan. Many fear that radical groups will get hold of the nuclear arsenal: when that happens, the shit hits the fan.

Another threat comes from the rising levels of piracy emanating from Somalia. Because of their lack of opportunities to make a reasonable living, Somalis have taken up piracy as a lucrative profession. Somalia itself does not have the political power and infrastructure to prevent this. Other trading nations that are affected by piracy have to act for themselves, with all of the conflicting power questions that go along with this. If this piracy is not stopped quickly, people in other lost regions might gain inspiration to follow the Somalis with this illicit activity.

What could help in lost regions is to promote economic growth from inside by means of using microloan programmes for the women. There is a saying that goes: 'Educate a boy and you educate only that boy. But educate a girl and you educate her entire family.' Especially in the Muslim world, which is dominated by men, there is room for women to have their own businesses. For example, from history we know that Khadija, the beloved first wife of the prophet Muhammad, was a self-made merchant who employed her husband for many years.

viii. Peaceful networks and diasporas

In the old world, most people were concentrated in certain regions where they originated. However, migration waves changed the way people lived. Even in the old world, we know of diasporas: people of one origin who were living scattered around the world. The Jewish diaspora started after the first temple of the Jews in Jerusalem was sacked by the Romans in the first century AD. This diaspora grew and became powerful all over the world, despite the fact that the Jews had to do without a homeland before the founding of Israel in 1948. The Tibetan diaspora was established but became bigger in the 1950s and grew further thanks to the support of Hollywood stars like Richard Gere. The Armenian diaspora started in the 1920s. There are more people of Italian descent living outside of Italy than within the country. Currently there are more than 60 million Chinese living outside of China, more than 35 million Indians outside of India, and more than 7 million Americans outside of the US. The gay diaspora of homosexual men and women has always existed, since between 5% and 10% of the people in the world is gay. Thanks to globalization and new media they were able to develop a global lifestyle and organize themselves into a powerful tribe. It seems that the global tribe of Freemasons has always been there, yet their power has always been hidden, as goes for the members of The Bilderberg Conference and the Mormons. In the new world, these tribes and diasporas of people, with multiple loyalties in parallel, will play an increasingly important role.

Powerful individuals will influence the world in more ways than the eye can see. Richard Branson, who finances inventors of new energy sources, may change the world in a more important way than we currently expect. George Soros influenced the Asian crisis a couple of years ago. In the future, thanks to new media like YouTube, new heroes will emerge more quickly than before and will gain popularity more easily than in the past. New professional networks and new virtual friends networks, like Myspace, CyWorld, MSN and others, will also become more powerful. All in all, this pillar of power will influence the world in more ways than one.

Managing multiple loyalties is difficult. European security agencies reported in 2007 that some Europeans of Chinese descent were arrested because they spied for Chinese companies. And the Indian IT company Infosys, working for the airline industry, reported that some Muslim employees tried to infiltrate their IT programs for Boeing and Airbus, in order to make bomb attacks on flights with these planes easier. On the other hand, double loyalties can also be used to smooth out differences and to build bridges.

ix. Angry tribes and networks

Angry tribes are groups of people that are unhappy with the way the world is developing. Some are white Westerners who have lost their jobs to immigrants; others are immigrants who are disappointed in their new homelands. Some are activists with a specific agenda that isn't in the mainstream (Earth Liberation Front, Animal Liberation Front). Some

are groups with a separatist terrorist tradition (such as the IRA in the UK or ETA in Spain); some have a political agenda, like the communists in India who attack multinationals; others have a more nationalistic or even xenophobic agenda. All of these tribes are opposed to globalization.

Traditionally, one-third of any population supports change, a third opposes any change and the remaining third is indifferent, as long as their own interests are not affected. The people who are against renewal are a varied bunch, voting extreme right, extreme left or not at all.

x. Technological industry

As already mentioned, the financial services industry has expanded massively over the past twenty years. In the opinion of Nout Wellink, head of the Dutch central bank, 'the development in the financial sector is technology driven'. Technology made people connected permanently and provided more mobility and flexibility than ever. In the future, technology will continue to be of crucial importance as one of the twelve pillars of power. It will cause the nature of business to be altered extensively. In megatrend 5, we will explain how this is supposed to happen.

xi. Religious and moral groups

We are living in times where religious demarcation lines are sharper than they have been in a very long time, and people are more conscious about their religious background. After a period of liberalization and secularization there is a recurrent call in the West for clear, compelling moral rules. Ethics is once again centre stage, mainly because it gives people the idea that they can come to grips with things again. In these hectic, unsafe and uncertain times, people long for a more orderly world that is characterized by respect and decency. The Kondratieff Wave Patterns also indicate that following a period in which the accent has been on increasing affluence, we then arrive in a period in which the focus is on increasing well-being, and in which ethics play an important part.

The moral views in this world are often expressed by worldwide organizations like Greenpeace and Amnesty International, organizations with considerable power through their influence on public opinion. A big part of the economy is ruled by emotions, and these moral organizations have a big impact on how people feel about a range of issues.

Although many people think that religion will be out of fashion in the new world, this is definitely not the case. Most parts of the world, including the most technologically advanced countries, are still religious, and the quest for morals and ethical boundaries will make people increasingly look to religions. This is evident even in high-tech regions such as Silicon Valley, where one technological whizz-kid recently stated: 'I don't believe in God any more, but I do miss Him'. More about this below, under megatrends 7 and 9.

xii. Financial institutions

The world is expected to become richer, with both the middle classes and elites expected to grow, according to the *World Wealth Report* of Merrill Lynch. Traditional financial institutions are expected to play a major role in financing the new economic world order. Banks, pension funds, credit card companies, accountants, lease companies, insurance companies and other financial bodies will play an important role in the future. However, they will have to share power with new players like hedge funds, private equity firms, sovereign wealth funds and even players from other lines of business. New coalitions and partnerships with companies from outside the financial sector will strengthen the position of this pillar of power.

The investment policies of the financial companies will be crucial in deciding in which direction the world develops. For example, their decision to invest in sustainability and in clean, alternative sources of energy would be crucial for the development of a new energy economy. Yet, within this pillar of power, we might expect shifting balances and a new lack of clear focus.

Conclusion: History returns

The twelve pillars of power described above will interact with each other and together will model and remodel the world and its people on the way to tomorrow. How will these pillars interplay with each other? Robert Kagan gives an idea in his book *The Return of History and the End of Dreams*. Kagan argues that the apparent triumph of liberal democracy in the 1990s was fleeting and that an era of renewed great power competition is upon us. That competition is marked by the tension between two political traditions: Western liberal democracies and Eastern autocracies, primarily a resurgent Russia and a rising China. He thinks that we are going back to something that looks more like the nineteenth century. However, in his opinion, we are not necessarily talking about isolation and confrontation.

China: superpower in the twenty-first century or a repetition of the mistakes of 1421?

The twenty-first century will be the century of Asia. Analysts are in complete agreement that India and China will become new Asian superpowers. But will China continue along its current trends? China is a world power. Several decades ago, that was inconceivable, but now it is a fact of life. It is a perspective that is rooted in history. There were times when China was as rich and powerful as it would now like to become. The Chinese, inhabitants of the oldest existing empire in the world, have a long memory.

China as former superpower

The first era of China's world dominance lasted from approximately 200 BC to 200 AD, during the period of the Han emperors. China expanded and conquered parts of Korea and Vietnam, as well as areas along the Silk Road. This route was used for trade by other nations, including the Roman Empire. But it was not only silk that found its way to the West: other Chinese inventions such as paper and porcelain also found their way along this route. In the West, we are taught about the might of the Roman Empire. Few learn much about China, which was just as powerful and prosperous in that period. China flourished for a second time in a period lasting from the seventh to the ninth centuries, during the Tang dynasty. Europe had been thrown back into the dark ages and China was superior in almost every field: economic, political, scientific and cultural. Printing – a Chinese invention – turned China into the first information society in the world. (There are still many in the West who believe that this honour fell, centuries later, to Gutenberg or Lourens Janszoon Coster.) At that time, Xian, the former capital of China, had around 2 million inhabitants and was thus by far the largest city in the world.

1421

With the advent of the Ming dynasty, which lasted from the fourteenth to the seventeenth centuries, China attained a new level of power. All China's neighbours, from Japan to Siam (Thailand), paid tribute to the Chinese emperor. China was by the far the most powerful trading nation in the world. It had trading settlements along the Indian Ocean right into Africa. At the start of the fifteenth century, when the Europeans still believe that the world was flat, the Ming emperor Zhu Di had a mighty fleet of hundreds of sailing ships built in order to map the world. He wanted to trade not only in Asia and Eastern Africa, but also in countries that had not yet been discovered, so that they

could be brought under his influence. In 1421, the fleet left China under the leadership of eunuchs (castrated men), the most faithful and loved allies of the emperor. The best cartographers, sailors and navigational instruments were on board. The fleet soon split up in order to discover and map various parts of the world. They reached the coasts of Australia, Antarctica, North and South America, and West Africa. They established some settlements there and took away native plants and animals to offer as gifts to the emperor. After two years of sailing and deprivation, the ships that had not been lost returned to China with a treasure of knowledge and maps of the whole world. But China had changed much in the time the fleet had been away. The population was threatening to rebel against the astronomically high taxes needed to finance the fleet and the building of the new capital, Beijing. To add insult to injury, a fire destroyed the imperial palace. Many believed that the gods were punishing the emperor for his arrogance in wanting to map the world and bring it under his power. In just a few years, China changed from an imperial superpower into an introverted giant which slowly fell asleep. World trade and distant expeditions became anathema. The maps and logs of the fleet were largely destroyed. Several maps reached the West by way of the Silk Road and were then adapted. They formed the basis for Columbus's 'discovery' of America: thanks to the Chinese, he knew exactly what he was going to find. The knowledge that could have been used to secure world dominance was largely lost. Europe took over the baton, and European powers would rule the seas for centuries to come. European cultures would dominate the world until the start of the twenty-first century.

China in the twenty-first century

China is now resurgent. The big question is how it will use its growing power in the twenty-first century. Will it this time be able to maintain its emergence and become a

superpower, or will it ultimately give up its imperialistic ambitions, as happened in the fifteenth century? Although China is building its large military force, it does not yet look as if it will use this force offensively. At the moment, China is moving mainly towards an economic and popularity assault on the Western world, largely directed at the leading superpower, America. During a visit by President Hu Jintao to Russia in 2007, the popularity of China appeared to be just as extensive as the anti-Americanism of the Russians. An opinion poll in Russia showed that the Russians consider China a good influence on the world and the United States a bad influence. This probably had a lot to do with the poor image of the Bush administration. It is expected that the new American adminsistration will gain more international popularity for the US. China is trying to make its most important cities as attractive as possible for Russian business people and tourists. The large numbers in this latter group in particular take positive stories back with them to their home country. The popularity and economy of China are both growing rapidly (despite some backlashes such as the human rights demonstrations during the Beijing Olympics in 2008), but the speed with which this is happening must be maintained.

The enormous growth in China means an increasing demand for raw materials such as oil for industry. This will have to be available for growth to be maintained. Similarly, in the area of human rights, something that is a fully accepted part of the Western world, things will have to change if the contacts between China and the rest of the world are to run smoothly. There is already a lot of change taking place in the legal field. Prosperity is growing in China, but if the whole country is to be and remain successful, this prosperity must be cleverly divided. This demands a good internal market system with well-organized banks. Employment must also be utilized cleverly and a good education must not be limited to the elite. Many Chinese in recent years have come to Europe to study. People with a technical academic background will acknowledge the large numbers of Chinese they see in lecture and study halls. (These Chinese, by the way, often spend much of their time in university computer rooms communicating via webcams with the people back home in China.) The tide, however, is turning. China is slowly learning the success formulas from the West and is combining these with its own knowledge and successes. Chinese students are now increasingly choosing a university in their own country. What's more, large groups of students from the West are now attending educational institutions in China. If China maintains its own qualities, adapts in certain areas to the values held in the rest of the world and ensures a good organization of labour, resources and capital, then there will be no stopping its development into a superpower. ☐

Brazil: From internal market to global market

Brazil today can be seen as a globalized country, not only according to the international meaning of the word, but also because it comprises an ethnically and culturally diverse entity – "globalized internally" by the Portuguese language and the continental nature of its territory, and by the ethnic and cultural mix of the populations of its major cities.

The country's internal cultural dialogue is in any event no longer territorially confined and circumscribed; to understand Brazil, it is necessary to comprehend some of the processes that have defined its structure and history over the past twenty years, and which will continue to define its history and world role for at least the next thirty years.

Brazil underwent a process of re-democratization in the mid-1980s and the beginning of the 1990s after twenty years of military dictatorship and an economic model characterized by market restriction. The economy was opened up at the beginning of the 1990s, resulting in the restructuring of Brazilian industry (which has also become more competitive) and Brazilian society in general. In the past ten years, the consumer market has embraced millions of people who were previously excluded from it. These new consumers come from multicultural and multi-ethnic groups in different regions of the country, and their dialogue with the market is not confined to mere trend-led consumption, but includes the diffusion of new demands and products into their own regional cultures.

In this sense, it is possible to discern in the current situation in Brazil a co-habitation of the global and the regional, and new factors will join those described here in decades to come.

Brazil will probably make full use of its potential to expand its participation in the global market in the next thirty years in a new process of industrialization similar to that experienced in the emerging Asian countries, which saw the widespread dissemination of their cultures and products. Examples that spring to mind are the urban art of São

Paulo and Rio de Janeiro, the electronic Bossa Nova, and the combination of African, Indian, European and Eastern cultures they represent.

This means that tendencies that were formerly regional in character will spread not only throughout the territory of Brazil, but also internationally. Artists, designers, brands and fashion houses often bring elements of Brazilian culture to Europe, the United States and Asia, creating a dialogue with the products of each particular external market. Brazil is becoming a location for important international events, such as São Paulo Fashion Week, and is the exporter of famous brands and products such as Havaianas sandals and the designs of the Campana brothers.

Another aspect that is developing in this society, and which will mark it out in future in the global market, is the enduring strength of its industrial sector, particularly in the area of fashion.

New, upwardly mobile social groups still to emerge will profit from this impetus in order to grow and be successful in Brazil, on the basis of the country's abundant natural resources, international competitiveness, free enterprise system and open market. From these groups will arise a new economic elite.

A class of culturally aware consumers and producers is also emerging, ready to seize the future moment as an important impetus for personal, social and communal change, and this class will expand its presence in the coming decades.

This new cultural elite is regaining and reconfirming cultural and traditionally Brazilian values in a merging of the contemporary and the old, the modern and the retro. This new class will maintain its involvement in cultural activities, and retain a sense of

social and ecological responsibility in its search for a new model of development. This new model will be embraced by a dynamic country in which wealth and poverty, the rustic and the refined, the new and the old coexist: a land of contrasts, emerging as a new industrial and cultural force, and asserting its economic and political presence on a global and a regional level. □

Arthur de Toledo Verga holds a Masters in Education Arts and Cultural History. He is professor of Industrial Design at Mackenzie University, São Paulo.

Megatrend 2

Towards major demographic changes in the world

George and Francis are enjoying their tea. They are celebrating George's seventy-sixth birthday. This year, the retirement age in the UK has been raised to eighty-five; ten years ago it was seventy-five and George had been expecting to retire at an earlier age but he doesn't mind having to work until he's eighty-five. Francis, who is ninety-seven, sits at home most days, bored. His VirtualMe says that his life expectancy is 112 years, so he will have to manage his boredom for quite a while before he can enter heaven. Last year his wife bought him a soundproof Yamaha portable studio and she now expects him to spend most of his days in it. He can use his computer, play with his toy trains and communicate with other people around the world when he's locked up in there. His wife bought this soundproof studio because she concluded Francis is suffering from Retired Husband Syndrome. Since his retirement, he had started complaining about the quality of her omelettes despite having always eaten them without complaining before. The Yamaha box has, since its invention in Japan in 2007, become a best-seller all over Britain. Francis decided to coach young George, who had been suffering from stress.

The almost total lack of privacy in this present time makes it more and more difficult for George to see his seventy-eight-years-young girlfriend in private; his wife can track most of his movements. He enjoys working, so overtime is a good excuse for his absence. However, his wife's VirtualMe can trace him. Francis asked his web community if they had ways of deceiving the VirtualMe avatar of George's jealous wife so he could happily enjoy his extramarital affair. One member of his web community – young Mr Grace, a spritely 115-year-old – found an ingenious way to fool the high-tech avatar, and George's stress has now been reduced to an all-time low. The two friends smile and enjoy the birds singing in the wind. Technology is fine, but nothing beats human naughtiness. ☐

World population growth slows down

Looking at recent projections from the United Nations, world population growth has slowed and it is likely that it will slow further. It's important to notice that this slowdown differs markedly between the so-called 'developed' and 'less developed' nations. Population growth has been much faster in the poorer countries than in those with high standards of living and wealth. Whereas the developed countries of Europe, North America, Australia and New Zealand accounted for roughly one-third of world population in 1900, and about the same proportion in 1950, those countries accounted for just 20% of the world's population by 2000. It seems likely, however, that the population growth of many lesser developed countries will slow during the present century.

World population has more than doubled in the past fifty years, and it has nearly quadrupled since 1900. Currently, world population is growing at a rate of 1.35% per year. The United Nations' most recent forecast, however, predicts a slowing in the growth of world population to about 0.33% per year by 2050. Forecasters are predicting that world population will top 9 billion people in that year. It is interesting to compare this with the UN's 1976 forecasts. At that time, it was believed that world population could climb to 15 or even 20 billion people around 2100! The one-child policy that China began in 1979 certainly contributed to the change of the forecasts. So, we should be happy with 9 billion and it might even be less. India, the second most populous country after China, might face similar government restrictions on number of births to keep population and their needs in balance. However, India is a democracy so birth-control has to come as free will. Another and more humane solution is to give women interesting lives. James Martin stated in his book *The meaning of the twenty-first century* that raising the quality of life of women will lower the fertility rate. This means that women need an equal place in society next to their husbands to develop themselves and have good lives. The example of micro-loans for entrepreneurial women in poor countries has shown that this can help in lowering birth rates and at the same time put underdeveloped nations on a course to a better future. For the time being, world population is still growing and this creates increasing pressure on the environment, climate, and availability of water and food recources. Unfortunately, this growth will mainly take place in the poorer countries, which are already struggling to cope with all of the negative aspects of a growing population. Up until 2050, the problems will only get worse unless technological innovations can relieve the pressure.

Increasing ageing of world population

Combining the slowdown of the world's population growth with improvements in life expectancy we will see a rapid ageing of the population, which is shown in the table below. A good summary measure of a population's age is the median age – an age such that half the population is older and half is younger. Over the past half century, the median age of the world's population has increased by 2.8 years, from 23.6 in 1950 to 26.4 in 2000. The UN forecasts median age to rise to 38.1 years in 2050. More developed countries are expected to have an increase in median age from 38.6 years to 45.7 years, and lesser developed countries from 24.1 years to 35.7 years. Using an estimate for 2005, Japan is the country with the oldest population, having a median age of 42.9 years. Japan is projected to have a median age of 54.9 years in 2050. Similar changes are occurring in Europe. Italy, with a median age of 42.0 years in 2005, is projected to have a median age of 50.4 years in 2050. The United States is not excluded from this ageing, although it remains somewhat younger. The median age of the US population is currently 36.0 years, and is forecast to be 41.1 years in 2050.

China deserves a closer look. Because of the one child policy adopted under Mao, population growth will slow down much faster than in any other less developed countries and even some developed countries. A substantial demographic change will take place. Between 2005 and 2050, the median age in China is projected to increase from 32.5 years to 45.0 years. These projections indicate that in 2050 China's median population age will be *above* that of the United States.

The world's fastest growing age group comprises people of eighty years and older. In 2000, 1.1% of world population was aged eighty or older. By 2050, this number is expected to be 4.4% of world population. In that year, twenty-one countries or areas are projected to have at least 10% of their population aged eighty or over. Japan is forecast to have 15.5% of its population aged eighty or above. In Italy, this figure is projected to reach 13.3% of its population while for the United States it will be 7.6%.

What's good to know about an ageing population is that they tend to spend more than they save. After all, they are in the autumn of their lives and often have guaranteed pensions. That is encouraging news for the economy.

Population projections

Country/Area	Median age 2005	Median age 2050	Percentage of population 65 or older 2005	Percentage of population 65 or older 2050	Percentage of population 80 or older 2005	Percentage of population 80 or older 2050
World	28.0	38.1	7.3	16.2	1.3	4.4
More developed regions	38.6	45.7	15.3	26.1	3.7	9.4
Less developed regions	25.5	36.9	5.5	14.7	0.8	3.6
Least developed countries	19.0	27.9	3.3	6.9	0.4	1.1
Africa	19.0	28.0	3.4	6.9	0.4	1.1
Asia	27.6	40.2	6.4	17.5	1.0	4.5
China	32.5	45.0	7.7	23.7	1.2	7.3
India	23.8	38.6	5.0	14.5	0.7	3.1
Japan	42.9	54.9	19.7	37.7	4.8	15.5
Europe	38.9	47.3	15.9	27.6	3.5	9.6
Austria	40.1	48.0	16.2	29.0	4.3	11.9
Belgium	40.3	46.2	17.3	27.1	4.3	10.7
Denmark	39.5	43.8	15.1	23.9	4.1	9.2
Finland	40.9	44.4	15.9	25.6	4.0	10.0
France	38.9	44.7	16.3	25.9	4.6	10.2
Germany	42.1	49.4	18.8	30.2	4.4	13.1
Greece	40.1	50.1	18.3	31.7	3.5	11.1
Iceland	34.2	44.6	11.7	25.4	3.0	9.6
Ireland	33.4	43.0	11.1	23.4	2.7	6.7
Italy	42.0	50.4	19.7	32.6	5.1	13.3
Luxembourg	38.3	40.4	14.2	19.5	3.2	6.9
Netherlands	39.1	44.2	14.2	25.2	3.6	10.4
Norway	38.0	43.7	14.7	23.8	4.6	9.0
Portugal	39.1	48.8	16.9	30.7	3.7	10.1
Russian Federation	37.3	45.3	13.8	23.8	2.1	5.8
Spain	38.8	49.5	16.8	33.2	4.3	12.2
Sweden	40.2	43.3	17.2	24.1	5.3	9.3
Switzerland	40.1	44.2	15.4	25.0	4.3	11.0
Ukraine	38.9	50.0	16.1	27.6	2.6	7.1
United Kingdom	38.9	43.4	16.1	24.1	4.5	9.2
Latin America/Caribbean	26.0	40.1	6.3	18.5	1.2	5.2
North America	36.3	41.5	12.3	21.5	3.5	7.8
Canada	38.6	45.3	13.1	25.7	3.5	10.0
United States	36.0	41.1	12.3	21.0	3.5	7.6
Oceania	32.3	40.0	10.3	19.4	2.6	6.8
Australia	36.7	43.4	13.1	24.3	3.5	9.3
New Zealand	35.5	44.1	12.2	24.1	3.2	9.2

Source: World Population Prospects: The 2006 Revision Population Database, United Nations Population Division.

Boys surplus

As well as the trend of people getting older, there is another trend in some areas of the world that looks quite worrying: 'boys surplus'. In the history of mankind, wars always erupted in times of a boys surplus according to Gunnar Heinsohn, sociologist at the University of Bremen. Every local economy has a market for only two sons in every family. In the past, the first son inherited his father's business and the second son became a priest or migrated. If you had more sons, you were in trouble as a family. All the testosterone in boys needs to be released in one way or another. They do not necessarily want to fight but if they don't have any economic opportunity, they will. Usually there are two scenarios. The first one is the 'kill each other scenario' in which the boys who are superfluous and redundant start to fight each other, until the society has got rid of the surplus of boys. Then peace sets in naturally. This happened, for example, in Rwanda in 1994, when about 1 million excess boys were killed – by each other. When the period of the boys surplus was over, peace settled in Rwanda. The second scenario is 'new ideology, new leader'. In this scenario there is a market for a new, violent ideology that provides the redundant and unloved boys an opportunity to set things straight. At least, that's what they think. This ideology always focuses on rich yet militarily weak enemies, which are targeted first in order to provide the boys surplus a quick hit of easily gained successes and money. Then it focuses on taking over power in the whole region. A smart leader who invents such an ideology and is able to mobilize the masses of redundant boys in the fighting age between fifteen and thirty-five is thus able to grab power. After coming to power, the leader gets rid of the boys surplus anyway, to prevent them bringing a rival to power in case he fails to deliver what the boys expect from him. Here are some examples. In the late nineteenth and early twentieth century Russia experienced a 'boys surplus'. Communism was created, with a strong leader, Lenin, and the boys surplus brought him to power. Yet communism could not deliver the boys' aspirations, so Lenin's successor, Stalin, got rid of tens of millions of the surplus boys. The same happened in China in the 1920s and 30s, where a boys surplus brought the communists to power under the leadership of Mao Zedong. After coming to power, Mao too could not deliver what his boys wanted, so he got rid of millions of them. In Germany at around the same time, nazism and Hitler came to power thanks to the boys surplus. The Second World War saw to it that Hitler's boys surplus was eradicated.

Today, it is possible to see a boys surplus in China and in the Islamic world. Within the Islamic world alone, there are currently 60 million redundant boys redundant in the fighting age range between fifteen and thirty-five. That is the main reason for the success of the relatively new and violent Islamist ideology, a natural successor to communism and nazism.   □

Consequences of the growth slowdown and ageing of the world population

Housing

Looking closely at the different areas of the world, you can see that there is a big variation in the population depending on where you live. In due course, Europe and Japan will face a decline in population. Russia will have a similar problem. Declining populations cause an emptying of regions, which is no new phenomenon. Europe has known many such periods of decline in the past: for example, there was the emptying of the countryside in France; likewise, Spain and Ireland emptied in the nineteenth century. Geographical shifts of important trade routes have also resulted in a decline in certain areas in the past. For example, the old Punta Arena on the Straits of Magellan in Chile lost its role after the construction of the Panama Canal. Similarly, Kutná Hora in a silver mining region of the Czech Republic was at one time the second city in Bohemia, rivalling Prague. The mines became inoperable and today Kutná Hora is a just small town with 20,000 inhabitants.

A decline in the population

has a number of advantages. Fewer people means less strain on the environment and lower energy and water use. There is more space per head of population, and that is a blessing. But there is also a downside to population decline. In European countries, the focus on the growth function is in such a way that long-term investments come under threat when the social costs for them have to be borne by fewer people. The advantages from economies of scale decrease, which means that the bills governments run up for municipal projects have to be footed by fewer people. Rents and the cost of energy and water are then increased. Tax income decreases and there is not enough money for new developments. This reduction in investment is to the detriment of those people that remain; they become the main victims of the decline process.

East Germany has a special history, and it is therefore difficult to compare it with other declining regions in Europe. Here, it is not only the rural areas that are emptying, but also the cities. The speed with which this is taking place is remarkable. For example, in the new city (in German, Neustadt) of Guben-Spruke, on the outskirts of an old industrial city in the Lausitz, a traditionally agrarian region in South Brandenburg, eighty workers leave every month. Because of this, the population has halved in the past fifty years. The Lausitz became an industrial region following political pressure in the German Democratic Republic (GDR), and grew to be a supra-regional energy centre for the GDR. Because of the enormous growth in the area, the use of industrial building processes became essential. The result was Plattenbausedlungen (prefabricated panel building): independent living complexes with a modern level of appliances, certainly by the standards of the time. They had hot water and central heating, things that were not readily available in the old cities. Thanks to this, the new housing was in great demand. The advantages of these new cities were clear to both urban planners and architects. Thanks to a combination of a high building density and an efficient infrastructure, the actual area on which the buildings were constructed was kept to a minimum, and there was a lot of green space left. The intended facilities, however, were frequently insufficient, or left out because of cost considerations, and the outside areas (and the planting) were seldom completed.

After the fall of the Berlin Wall in 1989, the economy in the region collapsed and many people left to move to the west of the country. Because of this, Lausitz is one of the most rapidly shrinking areas in Europe. In 2001, 12.5% of all housing in Brandenburg was empty.

Such population shrinkage will not take place solely in Germany. French and Italian rural areas are depopulating at a fast pace. In Italy, I have seen villages that used to boast 1,000 inhabitants and now have just twenty. The vacant houses are boarded up. Because so few people live there, there are ever fewer shops: fewer bakers, grocers, supermarkets, petrol stations, and even fewer schools and nurseries. At least the Italian countryside has the advantage of breathtaking beauty; the joyless new cities of East Germany merely beg to be demolished.

The picturesque Italian villages that are empty demand new types of living concepts. They might offer part-time living, as a country retreat for city-dwellers from all parts of Europe, or provide country residences for Chinese, Indians, or people from other strong economies. The village of La Palombara in Italy was deserted by all its inhabitants in the 1970s. Now, city people have moved in, eager to occasionally escape the incessant noise of traffic: they are called bio-regionalists. They do not stay for great lengths of time, because the sound of the wind becomes irritating! There will be more about part-time living arrangements in the future in the following chapters.

So far, various governments have provided subsidies to alleviate the worst problems caused by this depopulation of rural areas (and former GDR cities), but that will eventually stop. You can only spend a euro once. What's more, all these subsidies do not lead to a structural, visionary solu-

tion for the long term. Now that the shrinkage in the population is so drastic in many parts of Europe, the expectation is that, within the foreseeable future, uniform and decisive measures will be taken. It will no longer be enough to demolish unattractive flats of Stalinist design and replace them with municipal parks. Semi-abandoned cities can no longer become like Gruyère cheese, with flats and holes where flats used to stand. In future, whole cities will be razed to the ground and be replaced with areas dedicated to nature conservation, or they will have an 'entertainment' function for European tourists or for those from other countries (e.g. from countries in Asia).

For successful tourism, local inhabitants will, of course, have to become more positive and less xenophobic. There is much to be gained by that: it is, after all, about trade and employment, and for that people are generally prepared to reach some compromise. The buildings that replace those in the east of Germany must be German in origin – replicas of traditional German architecture or retro-building that is timeless – so tourists will know that they are in Germany. In France and Italy, the countryside has retained its authentic character to a much greater degree than in the former East Germany, and people find it charming. Renovation and a good brush-up will be sufficient in those places.

For most other parts in the world, growth will continue but at a slower rate. This means that pressure on finding adequate housing and commensurate infrastructure for everyone will continue. A huge challenge is to transform shantytowns into healthy and safe areas. Construction companies in Western countries, which are facing a decline in building activity, should look south and east. There is enough work for them in the poor countries in the coming decades, with nice returns. Because of the surplus of houses in Europe and Japan, people in other areas could be motivated to move into them. This could be done on a full-time or part-time basis. Openness towards foreigners is therefore important, but this is difficult for Europeans and even more so for the Japanese.

Infrastructure
Looking at Europe and Japan, it will still be necessary to have a good infrastructure but it will be used less intensively, which means that the costs per capita will rise. The same is true of electricity and drainage. Laying and maintaining roads will cost the same as before, but these costs will increasingly be borne by fewer people. It is essential that these people earn more in order to be able to pay for it all. The paradox is that, in this century, Europeans will work less. A smaller group of people will earn more money for shorter working hours in order to foot the bill for the infrastructure in rural areas.

Parking will become an even more important issue than it already is in municipal planning in the modern Europe. The 'rush-hour family' will become the cornerstone of society. The family will take care of partner(s), friends, extended family, children and elderly parents. Combining all this will demand mobility.

Most European cities adopt a car-discouragement policy, however, and that is understandable. But how is, say, a forty-year-old working mother supposed to get around with her kids, their toys, her shopping, and her elderly parents without a car? Policies to discourage or prevent car usage will have to become more nuanced in the future as demographics and lifestyles change. Otherwise, an increasing number of middle-class people belonging to the group of rush-hour families will leave the city and move to the countryside. They will take urban cultural habits with them, so that the rural districts will also become more urbanized. There will be a growing market in Europe for cheap cars, most of which will be imported from China and India, all aimed at greater mobility for the rush-hour family.

How different the picutere looks for the other areas in the world. How fast we can build new roads, railways, harbours and airports will be a main issue for policy-makers in those countries. Look at China, where at a tremendous speed airports are being built. Along with the rapid growth of China's economy, airport construction has achieved great development during the tenth Five-Year Plan period (from 2001 to 2005). By the end of 2005, China had 135 civil scheduled-flight airports in 133 cities compared with just a dozen airports in the 1970s (*source*: China Airport Industry Report, 2006–2010). While China leads in infrastructure investments, other countries are following as well. Brazil and India are expanding quickly, for example. Even parts of Africa, helped by investments from China and other countries, are making headway. In poor countries, there is a lot of 'dead capital' that has not found an interesting investment opportunity. This dead capital consists of people's savings and they simply do not trust most investment opportunies offered in their country. Governments in these poor countries should be aware of this and develop sound and trusted infrastructure projects in which people would dare to invest. The same goes for the local banks; they too need to build more trust.

Employment
In Europe and Japan, the 'grey pressure' is increasing: a shrinking pool of young people must care for a growing number of elderly. There will be more than enough work in the future and young people will not have to worry about mass unemployment because the whole entertainment and care industry for the elderly, not to mention tourism, will offer long-term, stable employment. For a continent that will be made up partly of retirement countries (Western Europe) and partly of productive nations (manufacturing and services in Eastern Europe), and which will have fewer young people, this is a challenge.

To ensure that all of this work is done, parts of it will be taken over by computers and robots. We will soon have computers that are ten times more 'intelligent' than people, and these will be able to take over the

work done by people as they reach retirement age. The relatively scarce group of young people will therefore not have to work excessively hard to compensate for their lower numbers. And, of course, we shall also see more robots like those that have taken on a lot of factory work over recent years (and which don't complain about hours or pay, and never call in sick).

Working animals will also play a role in the employment mix of tomorrow. Recently, a television programme showed how a trained Alsatian took virtually complete care of a handicapped woman. The animal collected her newspaper and shopping, helped her shower and dress, and was also a caring companion (but with more hair than her lady companions of the past). A dog like this can live and work for fourteen years without demanding any wage increases and is virtually never ill. In short, it is a blessing for a person needing care.

The working population of the future will thus be made up of young

people, computers, trained animals and, of course, robots. In this way, it is possible for a limited number of people to achieve a high level of productivity. This will be despite the 'greying' population, the decreasing number of young people, and the shrinkage in the population as a whole.

Other areas in the world will need to invest in new jobs as their populations will continue to grow and more people want to share in the wealth. China, India and Brazil are making good progress with this. However, in the near-term, emigration to the USA, Europe and Japan will be necessary to satisfy the demand for jobs that the workers' home countries cannot provide quickly enough.

Care tourism

The care industry will profit from the growing number of elderly. People cost much more in the final ten years of their lives than in their preceding sixty to seventy years. However, these costs will fall: medical technology is improving, and the elderly are more frequently adopting a healthy lifestyle.

What's more, an increasing number of the elderly are no longer willing to accept ailing all the time: no lengthy deterioration, dementia and other health problems, which not only reduce the quality of life but also create a burden for those around them. Who really wants their nearest and dearest to remember them as a demented, incontinent, incoherently babbling man or woman? More and more seniors will choose to decide for themselves when their lives should end. But, until they die, care is still essential, not only for major medical maintenance but also for routine things like pacemakers, replacement hips, cataract operations and so on.

Globalization of care will take off. The bulk of such medical care will take place in health centres in Dubai, Thailand, Turkey, Eastern Europe and other low-cost countries. The population in those countries will eventually also profit from this globalization of care. Regular treatment, particularly for the young, will still be concentrated in northwest and central Europe.

Financing

People have to be able to finance it all in Europe and Japan. The expectation is that, during the coming decades, the financing of, and policy regarding financing, the lifestyle of seniors will be the most important matter on the political and social agenda. In all countries, a struggle for pensions will erupt, a struggle between generations. Take the UK, where a time bomb is ticking under the pension system. The recent report of a commission under the leadership of Adair Turner, former chairman of the CBI, a UK employers association, advised that this can only be disarmed by decisive and politically controversial measures. According to the report, 12 million UK citizens (40% of the working population)

are saving far too little for their old age. Over the next three decades, pensions will drop by an average of 30% if no hard choices are made about raising taxes and national insurance contributions, obligatory additional saving and a rise in the retirement age. Turner says that UK citizens have, for many years, imagined that they will live in luxury partly because many pension funds are linked to the stock exchange index. 'Irrational behaviour' on the exchange and a 'delayed acknowledgement of a society becoming greyer' meant that many pension funds only took corrective measures towards the end of the 1990s. That was at

least twenty years too late, and the measures are still inadequate, claims Turner.

In Italy, France and Germany, the trade unions have protested, often with mass demonstrations, against any rise in the age of retirement. France has a uniform pension system. When the government recently wanted to raise the age of retirement from fifty-five to fifty-eight, it affected everybody. In Italy, similar circumstances prevailed, but there was an additional problem: people in the private sector had to work longer than their colleagues in the civil service. At the end of last year, the German government lowered the sum that the elderly receive from the state.

Oil-rich Norway will also be confronted with the financial consequences of an ageing population. Norwegians have become lazy because of this wealth, analysts claim. It is all to do with the income from the daily Norwegian oil production of 3.3 million barrels, which is deposited into a government investment fund. This recently reached 1,000 billion kronen (more than €121 billion), which makes it one of the richest pension funds in the world. However, the oil fund is not bottomless. The Norwegian central bank, which manages the fund, recently reported that it cannot pay more than a quarter of the Norwegian pension bill. Taxpayers will have to take care of the rest themselves. The Norwegian government has introduced radical reforms to the state pension system, which is now thirty-seven years old. It is considering raising the pension age from 62 to 67. At the same time, Oslo will cap the annual growth in state pensions.

Most European countries have set aside too little for pensions. In 2004, the European Commission published a report titled *Unequal Welfare States*. The report concludes:

- In almost all European countries, the population is ageing. Since pensioners in general have less income than those working, income inequality will show a slight increase over the next twenty-five years. Poverty will also increase slightly in most countries.
- A policy of lowering pensions will be beneficial to the financing of social welfare, but will increase income inequality and poverty.

Virtually all countries in Europe are facing growing costs for social welfare and private pensions. The ability to finance this can be improved by getting more people to work. This could be through, for example, letting people work to an older age or by encouraging more women to participate in the workforce. In the participation scenario, it is thus assumed that by 2010 all countries will satisfy the employment agreements reached in Lisbon in 2000. The aim is to have 50% of people between the ages of fifty-five and sixty-four, 60% of women and 70% of the total population in work. When more people continue working to an older age, they will build up more rights and their pension will be higher. Such a policy can reduce income inequality and curb an increase in poverty.

Another possibility is a decrease in pensions. This policy has positive effects on the financing of the social welfare system, but negative consequences for both income inequality and poverty. If the elderly receive a lower pension it will bring them closer to the poverty level. An analysis of the characteristics of existing European systems reveals five types of welfare state. The Scandinavian countries have, in general, a social security structure that is largely aimed at increasing labour participation: virtually all women work full time and the pension age is relatively high. The Anglo-Saxon countries (the United Kingdom and Ireland) have a system in which benefits are restricted to combating the worst forms of poverty. In several of the new EU member states (Poland, Hungary, the Czech Republic and Slovakia), the benefits system is fairly restricted. The Mediterranean countries (Italy, Spain, Portugal and Greece) enjoy a fairly generous pension system, but benefits to non-pensioners are still somewhat limited. The Continental countries (Germany, France, Austria, Belgium and Luxemburg) have, on the whole, good regulations for employees. Many of these regulations are based on the cost-winner model and stimulate early retirement.

Other areas in the world will have far fewer problems with financing the pension system as they have enough young people to bear the costs, although, of course, this depends on the condition that wages are high enough for part of it to be spent on pension costs. These countries can learn from the pensions experience in Europe and Japan. China, however, will need to make its pension agenda in anticipation of the strong increased ageing of its population.

Conclusion

The European and Japanese population is ageing and their total numbers are shrinking. This has consequences for the density of the population. An increasing number of ugly and uneconomical cities will be demolished in the near future. In their place will be nature reserves, or there will be facilities for the new European economic foundations, such as recreation. The new or renovated buildings will be historical, or will be replicas of traditional regional architecture. The depopulated rural areas will once again be populated, but now by part-time seniors and juniors who wish to enjoy the pleasures of both town and country. Since the new inhabitants will largely be from the cities, there will be an increasing urbanization of rural culture. Non-Europeans from Asian countries that are becoming more prosperous will purchase their rural retreats in picturesque parts of the European countryside. This will lead to greater industry in the countryside. Busloads of seniors and Asian tourists will come to see how things work in this 'human zoo'.

Migration will largely be from West to East. This will be due mainly to medical care tourism and the fact that real estate is cheaper in the East. A fear of further Islamization in Western Europe will also play a role.

The lifestyles and the way people fill their days will change too. Management of boredom will become an important economic pillar: maintaining a virtual 'family feeling' and 'regional feeling' and cultivating contacts with extended families will be important activities. In short: living with fewer people will, in fifteen to forty-five years' time, result in a lifestyle that is different from the one we currently know.

The other areas of the world won't be bothered by the problems that Europe and Japan are facing. They have to cope with growing numbers of people and how to give them decent living conditions. The countries that manage this well will experience a great economic boom like Western Europe had after World War II. Russia and China will have to be cautious because they might face problems of declining and ageing of populations similar to those in Europe and Japan but without having the levels of savings that have allowed the Europeans and Japanese to cope.

How to create a clean energy future

When I was growing up in a small fishing village in the north-west of Iceland, over 80% of the nation's energy production was based on oil and coal; fossil fuel was the only energy resource utilized in my village. Ocean-going vessels arrived from the European continent and Russia bringing this combustible cargo. My country had to spend a great proportion of the foreign currency available on such costly energy imports. Half a century ago, our position resembled that of most countries in modern times.

Today Iceland has become one of the leading clean-energy countries in the world. All the electricity generated in the country comes from hydropower and geothermal power plants. Houses are heated in the same way, making the energy bill for ordinary families among the lowest in the developed part of the world. Foreign corporations, aluminium smelters, information technology companies and data-storage providers see Iceland as a suitable venue for future operations due to the viability of its clean energy on a long-term basis.

How did this transformation come about? Was it a great governmental plan or the result of a comprehensive international treaty? No. The fundamental shift from oil dependency to a clean-energy economy was produced by a multitude of decisions taken in small communities and large ones, by local councillors and state officials, by village elders and national leaders. It was based on the innovations and technical know-how created by large numbers of scientists, engineers, innovators and thinkers who over the past decades have been inspired to seek new solutions.

In one small fishing town, what started as a minor local geothermal heating system has, through this piecemeal process and bottom-up initiatives, become one of the most technologically advanced clean-energy power stations in the world.

When humankind faces the threat of irreversible climate change and the oil riches of many countries will have disappeared or become minimized, the Icelandic story offers both hope and inspiration, and guidelines to success. Other examples can also be found all over the world.

- Denmark has harnessed wind power on a large scale, so making that small country a leader in energy technology.
- Households in many American cities have demonstrated how urban life can be based on a more sustainable system and thus help to give the US the chance to lead the world if the new Administration encourages local efforts.

- In India, a group of technicians has developed a small and cheap solar lamp, which can bring light to the poor, the billion people who otherwise would have to burn wood to see in darkness. The total cost of bringing such clean energy to one sixth of mankind amounts to but a few weeks of military expenditure by the global superpower.
- In Singapore, the new national library utilizes less than half of the energy normally consumed by similar buildings, demonstrating how energy efficiency can transform urban centres.
- Abu Dhabi is planning the zero-emission Masdar City, utilizing a multitude of new energy technologies created locally in other countries.

The list of initiatives is longer; in fact, endless. The message everywhere is the same: a clean-energy future will be created by encouraging personal initiatives, local enterprises and individual innovators. It will be a combination of democracy and enterprise, the will of the people becoming the ultimate force of transformation.

Ólafur Ragnar Grímsson was inaugurated for his fourth term as President of Iceland in August 2008.

Megatrend 3

Towards new tribalizations

Tim and James take the tube together to their jobs in the City. They chat about life, hobbies, work and society. Both of them are in their early thirties and they generally enjoy life. They work in the creative financial industry and live in the brand new apartments in the Usk Complex. Built in the popular art deco style, yet with all the mod cons of the twenty-first century, the apartment building is everything they both dreamed of. It was designed by a real-estate developer who mixes retro building techniques with high-tech finishing. Everybody who lives in this apartment complex has the same lifestyle. Tim and James only mix with people like themselves, who think, feel and live like they do, whether they live in the same apartment building, or in other places in the region or around the world. Their tribe connects through the internet, parties, VirtualMe avatars and, of course, through work, although the mixed work–life balance of the new century makes work much less of a chore. In the post-material economy in this 'people's century', life is about living and experiencing passions. Their multisexual lifestyle, typical for a metropolis, makes bisexuality normal; all other sexual deviations are looked upon with a humorous indulgence. They have no kids, which is the norm in their tribe. Kids are too much of a hassle anyway. They ignore people of other tribes.

'The only way to find your way in the post-modern world, where globalization and Europeanization have unified the un-unifiable, is to have a strong identity, rooted in your own community,' says Tim. 'This community of our friends and family members, with the same culture, attitudes, tastes, values and lifestyles, gives us such a strong sense of identity, as a village in a fast world, an oasis of peace in a fast moving environment. It's great!' Forever young is the norm in their tribe, whereas in some other tribes the norm is totally different. In the apartments in the next building, the people are more attracted to nature and natural living, James typecasts them as the Nature tribe. 'They only wear clothes of natural fibres, not the ones we prefer that protect us against bullets or knifes, since the nanocells in our clothes function as a harness. They only eat natural foods, straight from the farms, and they are very happy about all this, totally vegetarian, no leather shoes, no furs, no alcohol, no fat in their food. They breed a lot. An average family in this tribe has two to four kids.' People belonging to other tribes live in the other neighbouring apartment buildings. Just in their part of town, Tim and James count about fifty different tribes. In the tube the tribalization is clearly visible: people only talk to members of their own tribe or exchange text messages with tribe members outside the tube, while ignoring the other people in the carriage. Tribalization is here to stay! ☐

Introduction

After the Second World War, the USA, Canada and Australia experienced high levels of immigration. Europe had the same experience when former colonies became independent and when its economy needed more employees than could be found within Europe during the 1960s. These countries now have populations with a diverse mix of cultures and ethnicities. Amsterdam, for example, has the highest number of different nationalities of all cities in the world: in 2006 it was home to nationals from 176 countries. Conversely, during the same period, the other areas in the world saw many of their people emigrate but didn't experience any immigration. They have thus maintained a very homogeneous population.

Inhabitants of previous European colonies moved to their former colonizer: the Congolese to Belgium, North and West Africans and Vietnamese to France and Belgium, Surinamese and Indonesians to the Netherlands, Indians and Pakistanis to the UK. In addition, various diasporas have been witnessed in Europe: Jews can be found in all European countries and so too can Chinese. A large Turkish diaspora can be seen in many European countries, such as Germany and the Netherlands. Muslims are present in virtually every European country, although there are fewer in the eastern nations. Gypsies (Romanies) live in various places spread over the whole of Europe.

Seniors are also on the move. An increasing number of European seniors choose to live, full time or part time, in other regions or countries. Sometimes, it is an individual choice but often they live in groups. The number of people over sixty-five who enjoy their old age in Eastern

Europe is increasing. Houses there are (still) cheap and the cost of living is three to five times lower than in the West. However, the majority of pensioners still live in France, Spain and Portugal. Three months a year, Benidorm is populated by young people; for the rest of the year it is literally grey. There is even a stretch of sand there that is covered with a wooden deck so that people in wheelchairs can enjoy the sea air. For those who wish to venture further onto the beach, there are wheelchairs with large yellow plastic tyres: broad and without profile, they are perfect for pushing an adult through the sand. The terraces offer walking sticks, rolling pathways and other aids. Yet, strangely enough, all this doesn't seem out of place. Life on the boulevard is far from dull. Every morning, gym lessons are held at various places on the beach, one of them taught by an eighty-year-old. Anybody who wants to can join in. People jump up and down on the balconies with a view of the sea. There is live music in a number of bars. Old men in smart white suits sing Frank Sinatra and Bing Crosby standards, accompanied by a tape or synthesizer. If a band is performing and the music is infectious, people dance. They chatter and flirt, admire and show off. It is a grey paradise.

Benidorm, famous for its white sands, has long been a place for people, largely British and Dutch with a limited budget, spending the winter in a kinder climate. It proves that the democratization of the elderly works: it is not just the more affluent European elderly who are able to enjoy part-time living in two places, so too are those with lower incomes. In the near future, this phenomenon will certainly increase, with Turkey becoming a particularly popular destination. The Turks have already built a replica of Amsterdam especially for these groups.

Not a 'melting pot' but a 'salad bowl'

Tribes have come into being throughout Europe and the USA – groups of people who share a culture, religion or life-style, who have spread far afield yet feel a strong cohesion. Europe and the USA have, in fact, become an enormous salad bowl inhabited by large groups of people,

dressed with a Western sauce. In the other areas of the world, tribes also exist but in much smaller numbers than in Europe and the USA. In the twenty-first century, the number of tribes will increase and the size of most tribes will also grow. The tribes manifest themselves increasingly as simultaneous partners and rivals. Sometimes they work together, if their interests demand this, while in other cases they are (economic and/or political) opponents. The characteristic that distinguishes these tribes from the 'mainstream' is that they live in several places. They are people who live part of the year in their homeland and elsewhere for the rest of the year. They are world citizens who really do not need a homeland.

In this way, the distinctive experiences and lifestyles of traditional nation-states disappear, although those various nation-states continue to exist and retain their importance as government-legal entities. There are an increasing number of economic, financial and political cooperative agreements – that's logical in an integration process – but it is unlikely that national governments will allow themselves in the future to be degraded into vassals of a world or regional government, as happened, for example, in the United States. There, although the individual states retain control of a number of important functions (every US state, for example, decides how best to organize its welfare system), government is dominated by the Federal administration, which has powers laid down in the US Constitution that are far greater than those of the European Union. It is naturally unavoidable that in Europe, too, central authority will grow stronger in the coming decades. Although the 2005 rejection of the draft European Constitution by France and the Netherlands offers little hope that it will now be adopted, the influence of the European Commission and the European Parliament should increase as time passes. A European head of state is also a possibility. He or she is unlikely to have anything like as much power as the president of China or the United States, but they would have an important symbolic function. A charismatic, multilingual European president, whose prime function is to act as an ambassador, can help establish European integration firmly in the hearts of both mainstream Europeans and the tribes.

'Glocalization'

Increasing globalization, as evidenced in trade law-making and the disappearance of some borders and import duties, is perceived by the world population as easy and comfortable on the one hand but as increasing anonymity and alienation on the other. As the importance of globalization continues, many fall back on regionalism.

People will cultivate their regional identities and invest in them, learn or revive regional languages and acquaint themselves better with the history and culture of their local area, even if they were not born there. Regionalism will rise above borders. In some areas it has existed for some time but has now been given a new impetus. In others it is totally new. Examples of old regionalism are the Basques (France/Spain), the Catalans (Spain), the Frisians (the Netherlands), the Flemish and the Walloons (Belgium), the Lapps (Scandinavia), the East Frisians (Germany), the Kurds (Turkey, Syria, Iran and Iraq), the Laz (Turkey) and the Aboriginals (Australia).

Pure nationalism will become a thing of the past, since it constrains bicultural thinking and action, it restricts the ability to entertain more loyalties simultaneously and it disturbs the distance between the nation-state and the region (all of which are vital factors for success in the new era). And yet nationalism will not disappear completely; it will assume a different form that can be typified as 'glocalization'. Alongside the globalization that is embraced, there is a revaluation of local, regional and personal identity. In practice, these two can go perfectly hand in hand: you act as a globalist, you feel yourself a nationalist or a regionalist. This is the attitude of the future: ultimately, we are all world citizens.

What makes tribes so attractive is that tribes form networks. Tribe members in all parts of the world are connected to each other and put business each other's way. Thus they form an economy that is separate from a nation-state. Chinese and Indians create high GDPs outside their home countries. In the past, the Jews and Armenians did this too, and now the idea seems to be taking root throughout the world: tribalization is taking on major dimensions. This übertrend will have consequences for Europe in a whole range of areas.

Different people, different wishes

Every tribe has its preferred way of living, and this gives rise to new trends. For example, there is something that could be called 'Florida-ization', a phenomenon named for the migration of American seniors to the state of Florida. It is the result of people wanting to go somewhere different when they retire, preferably somewhere that is warm and pleasant, where there are good facilities, and where they can enjoy themselves. Because of the ageing throughout Europe, Japan and USA, an increasing number of people will be going into retirement. This is certainly not unexpected. The baby-boomers, people who were born soon after the Second World War, are approaching the age of retirement. They are generally well educated, have had good jobs, have money, and are healthy. What's more, they are adventurous and are certainly not aiming to spend the rest of their lives tending window-boxes. They can be called YEEPIEs: Young Energetic Elderly People Into Everything. Although members of this tribe will retain their roots in their homelands, they will increasingly spend long or short periods abroad. Seniors from north-west Europe will settle en masse not only in Europe's sunbelt (southern France, Spain, Portugal), but also farther afield in such places as Thailand, Uruguay, Argentina,

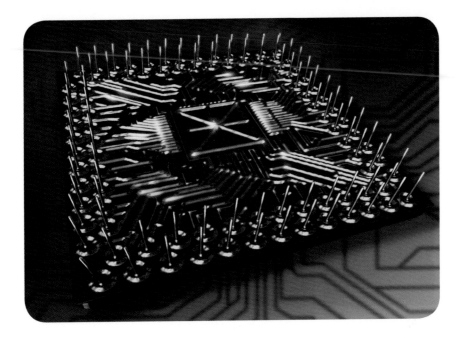

Brazil and South Africa. These seniors are creating a 'part-time living' trend that is also being followed by young people. This is matched with a lifestyle that could be called five-star living. We have become accustomed to this partly through holidays in countries such as Bulgaria and Turkey where the cost of living is much cheaper than in our own countries. The five-star lifestyle means luxurious living in an urban environment, in a security protected apartment near to all of the shops and facilities. This is combined with owning a house in the countryside where people can enjoy rural life and tend their gardens, giving them the best of both worlds simultaneously. Part-time living and five-star living are, of course, possible in your own country or region: you have an apartment in Berlin, for example, and a country house near the Polish border.

Luxury apartments in cities or other places are increasingly exploited by five-star hotel chains. You can live in the centre of Vienna or Paris in a Hilton apartment. It is your own apartment in a luxurious, safe complex in the centre of town. The Hilton personnel can, if you want, provide room service, and you can make use of the hotel facilities such as a swimming pool and exercise area.

Doing the shopping will also change: anybody who lives in two different places will no longer do a weekly shop on Saturday. Thanks to this, there is a market for multinational supermarket chains that can carefully monitor the border-hopping consumers with the latest customer relationship management (CRM) techniques. Example: you are citizen X who spends eight months of the year in Cologne and four months on Majorca. You will certainly appreciate a supermarket with branches in Cologne and Majorca that offer an assortment of products to match your lifestyle and your needs in this period of your life. Such a supermarket can supply these needs since it can monitor the target group. It can streamline its purchasing, and be efficient, effective and profitable.

At the same time, there is a market for local shops, as long as there is a large enough supply of consumers. For instance, it would be nice to be able to buy local bread, local jam and local ingredients in Majorca. In the framework of the experience economy, you enjoy two totally different experiences in one year. In Majorca you live as a (German-speaking) Spaniard in the countryside; in Cologne you live as a busy town-dweller who consumes German urban products and lifestyle. The expectation is that in areas that are more densely populated, and where it pays marketing-wise, there will be more local immigrant facilities, shops and products, while in 'emptier' areas there will be more pure local supermarkets.

In all cities, neighbourhoods will grow where tribe members live together, following the American example where this first started.

Cities will have a Chinatown, a Little Moscow, a Little Rio, a Little India, a gay neighbourhood and an older people's neighbourhood.

Though most examples of this are to be found in USA, countries such as Brazil and South Africa have their own old tribal areas. The city of Sao Paulo, for instance, has a Japantown called Liberdade. Some 1 million of the

16 million inhabitants of Sao Paulo are of Japanese origin. They arrived in the first decade of the twentieth century when Brazil needed them to work on the sugar and coffee plantations that could no longer use African slaves after the abolition of slavery. At that time, Japan itself was a poor country. While the total number of Japanese living in Brazil is barely 1% of the population, they make up 15% of the Brazilian student population, which makes them a very successful tribe. In south Brazil, there are German tribes that have been very successful. They even have their own city, called Blumenau, where an enormous beer festival is held, second only to the Oktoberfest in Munich. In Durban, South Africa, they have little India. Mahatma Gandhi was born there.

An ever increasing number of languages will be spoken, even in those areas where traditionally only one language was spoken. In Provence you will hear more German and English, just as you will in various Italian rural areas. Estate agents that sell property in new EU countries such as the Czech Republic and Hungary will do a roaring trade. In a Dutch newspaper, I read about Bas (66) and his wife Margo (52) who left the Netherlands for Hungary in 2004. Their new home is in Tiszaders, approximately

160 kilometres to the east of Budapest. It is a beautiful area, close to the enormous Hortobagy Puszta national park. They had been going there for years, having purchased a holiday home there ten years previously. Friends who live down the road bought a gigantic house there four years ago for just €20,000. You don't have to be rich to buy a property there, but the prices are starting to rise. There are a growing number of Germans in the area and it is becoming more and more popular. This migration to the east will increase in the coming decades. More and more seniors from the western part of Europe will move to the eastern part, which will give the area an economic boost.

Despite the problems with pensions and the fact that people will have to work to an older age in various countries, demographers expect that grey emigration will persist. More and more seniors have purchased a second home before they reach retirement age, and, once they stop working, they will move there for good. And as so often happens, the first to do so will act as an example that many others will follow. The growth of 'two-pension households', where both partners enjoy a pension, will ensure that there is enough money to undertake such a step.

As seniors spend more time abroad, there will need to be good travel facilities. After all, they will want to see their children, grandchildren and other family and friends on a regular basis. They will, of course, maintain virtual friendships via the internet, webcams and increasingly cheaper telephone services (including telephony via the internet). It is unthinkable that budget airlines will disappear from the air for some time to come.

Intersections

Because people want to live in several places simultaneously, and transport between their chosen locations becomes much more important when they commute rather than just visit a holiday home once a year, new intersections will arise in the infrastructure. The areas around train stations will become important residential intersections for people who live part time in the city and part time in the country, but these will also become important places for pieds-à-terre. Stations that serve high-speed trains will in particular become new urban intersections; for those who live there, travel to their country house in some other European country becomes a lot less complicated. Changes will arise in logistics and transport. The phenomenon of the coach trip has a healthy future, and there will be more opportunity for various taxi concepts, car sharing, car rentals and so on.

European roads will not become less crowded, because the many tourists who come here will also need to get around. In addition, increases in city breaks, short holiday getaways, day trips and so on for groups of bored, fit seniors, plus the fact that we will work less and have more spare time, will mean that the roads will be as busy as ever.

Building

In the future, building will become increasingly concentrated. We will live closer together, and this even counts for Europe and Japan where there is a decline in population. For those who live in the city, this will imply that they live close together in dwellings that are built on top of each other. They will be safe, with many facilities and a large number of shops. Despite the fact that we will shop more on the internet, physical shopping will remain an experience that we would not like to do without, if only because it provides an opportunity for showing ourselves off and looking at other people. There will also be lot of entertainment in these urban concentrations. People want to have fun, and want it in all shapes and sizes: concerts, shows, museums, temporary exhibitions, sing-songs, spiritual meetings, revues, cabarets, stand-up comedy, theatre, real-life soaps – you name it.

The city becomes the backdrop for people's lives. This life takes place largely in the old city centres and the nearby urban areas, which will be renovated in the coming period if they have become run down. The lower classes that currently live there will leave the area, either voluntarily or under pressure. Empty areas in city centres (such as the City of London and the centre of Brussels) will have new life breathed into them so a greater return can be achieved from the expensive land.

Products for the elderly

Although the elderly are increasingly active and want to measure up to the younger generation for much longer, they will still desire products that are geared to their wishes and limitations. The ageing of the population will initiate major changes in the design of packaging. For instance, we will see fewer pastel colours being used in the package designs of food and other articles for supermarkets because the eyesight of older consumers demands clearer colour schemes, as a recent survey by Trend Office Bakas shows. Bottles, cans and food packaging should be designed in new ways that enable people to open them with less muscle power. The survey by Bakas revealed some of the items that older consumers use to open bottles, cans and other packaging: a pair of pliers, screwdrivers and scissors. Teeth are no longer used to open packs containing snacks.

Targeting women: tomorrow's most powerful consumers

The economic crisis is hitting men hard. In contrast employment amongst women is rising. This means that if anyone is going to spend during these times, it's going to be women. In America, where female consumers make more than 80% of discretionary purchases, according to *The Economist*, companies have started tailoring their products and messages to appeal to women, in an effort to boost their sales. Frito-Lay, a snack-food company owned by PepsiCo, has launched a campaign to convince women that crisps and popcorn are not just for male, beer-guzzling sport fans. OfficeMax, America's second-largest office-supplies company, has redesigned its notebooks and file-holders to appeal to women and has run advertisements that encourage women to make their cubicles more colourful. For the first time, McDonald's was a sponsor of New York Fashion Week in February 2009, promoting a new line of hot drinks to trendsetting women.

Feminization and the economic crisis

It has taken the economic crisis to get companies to focus on women, and it has prompted companies to rethink their approach. Bosley, an Amsterdam based advertising and marketing consultancy firm that helps companies including Daihatsu and Sony to reach women consumers, has tripled its number of clients since the crisis began. Some women's magazines, too, are benefiting as companies that had never before expressed interest in advertising with them are now doing so. Eveline Posma, managing partner of Bosley says: "Aside from their greater purchasing clout, women are valuable customers for three reasons. First, they are loyal, and more likely to continue to buy a brand if they like it. Second, women are more likely than men to spread information about products they like through word of mouth and social-networking sites. Third, most of the lay-offs so far have been in male-dominated fields, like manufacturing and construction. This means women may bring home a greater share of household income in the months ahead and have even more buying power".

Does female marketing and advertising exclude men? Eveline Posma: "On the contrary. Products don't have to be painted pink and it is rarely necessary to present a proposition to the market that is designed exclusively for women. But it is crucially important to take a human and

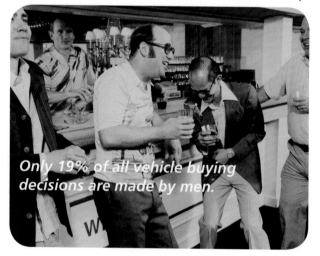

Only 19% of all vehicle buying decisions are made by men.

empathetic view. To pay just that little bit of extra attention to all the details. But that sounds much simpler than it is. Because it demands carrying out our profession in a fundamentally different way than we have been accustomed to over the past decades. Making a product or service more attractive for women will soon make it more attractive for everybody. Or as they say in America: 'If you please a man, you just please a man. If you please a woman, you please everybody.' And that's good news for every marketeer".

Feminization in the financial industry

Financial services providers are experimenting with products for women and there is a lot to be said in favour of this. Women are becoming an attractive target group for financial services providers. They are better educated and make the most important purchase decisions. In fifteen years there will be more female than male millionaires in the UK.

Women take a much more holistic approach to the buying process. Men settle for "good enough", while women want maximum choice. They want to be able to compare all their options and discuss their choice with others. They want all their senses to be stimulated, so tone of voice and look and feel are also important to them. In short, the overall picture has to be right for women. This also has been the experience of Bosley. 'A man who needs a vacuum cleaner walks into a shop and buys one,' says Eveline Posma. 'A woman walks into the shop, goes home and calls three girl-friends, finds information on the internet and then goes back to the shop. Word-of-mouth advertising works eight times faster among women than men.' Nearly all the pieces of wisdom found in popular women's magazines turn out to be true in practice. Men look for a solution; women also want empathy for their situation. Words such as better, stronger and bigger are effective with men, while women look more for similarities and like to talk about them. Posma: 'Give the company a human face, use real people in the communications and make sure there is interaction and details. That's what women like.' Posma says there is tremendous interest in female marketing in traditional male product groups such as automobiles, electronics

90% of all buying decisions concerning financial products are made or influenced by women.

and financial products. Bosley has calculated that women decide or dominantly influence 91% of all electronics purchases. Research conducted in the US reveals that women share their experiences with 21 other women, while men share their experiences with only 2.6 other men. Other studies show that women eventually make eight out of ten automobile and mortgage purchase decisions. Posma comments that only fifty years ago women still needed a man to be able to purchase a financial product. 'Today they pay and invest, but women still have a number of remaining insecurities that they must resolve. The key question is: How do you help them to overcome these insecurities, without being patronising or pedantic? And can this be achieved with a separate female proposition or not?' The US bank Citi opted for a platform for women. Women & Co provides women who are under 55 and have disposable capital of more than $ 100,000 with training and a network of resources. The French AXA Financial takes a different approach via an internal programme designed to ensure that all marketing and communications are female-friendly. The feminization of the financial industry is therefore set to gain more and more ground. This industry is not yet very adept in thinking in terms of target groups, but the current shrinking margins have necessitated this development.

Feminization: the Daihatsu case

It is customary for car brands to address men. This is preferably done through the television and frequently includes a great deal of information about the performance of the cars. And when a car brand does address women, this is usually done in a stereotypical way; 'a perfect little car for the city, to have as a second car, to go shopping in.'

Women are responsible for 60% of new car purchases. For that reason, it is worth ensuring that communication is better tailored to this large and, in particular, financially strong target group.

Daihatsu was the first car brand that decided to improve the way in which it tailored its communication to its chiefly female buyers, which was in 2008. Along with advertising agency Bosley, Daihatsu carried out extensive research amongst both women and men. Armed with a bag full of insights, a campaign was created which clearly speaks a different language compared to what we are familiar with in car campaigns. Daihatsu now presents itself as an accessible and friendly brand that acts as a sort of everyday companion. Daihatsu doesn't, as is often the case when car brands specifically address women, characterize the models as typically feminine. The company addresses men and women who have both feet firmly on the ground and who are averse to status symbols.

Feminization: the Sony case

Women are responsible for a significant portion of consumer electronics purchases. This is reason enough for Sony to enter into a dialogue with

Women take or influence 91% of all buying decisions in consumer electronics

the female consumer. The first step was recently taken in that direction. This time, there will be no images of Sony equipment with mention of superior performances, as that is not exactly captivating for women. Women want to know what a product could mean to them, what its worth is to them and whether it will improve their lives and make their lives easier. To that end, four promotions were developed, which called on women to set to work creatively. By means of editorials in the similarly named magazines, Sony provided them with tips and tricks and informed them in a fitting and relevant manner about the Sony equipment. This information immediately generated the prizes that could be won. It was possible to win cameras and laptops in the Cosmopolitan photo promotion, and in another photo promotion, Sony Alpha lens reflex cameras could be won. Especially for the promotions, microsites were set up for each title, to which entries could be uploaded and where visitors could vote on the entries. Public attention was held for a longer period of time (3 months) through announcements relating to the above appearing in magazines and on websites, and this created a significant amount of awareness and feedback. Additionally, this afforded Sony a considerable insight into how women deal with these types of products.

The future of feminization is now

Many companies still target their marketing and communication activities to the traditional 18-34 male target group. A target that rapidly decreases both in number and buying power. Tom Peters, one of the world's leading management consultants calls upon corporations and marketeers for years now: "don't be mistaken, women are not an 'initiative', women ARE the market".

Conclusion

The USA and Europe will become a 'salad bowl' of racially and nationally diverse groups, and that is a good thing. Other areas in the world will follow at a rate that depends on their economic success and openness to foreigners and different lifestyles. Everybody will more and more come into contact with other cultures and other lifestyles, and this will promote integration. Of course, this will also have consequences for local and regional cultural expressions. To prevent these disappearing altogether, people will increasingly search for their identity: the continuing existence of separate cultures, customs and lifestyles will thus be safeguarded. More than ever, we will live here, there and everywhere, and thus take our needs with us wherever we go. This will have consequences for day-to-day matters such as housing, shopping, logistics, medical care and financing. Smart business people can profit from this and try to satisfy the various needs. The inhabitants of the salad bowl will be an interesting market.

Architecture and globalization

Of all the activities that humanity has developed throughout history, architecture is in my opinion the one that gives the best and most complete view of reality. I say this, of course, from my position as an architect, and thus from the basis of all the knowledge that has formed me. Undoubtedly, other people could make similar proposals concerning their own area of expertise, but this is not the place for such a discussion. Everything that is built is an architectural expression of culture; people should not immediately wish to make a value judgement on whether it is beautiful or good. From here, we can see in architecture the value of the combination of a creative mind – and artistic and philosophical heritage – economic industry, social activity and technological development. The balance between these various elements can help us discover whether a building is good or not. In general – and still from the point of view of everything that has been built – we discover, until the beginning of the modernistic movement, a close relationship between location and architecture. We could go further: the expansion of the classic empires (of Greece and Rome) and the more recent empires (those of the United Kingdom, Spain, the Netherlands, Germany) and the extensive migration that this brought about resulted in the architecture of the homeland being reproduced in the conquered areas, for both houses and more symbolic buildings. However, the building style also adapted itself to the location. In some cases, this created an aesthetic and technological symbiosis with remarkable results, such as the Dutch building style and its application in Indonesia.

Since the arrival of modernism, a new situation has emerged. The expansion of the fundamentals of modernism and the technology that allows it to develop have resulted in architecture that is similar wherever you go. The same patterns are applied everywhere in the world. Whether a building is in Moscow, Paris or Cape Town, one encounters extremely uniform solutions. Only in concrete cases by exceptional builders (such as Alvar Aalto or Alvaro Siza) is the theory of modernism successfully expressed, and this raises their work to the level of masterpieces. One of the fundamentals of this expression is the relationship that the buildings have with their location, in every possible perspective. Siza also involves the political circumstances under which his work is achieved.

The process of globalization in which we are immersed means (in many cases) a step forward. On the other hand, however, globalization ignores not only the characteristics of the location, but also those of the culture, economy or production forces of the places it enters. In its constant attempts to find consumers and attract their attention, it reacts exclusively to commercial considerations or image. Certainly, globalization forces many architects to extend their working arena to far from their own homes – in China, the Middle East, the US, Europe or some other place in the world. Nevertheless, it is quite clear that their architectural production would result in a higher quality and

improved understanding (and thus greater appreciation) if they adhered more closely to the local culture, economy and technology. This leads me to believe, I repeat, that architecture is a tool that can build bridges – both literally and figuratively – between various societies and cultures, and thus enrich the heritage of humanity. □

Albert Vidal is an architect, based in Barcelona. He works around the world, predominantly in southern Europe and the Middle East. He specializes in designing retail spaces, most recently in Saudi Arabia, and in private homes.

Megatrend 4

Towards new perceptions of security, privacy and terror

Saddam Hussein, Stalin, Mao Zedong and Adolf Hitler are playing scrabble together in Hell. During a break they watch BBC World's TV coverage of how the French police prevented a major terror attack in Paris. They watch in amazement as the BBC journalist unveils how the plotters were deceived by their VirtualMe avatars and the new technology of the security agencies in France. 'What a world of wimps it has become without us,' Saddam says, sounding upset. 'Why are there no real men anymore, like we used to be? How can they let some piece of technology with a damned Hindu name – avatar – prevent them from their manly work of terror? The whole world has become degraded. The real men out there must really miss us. Shall we ask the Devil if he could reincarnate us?'

The future of security

Not everybody embraces the future as it is currently developing. As already noted, several groups are angry about the the direction the world is heading. 'Men love wars and women love soldiers' is an old saying. With major wars going out of fashion – the current ones in Iraq and Afghanistan will probably be the last big wars in a long time – this saying is also going out of fashion. In the new world order, terrorism and small-scale wars, fought within cities, will become much more important. Therefore, armies have to change their organization, weaponry, intelligence and infrastructure. Superpowers and power blocs will use military force to protect their interests and to threaten enemies and rivals, but it is most unlikely they will use all their weaponry and large armies to fight full-scale major wars or even world wars in the way they used to in the past. Since all major economies are now integrated, it is in nobody's economic interest to fight big wars anymore.

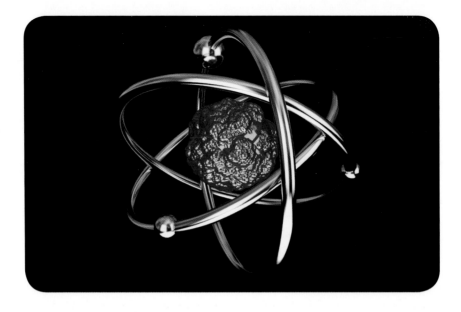

Growth of terrorism

Although the risk of large-scale wars is diminished, we will witness the growth of terrorism. Animal rights activists, Islamists, communists and classical terrorists like ETA in Spain and the IRA in the UK will continue to fight what the world is developing into. Terrorism may hit us anywhere, in our own cities or abroad. Terrorists will become more creative, inventive and they will use more high-tech methods than before. Several independent terrorist networks will form coalitions with each other, as ETA and al-Qaeda did in Spain. Terrorists will find new ways of attacking others, as we see with the animal rights activists who try to threaten financial institutions and the people who work there in order to put pressure on them not to finance companies who, in their opinion, don't treat animals as they should.

We will also see that terrorism is linked to media coverage. Many modern-day terrorists are young boys who are hungry for media attention focused on their acts and don't mind dying to get it. In the past, terrorists wanted to avoid their own death at all cost; nowadays they crave death as their path to martyrdom. Media attention is all part of it.

The Israeli security agency Mossad recently developed a camera that can film through walls for use in cases of hijacking or kidnapping. This way the security forces can see where the terrorists are located and work out how best to attack them. New innovations like this one will help police and armies to fight terrorists.

Terror and the 'boys surplus'

Terrorism is related to the boys surplus, as mentioned earlier. When there are too many boys in the fighting age between fifteen and thirty-five in a certain region, they always start to fight and look for a reason to fight. All their testosterone needs to be released, especially when they suffer from pent up sexual frustration. That is why there were so many guerrilla wars in South America from the 1960s up until recently, and the reason why most of them ended is that the redundant boys had killed each other, so ending their guerrilla activities.

Terrorism is also related to passive or active support from the communities from where the terrorists emerge. State-sponsored terrorism, as we know from Libya in the 1980s and now from Iran in the beginning of the twenty-first century, provides terrorists with a certain degree of legitimicy. So, too, does passive support from communities strengthen terrorism. Even the silence of those communities involved bolsters the terrorists. Look at what happened in the Indian city of Mumbai in November 2008. Ten young Pakistani boys took a boat from Pakistan to India, executed more than 200 people and caused mayhem. What would have happened if ten young Hindu boys had taken a boat to Pakistan and murdered 200 people over there?

Condemnation of terror

After the Danish cartoons of Muhammad were published, we saw demonstrations of angry Muslims everywhere in the world. Did we witness any demonstration of angry Muslims against the Muslim terrorists, who came out of their midst and who, in the name of Islam, murdered all those people in Mumbai, London, Madrid and New York? No, Muslims stayed quiet. Therefore, the terrorists in their midst believe that they are supported by the large majority of Muslims. The best way to prevent Muslim terrorism from growing further is for Muslims all over the world to strongly and publicly condemn the acts of these people who have hijacked their religion. I hope they will soon denounce these fanatics in the strongest terms. I know they can.

Wise procreation, sex and terrorism

Given that terrorism is linked to a surplus of boys in the fighting age range, the best way to prevent it is therefore to reproduce wisely. A classic example of inappropriate reproduction is that of the Palestinians in the Middle East. An average Palestinian woman has eight children in her life, the majority of them boys. No economy can support more than two boys per family. The population of the Netherlands grew from 12 to 16 million people between 1960 and today. If the Dutch had bred like the Palestinians, 48 million people would currently live in Holland. Likewise, 240 million people would now be living in Germany instead of the current 80 million, and there would be some 180 million in the UK rather than the current 60 million. The Palestinians never missed an opportunity to miss an opportunity. Smart breeding would have enabled them to turn Gaza into another Singapore. The current boys surplus there prevents peace from ever being possible: the redundant boys know that peace won't bring them economic participation, and therefore they will keep on fighting. The fighting will only stop when the redundant boys are all dead, as happened with the guerrilla wars in South America.

A major problem within the boys surplus is sexual frustration. The girls have to stay virgins, and can only enter marriage as virgins. Sex before marriage is taboo, as is gay sex. Marriage is only possible if the boy has a steady job and can support the girl according to her family's wishes. However, it's impos-
sible for them to get a job with so many male rivals around. Prostitutes are too expensive and wanking all the time is boring. So, what to do? Have secret sex with other boys or become a terrorist. Legalizing gay sex and gay marriages might help to relieve the pent up sexual frustration amongst all these redundant boys, who are not loved by anyone, only used by others. In a revealing interview, a former bodyguard of Osama bin Laden told a Dutch journalist about routine gay sex amongst the Islamist terrorists. And another Dutch journalist told me about the many boys brothels he visited in Gaza and the West Bank. The reality behind the screaming headlines about the conflicts in the world, and the Middle East in particular, is truly fascinating.

The end of the open society

Open societies – and most modern societies are quite open – are more vulnerable to terrorism than closed societies.

In many open societies, security was not a major issue during the last few decades of the twentieth century. Security of hearth and home was relatively high in most open societies and it wasn't necessary for the middle classes and the elites to construct high fences around their properties, to hire bodyguards (as protection against kidnapping and other threats), install elabourate alarm systems and arrange other security measures to protect their property and possessions. But, thanks to Google Earth, now everybody can see how and where you live, and how large your property is. The internet enables any indiviuals to collect data on you and to form a coalition to attack you. A whole new form of criminality is growing: internet crime. More about this later.

Times change. At the start of the twenty-first century, there is a new perception of security risk that is at times almost obsessive. This covers security in its broadest sense: security in the home and security on the streets; protection against multinational gangs and against kidnapping and terror.

Becoming more suspicious

People will soon take leave of their open society and become increasingly suspicious of each other and even more suspicious of outsiders and foreigners. Governments will run more campaigns and other initiatives to alert citizens to potentially suspect people, packages and so on. Awareness of terror is thereby increased. Since more use will have to be made of the expertise of countries such as Israel and India, the image of these countries might improve throughout the world.

In the times ahead, representatives of several terror movements will infiltrate mainstream organizations more and more efficiently. Old and new terrorists will come together and cooperate with each other. As mentioned earlier, there are strong indications that the attack in Madrid in 2004 was a joint venture between the Islamic al-Qaeda and ETA, the Spanish Basque separatists. More such collaborations are being forged, not only in Europe but also in South America, where al-Qaeda works together with local terror groups related to the drugs trade. This form of globalization will increase in the near future, now that terror is primarily becoming nihilistic by nature and less ideological. 'Terror education' is also becoming more global. Terror organizations no longer need to set up training camps and education centres; the internet offers increasing possibilities for achieving these aims. It is easy to put the blueprints for making a bomb on the Web, and ideological support is also taking place online.

The end of privacy

Because of all of these security fears, privacy is becoming a thing of the past. More security cameras are appearing in high streets and other public places. Events, city-centre malls and public transport hubs are kept under surveillance more often and more intensively than ever. The cameras that used to be considered as an invasion of our privacy have become our friends, equipment that safeguards our security. We have become increasingly prepared to give up our privacy. We are prepared to have our bags and bodies searched at public events, museums and shopping centres, just as those people in countries where terrorism is commonplace have been accustomed to for so long. The terrorist threats engender new forms of xenophobia. People will feel this in the body language of other people. This will also lead to greater difficulty for several groups of people to obtain visas and residence permits. A new apartheid will emerge. Several tribes will increasingly live and work separately from other tribes. This separate development will result in less tension. Various groups of people will also leave what they consider to be a new battlefield.

In these periods of distrust of each other, we can expect massive investments in security measures, particularly at harbours, airports, important buildings, railway stations and major events. These measures might not necessarily increase security but will increase the perception of security. They will also cost a lot of money and will thus count as an attack on the economy – one of the most important objectives of the terrorists. Causing economic depletion and heightening fear is just as important as shedding blood.

More gadgets

There are more and more gadgets and technical tricks that claim to guarantee security. Some are for private individuals, others for professionals in the security industry. As I write this book, there are reports of trained flies and wasps that can track down terrorists carrying bombs! However, a new generation of bombs (made of plastic rather than metal) will indeed require new detection methods to replace metal detectors. The security services can look forward to golden times as citizens spend a lot of money on their security, in common with areas where self-respecting individuals have gas masks in their homes. Clothing will appear made from materials that stop bullets and knives, as is currently

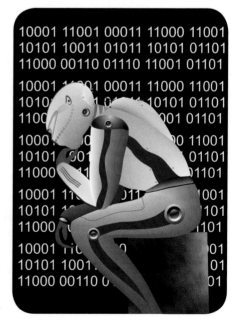

found in Colombia and Israel. And do-it-yourself terrorist protection kits will become available, together with civilian gas masks and water filters to counter the danger of water being poisoned.

The threat of terrorism has other consequences. Public transport, for instance, will suffer tremendously as a result of increasing terrorist attacks, because fewer people will make use of it. In addition to regular taxis and shared car ownership, demand will grow for new forms of individual transport, like one-person taxis in the form of bicycles or running on electricity.

Harsher sentences

Sentences and new legislation will also become much harsher. Existing laws and rules will be eroded. There will be new laws that allow the deportation of hate-preaching imams and that restrict freedom of speech. There will be stiffer sentences. Terror will also cause the demand for the reinstatement of the death penalty to become more insistent. Although this will do little to dissuade suicide bombers (who believe that, at the moment of their death, they will be able to enjoy the pleasures of dozens of virgins), the law will appeal to the feelings of insecurity that exist among the population. Among the youth population, there are already large

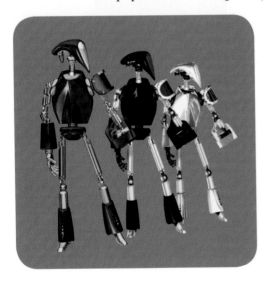

numbers who support the reintroduction of the death penalty; among older people, particularly the baby-boomers, the majority are still against it. The emotions of groups within the population will be mobilized.

The 'war on terror' will change slowly but surely into 'negotiating terror'. On the one hand there are an ever-growing number of security measures taken in the light of a war on terror; on the other, people are aware that they cannot win such a war and there will be (at first privately, and then publicly) negotiations with the terrorists.

Terror, integrated in amusement

To give terror a proper place in our lives, it will be integrated into entertainment, as has happened earlier in our history. Many films were made about the war in Vietnam. The same is true of the Second World War. In Israel, there are comedies about Palestinian suicide bombers and there are countless jokes about them doing the rounds. (Example: two vain Palestinian women, bombs concealed under their scarves and dresses, are waiting at a bus-stop in Tel Aviv. One says to the other: 'Do I look fat in this dress?') In the future, we can expect al-Qaeda comedies, musicals and suchlike. Terror entertainment will have arrived – terrortainment.

The creative and security industries will increasingly join forces to combat terrorism. In the United States, after the attacks of 9/11, film directors from Hollywood were engaged by the security services to dramatize the terror. New collaborations arose between security experts and the creative industry to allow them to get under the skin of the terrorists and

put them a step ahead. In Germany, a nazi comedy is currently a big hit. In Europe, too, we can expect collaborations between the security and creative industries in the near future. Novelists, game developers, (film) scriptwriters, film makers, playwrights, actors, fashion designers and others will increasingly contribute to the development of new security concepts. This new coalition is uniquely capable of 'out of the box' thinking, and can thus combat the enemy in a creative and original way.

All these trends have one thing in common: they are all directly connected to the expectation that there will be more terrorist attacks in the future, all over the world. Cells of terrorists are spread throughout the world and where the attacks will take place is anybody's guess.

Use of technology

New technology will also fall into the hands of terrorists. It is no longer the threat posed by nations that dominates our thinking – with some exceptions – but the threat from groups that represent no formal power. Futurologist Wim de Ridder says: 'The power of such groups is so great because the means at their disposal allow them to unleash widespread terror. It is almost impossible to prevent the threat of anthrax. The threat that computers will be used remotely for an attack on the internet will be greater in the future than it is now'. Marcus Sachs, director of the American SANS Internet Storm Center, which tracks down storms on the internet like a cyber-meteorologist, thinks that the internet at the start of the twenty-first century is a mess: 'I would dare to state that almost every computer with an internet connection is confronted with an infection, whether successful or not. Every week, we encounter new digital zombie armies, each one more ingenious than their predecessors. They are used for espionage or they smother companies by visiting websites en masse and bombarding them with emails, sometimes for extortion – a company that does not pay up is simply shut down. Alternatively, the netbots send people emails that look like official bank correspondence. Those who reply and give away their banking details can expect their bank accounts to be plundered. The user of the computer often has no idea at all that the computer has been taken over by criminals: it generally happens at night, when the owner is in bed'.

Genetic technology

In addition, the assumption is justified that genetic technology developed for commercial use can also be used to kill plants, animals and people. This fear is largely thanks to the knowledge that the raw materials for this are readily available. A laboratory can be fitted out using equipment that costs no more than US$10,000. Thousands of students throughout the world have worked with such equipment and materials. There is also a fear that, should certain viruses be used by terrorists, it will be impossible to eradicate them from the environment. Attention is also being given to recombinant DNA designer weapons, which can be used selectively (e.g. such weapons can be developed that only attack specific ethnic groups, or that affect the mood and behaviour of people). It is hardly surprising, then, that the fear of chemical and biological weapons is so great.

In 2003, the most-read book in the world of futurology was a study by Martin Rees published under the title *Our Final Century*. His conclusion is that the chance of our civilization surviving until the end of the current century is no larger than 50%. In short, the technology of the twenty-first century can, whether or not by accident, seriously threaten life and bring it to a premature end.

Police and technology

Eavesdropping bugs, covert cameras, datachips, messaging barrages and intelligent tracking systems keep many dangerous sections of society under control. Actual detection work increasingly takes place at a computer terminal or in a laboratory instead of at the Crime Scene (CS). If necessary, a digital 'copy' of the CS is made using, for example, a *3D-PD Scanner*. The European police officer will not become a Robocop (half man, half robot), shopping centres and streets will not be patrolled by agents that look like cyborgs and we won't see computer-system implants and self-directing harnesses with built-in laser cannons. However, the 'collaboration' with robots and associated techniques will become much more intensive. The application of technical and scientific insights is not just a desirable way of augmenting police work, it is a necessity. Every new development in technology must not only be followed, it must also be under the control of the law enforcers sooner than it is under the control of the criminals.

Criminality is becoming increasingly complex, just as society is becoming more complex and flesh-and-blood police officers are finding it almost impossible to carry out all the detection and enforcement work by themselves. Computers and other pieces of equipment can quickly and reliably take over large amounts of work from the officers. Each new technology, however, creates new possibilities for criminals. There are, for example, more (luxury) goods that are interesting for thieves

and these items are often smaller and more expensive. The range of instruments of interest to the police is very large, and will only increase in the coming decades. That certain technologies are not currently used, even though they exist, is in many cases a question of technophobia. At police board levels, traditionally many positions are held by gamma and alpha thinkers, such as economists and lawyers: more betas must and shall have a place in the top levels of the European law enforcement organizations. The fear of using technology will then quickly disappear.

Combating terrorism
One of the most important areas where the police will employ new techniques is that of combating

terrorism. At airports, metal detectors will be replaced by gates which do not only react to metal, but also to drugs or, for example, biological weapons. At Amsterdam Airport, Schiphol, scan equipment was installed in 2007 which could scan right through clothing: the security scan. The labour intensive and sometimes intimidating body searches may soon belong to the past. The equipment looks through clothing, in search of suspicious items, but the travellers remain anonymous. In the coming decades, use will also be made of *smart dusts*. These are silicon chips, the size of a dust particle, which can be added to drinking water so that the water can be tested for harmful substances. Tracker dogs are gradually being replaced by ichneumon wasps and electronic trackers.

There are other examples of intelligent technologies that can take over the analysis of situations from police officers. There are cameras that are specialized in *object pattern analysis*, a pattern recognition system. If somebody spends an inordinate length of time at an automated teller machine (for example, to empty it or to fit a card-copier into the slot), he or she will be immediately signalled as a suspicious person and can be placed under observation or arrested. 'Big Brother' officers keep an ever-more watchful eye on us in shopping centres and social and entertainment areas, but in the future they will also keep their eye on other areas. Lampposts are frequently fitted with a camera, although these are often non-active units, intended as a deterrent: cameras are primarily a preventive measure. At certain large events or during terrorist threats, intelligent camera systems can be fitted to unmanned planes or helicopters. In Great Britain, some cameras do more than just observe and record. If people are spotted behaving badly, the camera tells them that their behaviour is not acceptable. The talking cameras are intended to remind people that they are being observed.

The future of identification
Identification will become more and more important, and the technical possibilities for identifying people will grow in number. In many European countries there is already an identification obligation. Until now identification cards have been sufficient, but the biometric passport is coming, and iris scans are already being used. Even these new passports

might not suffice. By 2020, every police station will have the technical means to identify a suspect not only by using biometrics but also through his or her DNA.

Car theft will increasingly become a thing of the past. The GPS systems and car tracking equipment already available make it possible to trace and follow stolen cars. New identification systems will also ensure that every car part is numbered and marked, and thus stealing cars and breaking them down in order to sell the parts throughout the world will also be an extinct crime.

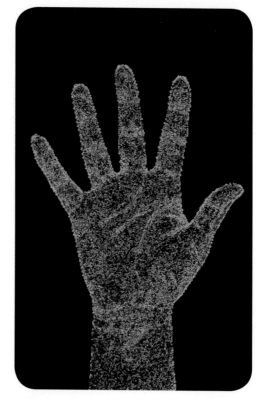

The same ID technology can be used in the cause of road safety. For instance, cars can be rigged up so that they will start only when the driver has shown, using an electronic breathalyzer, that he or she is not under the influence of alcohol. This new ignition breaking system is already in use in Canada.

Chips can also be fitted in other products that are susceptible to theft. For example, cracking bicycle locks is generally a piece of cake for the experienced bike thief and stolen bicycles are easily concealed. However, a built-in chip makes it possible to track them down so that they can be quickly returned to their rightful owner.

Terror scenarios

The US Department for Homeland Security has developed a number of disaster scenarios that could apply not only to the United States but also to other regions in the world. The scenarios show that the 'universal adversary' (UA) can attack in a variety of gruesome ways. And the big question is whether security services measure up to such a threat. The second question is how far we will be capable of handling the consequences of the inevitable attacks – a major run on hospitals, the environmental effects. The answer is we do not yet know the scenarios well enough to prepare ourselves for them.

The Department of Homeland Security works on the assumption that ten times as many people will rush to the hospitals after an attack than is necessary, but that's a convenience figure that cannot be established accurately. When al-Qaeda attacked the Twin Towers on 9/11, the hospitals in New York were clogged up in no time, not with the wounded, but with the stream of people – fifteen times more than those injured – who went to hospitals demanding examinations because they had breathed in smoke. That had a paralyzing effect. The terrorists could not have asked for more. In Tokyo, this effect was already well known. In 1995, members of the Aum Shinrikyo sect spread nerve gas through the metro system: not much, but enough to cause a rush on clinics that offered front-line medical treatment.

Identifying disasters

In 2004, the American government ordered that the consequences of such attacks be better identified, for it was clear that the United States did not have adequate contingency plans. The Department of Homeland Security developed fifteen disaster scenarios, which were published for a short time on the website of the Department of Defense in Hawaii. A telephone call from Europe alerted the mega-department in Washington and, on 16

March 2005, the National Planning Scenarios disappeared. However, for a brief while it was possible to download the information from this site. The report did not predict where, when or how al-Qaeda would strike; it calculated what would happen if an attack took place. It also calculated the consequences of a few natural disasters, such as a major earthquake, a hurricane or a flu pandemic. In addition, the document gave twelve examples of attacks. The report did not mention any terror group by name, but talked instead of the UA. What that adversary can do is terrifying, and it could happen anywhere.

- The UA steals uranium in Russia and uses it to construct a nuclear bomb, which is smuggled into the country. The ten kiloton weapon is exploded in a business district. Everything is destroyed within a radius of one kilometre. Flying debris causes thousands of casualties and damage in a radius of six kilometres. Electrical appliances in the city no longer work because of the electromagnetic shock wave. Almost half a million people run through the streets, and the effects of the radiation and fall-out are felt to a distance of 250 kilometres. An area of 8,000 square kilometres has to be cleaned up, something that costs billions of dollars. The economy is hit hard; it will take years for the country to get back on its feet.
- The UA drives a truck through five cities and spreads clouds of anthrax. After a couple of days, spleen fever breaks out and the hospitals are overrun. Problems arise because the symptoms are not recognized instantly, and medications run out. The population is alarmed and pharmacists are terrorized. About 300,000 people are infected; 13,000 do not survive.
- The UA succeeds in releasing the plague virus in three places simultaneously: a railway station, the toilets in a large airport, and a sports stadium. The operation only takes a few hours. Within three days the disease has crossed the ocean, carried by travellers. A day later, eleven countries raise the alarm, following the United States and Canada. Then 8,000 people die. The fear among the population keeps people locked away in their homes. Banks, offices and factories collapse. A few weeks later – and after a further 2,500 deaths – life gradually returns to

normal. But the trauma and invalids remain.

- The UA flies an advertising plane over a major football stadium and for five minutes sprays a mixture of mustard gas and lewisite into the air. The spectators experience respiratory problems and flee in panic. There are more than 150 casualties; 1,000 people have to be treated. Many of them suffer from permanent lung damage and blindness; the mustard gas can also cause cancer. The damage (destruction, detoxification) amounts to half a billion dollars.

- After two years of preparation, the UA lands helicopters in the grounds of a major oil refinery, launches rockets at the oil tanks and places several explosives. Two nearby oil tankers are attacked, catch fire and sink. It takes days to put out the fires. Downwind, panic breaks out among the population. A few hundred people die as a result of poisonous fumes and accidents; the hospitals are full to overflowing; 700,000 people lose their homes; the pollution is on a massive scale. The economic damage runs into many billions.

- The UA releases the nerve gas sarin in three places into the ventilation systems of large apartment buildings (twenty floors, 2,000 people) in a major city. The terrorists have taken six months to prepare this attack, which takes just ten minutes to carry out. There are 6,000 deaths, largely among the tenants, but also among the emergency services, because the gas is odourless and works quickly. The panic will be extreme and the direct economic damage runs into the hundreds of millions of dollars.

- The UA explodes a bomb in an industrial area near a tank of liquid chloride. Downwind, panic takes hold of the population. The chloride gas that is released is poisonous and causes 17,500 deaths and tens of thousands of serious injuries. Nearly half a million people rush to the hospitals for treatment. There are also casualties in the resulting

traffic chaos. It takes weeks to restore order.

- The UA makes 'dirty bombs' from dynamite and radioactive caesium-137. The components can be picked up anywhere. The bombs are exploded in three medium-size cities. The areas within a few kilometres of the explosions are contaminated with fallout. The dust also penetrates the metro system and large buildings through their ventilation systems. Fires break out, caused by burst gas pipes. The explosions cause relatively little physical damage: initially thirty-six housing blocks are damaged. However, 180 people die in each city and the panic is intense. The material damage goes on to become enormous because large sections of the city have to be demolished, decontaminated and rebuilt. It takes years before the cities are once again fully functional.

- There are simultaneous bomb attacks on various targets. The UA explodes car bombs and several improvised bombs in a sports arena and its underground car park. A few suicide bombers take care of the metro system. When the transportation of the wounded gets underway, a large car bomb is exploded near the entrance to the major hospital. To disrupt the rescue efforts even further, the terrorists use an ambulance for one of their bombs. There is complete chaos and the terror is enormous. Around 100 people die.

- The UA carries out an attack on a meat factory and a processing plant for orange juice. Meat and juice are contaminated with liquid anthrax by terrorists who are employed in the factories through local temporary employment agencies. The anthrax spreads rapidly throughout the country via the distribution networks. Three hundred people die, a far greater number become ill, and thousands of people rush to the hospitals for check-ups. The meat and juice industries collapse, and the fear virus affects everybody else in the food industry.

- Spies working for the UA select suitable cattle markets and livestock haulers as targets for spreading foot and mouth virus; the virus spreads rapidly throughout the country. The terrorists are not concerned so much with causing human casualties as with causing disruption and economic damage. The greater the area of infection, the greater the problems caused by transport restrictions, the culling of livestock, and the resistance to controls. The public is afraid of eating beef, the export of meat stops and the damage runs into the hundreds of millions. It takes many months before the foot and mouth crisis is under control.

- The UA succeeds in letting a number of hackers make a cyber attack on a number of vital computers. Millions of credit cards become worthless, or are misused because the PIN codes are deciphered. Cash registers and giro systems are unusable, if only because the public no longer has any faith in them. Salaries are not paid on time, foreign speculators no longer trust the US dollar and the financial markets are plunged into crisis.

Homeland Security was not concerned with listing all the possible risks. Plane hijacking is not mentioned, because terrorists have done this so often it has been replayed countless times. Some attacks in the report cause human casualties, others cause economic damage. Some, despite all the suffering, are local; others spread themselves rapidly. All the scenarios, however, have one thing in common: the enormous disruption that follows. Panic, hospitals overwhelmed with wounded and people who want to be examined as a precaution, and loss of consumer confidence can completely paralyze a society. Terrorists know that. And we know that

terrorists know that. That causes a general feeling of unease in Europe. In fact, that's putting it rather mildly. We are scared: we feel unsafe in our own continent, in our own country, city, neighbourhood. And that will not improve during the coming decades.

Change in war and security

'All this changes matters about war and security,' says the Israeli security specialist Martin van Creveld, author of *The Transformation of War*. He predicts that major wars will slowly but surely fade into history and be replaced by what he calls LICs (low-intensity conflicts). These will take the place of wars in which states fight against states. In the major wars, the cost in terms of human lives is enormous. During the Second World War, 30,000 people died every day – and that went on for six long years. Compare that with the nearly 3,000 deaths in the WTC attack in New York on 9/11 – it's peanuts. Van Creveld studied 3,000 years of war history, from the Sumerians to the present day. In his opinion, terrorism is not a new phenomenon; it's ancient. A characteristic of terrorist attacks is that small units can cause enormous damage. The price–performance ratio is extremely favourable. Battles in which enormous armies face each other are a relatively recent occurrence. With the erosion of the modern state, we are witnessing a rediscovery of old ways of waging war – for example, those that reached their peak in the Middle Ages – that had since been forgotten: deception, betrayal, ambush, anarchy and all kinds of terrorism. According to van Creveld, it no longer makes sense in this century to invest large sums in classic war materials. He says: 'We must fight terrorism with the weapons of terrorism.' If you want to fight terrorism efficiently you must, according to him, train proficient commando units who can penetrate to the core of the enemy, attack swiftly and disappear again. Security services will become increasingly

important, and will concern themselves increasingly with our private lives. In exchange for safety, civilians will have to give up some of their freedom and privacy. 'The Middle Ages are returning. At that time, the feudal state was based on barter trade: the lords offered protection in exchange for a part of the harvest. That is now returning, albeit in a modern guise. In countries such as Somalia, it is already the case: the warlords have taken over this task from the state and are lords and masters in their own limited zone'.

Growing security industry

On the back of all these fears, the whole security business has mushroomed. Security is a commodity, a raw material that has to be purchased with hard cash. Citizens will have to take care of their own security, or will have to pay a lot for it. Van Creveld believes that terror and anarchy will become  commonplace; we will have to learn to live with them. He prefers that situation above major conflicts between states, which have always cost a great many more lives. He despises the state, which according to him is a monster that fortunately does not have a long life ahead of it. In his book he writes, 'War is the soul of man, written in large letters.' That metaphor that is taken from Plato. War is, according to him, the naked human soul in its most extreme, its most sublime, but also its most terrible form. For von Clausewitz, the Prussian general and strategist, war is a matter of politics, but van Creveld invokes words such as pride, games, the pure desire to win. Etymologically, the word 'war' actually means play. Children play at war. Adults also in fact do so, in their cruellest, most sublime, most authoritative and most terrible way. Van Creveld comments: 'Just look carefully at the way Palestinian boys throw stones at Israeli soldiers: there is a lot more sport and games about it than you think.' About Islam in Europe, he says: 'I know very tolerant Muslims, even here in Israel: people who are opposed to all forms of violence, genuine pacifists. I know Muslims who are rightly indignant about the WTC attack. In itself, Islam is tolerant – I do not know any other religion that intrinsically contains such a love of peace. But in the situation that exists today, I would not wish to live in any Islamic country, either as Jew or Christian.'

Gated communities

I have discussed security at a macro level, but the theme is also relevant at a micro level, the level of the household. A clear result is the growing market for various forms of gated communities being experienced by European project developers. These are 'protected' housing estates or

flats, where people live with 'people of their own kind'. Ethnic or socio-economic diversity is not desirable, for this only causes unrest. There is maximum security in these protected areas, including surveillance cameras, alarm installations and guards supplied by security companies. While people stay in their own gated community, they do not have to worry about their safety or that of their children and property. Theft, burglary, muggings and other possible attacks therefore become things of the past.

Apparently, more and more people think there is money to be made from such a concept. Some apartment buildings are already gated communities, and this concept of protected living will grow to large proportions in the future. This is also a result of 'part-time living'. Because people live in several places at once, it is important that their houses and possessions are safe when they are elsewhere. They will therefore invest more in new security equipment, surveillance cameras, all types of (silent) alarms, neighbourhood watches and private security officers. In France there are small companies that take care of the maintenance and security of holiday homes belonging to North Europeans who live there part time. These houses are frequently a target for burglars.

There is burgeoning enthusiasm for gated communities among the prosperous classes, and it will not be long before the concept is common in many cities. Little can happen to people at home in their own fort, and all that security equipment will give a feeling of safety. A good example of this is the inclusion of an extra-secure room in the house where residents can go if thieves break in. The thief cannot get to them while they are in there, and they can use a dedicated telephone to call for help, and make use of emergency food rations and lighting in the event of having to stay there for a longer time.

Cocooning

New technology is being used to give apprehensive civilians a greater feeling of security in and around their homes. Because most injuries in a bomb attack are caused by flying glass, windows will be covered with a special foil which ensures that if the glass is shattered for any reason, it is held in place, stuck to the foil, and simply crumbles. Seniors, who are traditionally more easily scared than young people, will stimulate the demand for new security concepts and equipment. Very soon, we will be able to buy security equipment at the supermarket. Security-conscious seniors can form virtual communities and warn each other if there are problems, a form of grey power.

Cocooning will increase, particularly among seniors. If, in the perception of citizens, it is so unsafe outside, it is better to seek entertainment at home. People will make fewer visits to the cinema and instead download films from the internet and enjoy them at home while cameras keep watch on their doors and windows, and security systems safeguard them and their property. Security guards in the lobby prevent hooligans from getting in.

Cash becomes less common

Because of feelings of insecurity, cash will become less common. In countries with high levels of insecurity, such as Brazil, people even purchase a tube of toothpaste costing €1 with a credit card. In Brazil, it is not possible to withdraw money from an ATM after 11.00 p.m. ATMs in Brazil, and also in India, Indonesia and South Africa, are generally guarded by armed security employees of the bank. In Europe, payment by credit card, PIN-protected direct debit card, and other plastic payment methods will increase in response to concerns about security. For seniors, there are already ATMs inside banks; and a card is required to get in. New identification methods and new ways of protecting credit cards and direct debit cards will replace the PIN, partly with forgetful seniors in mind. Iris scans and fingerprints are obvious choices. In places where people feel at greater danger than elsewhere – for example, at ATMs in very busy or perhaps very quiet points in big cities – there will be increased security, with either cameras or security personnel.

Increasing private security

Private security will increase; the role of the police will decrease. To turn countries into police states is costly and extremely labour-intensive, as was shown by the Eastern European countries during communist times. Ageing and a reduction in the population will decrease the labour pool in many areas in the coming years, but technology offers possibilities for new types of security. Armies and police forces will not grow larger in years to come. We can expect, however, a growth in intelligence services.

Private security firms will also increase. In Germany, the Netherlands and various other European countries, more people are employed by private security firms than by the police; the same is true in India. There will be an ongoing growth in the market for bodyguards. The elite and upper middle classes will make use of them. Job integration will also increase. Professional chauffeurs to anyone who is anyone will receive training in how to get the car and its occupants to safety if there is a kidnapping threat, and how to react to gunshots being fired at the car. For the elites, there will be a growing number of armoured cars on the market. In the future, the use of new materials will make these lighter and thus more fuel-efficient than the current generation of armoured vehicles.

Bulletproof fabrics and accessories

Bulletproof fabrics are also appearing. As we already mentioned, recent fashion shows in Colombia and Israel included a new generation of fabric that is bullet-proof but looks just like cotton. A summer dress that looks as if it is made of muslin but is nevertheless bulletproof will be available soon in Europe. Stab-proof clothing is also appearing.

Since there will be an increasing use of man-made fibres, natural materials will be used much more for accessories. This will allow someone to be both a well-protected city slicker but with a splash of 'back-to-nature' country girl at the same time. People want to spend less time walking in the street.

In the perception of the citizen in the twenty-first century, it is dangerous to walk on the streets of a city. They believe they can only go out on the streets if they are armed to the teeth in order to protect themselves from danger. An increasing number of women will carry pepper sprays with them in order to fight off attackers, even though it is legally prohibited in some countries. New ways of frightening off or disabling attackers are now being developed and will soon appear on the market. The mobile telephone is also a security accessory that can be used to sound the alarm if danger occurs (the new generation of phones will include this facility) and the built-in camera is useful for photographing attackers, which will allow them to be identified and apprehended.

Security gurus as pop stars

Security gurus will achieve the status of pop stars. As they gain in stature, they will become media stars and will frequently be guests on talk shows. They will have their own programmes on radio, television and the internet, will write regular columns in newspapers, and their blogs will attract many visitors. Some of these gurus might even make the transition into politics. They offer the electorate a certain feeling of security, and that makes them attractive as politicians. This has happened in the past – General Eisenhower became president of the United States and General de Gaulle president of France. In the near future, it is therefore not completely unthinkable that security gurus (from the police, military or security agencies) will become political leaders.

It will naturally make a big difference if the rapidly progressing gene technology succeeds in eliminating the gene that causes criminal behaviour. How wonderful it would be to implant in the brains of every criminal a chip that prevents any criminal impulse being carried out by the body. Just imagine: your brain thinks about stealing that little old lady's handbag, but before you can put this into action the chip springs into action. Stop! Don't do it! It's not your handbag; help the lady across the road, you naughty boy! And obediently you follow the new orders that have been issued by your chip-manipulated mind. There are people seriously brainstorming such possibilities in think-tanks made up of psychiatrists, criminologists, gene technologists and people from the security industry.

Major non-terrorist criminality

Major criminality will increase in the future and the following trends can be identified. The number of multinational gangs will increase. Roma networks will emerge, largely in Eastern Europe, and will join up with the Roma networks that have long existed in Western Europe. Serbs and Chechens will also have important functions in these networks. This cross-border collaboration will result in successful criminality with PIN theft and debit and credit card fraud, which is already largely dominated by the Roma.

Drugs will effectively be legalized and major users will increasingly be spared from prosecution. Many drugs – cocaine and ecstasy, for example – are used in Europe by people from the higher classes who are generally able to deal with them. They pay good money for them, which is one of the reasons this industry will continue. There is something to be said for legalizing drugs globally, as is already the case with alcohol in most regions, but a tolerance policy is much more likely. The drugs business is lucrative and will remain so, and it will not be prosecuted as aggressively as it should be (given that drugs provide a source of finance for terrorists) because attention is mainly focused on the fight against terrorism.

Black and white economies will increasingly coexist and intermingle. Income from drugs and other regular criminal activities is traditionally ploughed back into the regular economy. In most regions, that has always happened discreetly, although in some countries it is done more openly. In India, for example, legal and criminal funds go hand in hand in the Bollywood film industry. Films are financed simultaneously by criminal and professional film financiers. Extortion of money from the rich is prevalent in many regions, but until now it has been limited in Europe. In the future, this will also be affected by globalization. Asians from emerging economies who are facing extortion or blackmail scams in their own countries will settle in Europe – on either a part- or full-

time basis – and will, in turn, be bothered here by their much-travelled criminal persecutors.

Bribery and corruption will make growing inroads into international business transactions. In Mexico, the drugs cartels are getting so strong that the government is no longer able to resist their power. This will have all manner of negative effects on national sovereignty.

Crime networks

The major crime networks mentioned above will increasingly finance terror. Up until now, the various criminal groups, like the drug trade, have had no links with terror organizations (with the exception of Colombia, where there are links between drug dealers and terrorists). They were independent. This was also true of those who copied designer clothes and other luxury items, which is big business in the European market, from where many of the top fashion and cosmetics brands originate. However, these counterfeiting organizations are today increasingly allied with terrorists.

The so-called hawala banking system is nearing its end. This centuries-old form of banking, which originated in Asia, is a means of transferring cash. Because hawala banking is unregulated and has no formal records, it can only too easily be used by the criminal gangs to further their own ends.

Border controls will return. They were abolished between the Schengen countries in Europe, but border control will be reintroduced as a result of the new thinking about security and fear management. The arrival of asylum seekers will increasingly be obstructed. Ideas from places such as Libya to create a European asylum-seekers' centre there will win support. Human rights will become subservient to security issues: what some see as the exaggerated rights of criminals and detainees will come to an end.

One can expect that, if governments prove incapable – or insufficiently capable – of guaranteeing the security of their citizens in the face of the criminal gangs and terrorists, 'warlords' or private anti-terror units will emerge, as has happened in other countries. In India, police often shoot and kill many criminals (murderers, drug dealers, extortionists, black-mailers, kidnappers and terrorists) during 'encounters'. That the death penalty formally does not exist in India is a mere detail; nobody bothers about that. De facto, the death penalty does exist; it is carried out by the Indian police, without intervention from a judge. The CIA does the same; so too does the Israeli Mossad; and groups of off-duty Brazilian police agents operate as 'death squads'. All of this goes on without it resulting in lawlessness and a complete lack of justice. In Europe, we are not yet familiar with this phenomenon, but we will be confronted by it in the twenty-first century.

Towards more virtual piracy

Cyber crime is on the rise. Every year a staggering 25 percent more cyber crimes are committed, not only in the virtual realm but also in the physical world, where crimes are carried out or covered up with the help of modern information technology. That makes cyber crime (or high tech crime, as it is sometimes referred to) the fastest growing criminal industry by far. One of the most frequent forms of cyber crime is digital piracy: the illegal copying and distributing of copyright protected content through the internet. In the coming years we will see more and more of this and we will also witness on a large scale the negative effects of digital piracy.

Already millions and millions of people around the world download unlicensed movies, music, games and software from websites or through peer-to-peer networks, either for free or for a price far less than what they would cost in a legitimate store. Millions and millions return from vacations or business trips to Cyprus, Istanbul, Moscow or Peking with luggage filled with Hollywood's latest blockbusters and the newest albums by Madonna or U2, material quite often not even available yet on the European or US markets. All acquired for less than nothing in a shop, on a street market or from the boot of a car. And although almost everybody instinctively knows it is wrong, hardly anybody seems to care. In fact, quite often we boast about all the things we manage to get cheap on the internet and we advise family and friends on how to do this as well. We don't steal, we are simply modern Robin Hoods, taking from über-capitalist companies like Microsoft, Warner Brothers or Sony what we consider to be rightfully ours and we distribute it amongst our peers. And in many countries around the world – e.g. in the Netherlands – we do this with the silent approval of our governments which do not consider copyright violations to be criminal acts but merely economical offences, i.e. not something criminal investigators should be bothered with. But how wrong can we be?

According to the Motion Picture Association, that steps up for the rights of the American movie industry, the individual companies it represents in Europe suffer damages of at least 120 million dollars a year because of illegal copying. Worldwide the amount may be three times as high, and that is just for movies. Add up the costs for the software industry, book publishers, record companies and the gaming industry and we are probably talking billions of dollars a year. Now there is an economic offence for you! Since most copyrights and patents are held by American companies it is no surprise the United States is one of the few countries to take copyright violations seriously. Organisations like the Motion Picture Association and the Recording Industry Association of America work closely together with the FBI and other investigation services to fight digital piracy. More and more they try to do this on an international level, far outside the borders of the United States. After all, that is where most of the perpetrators are to be found. Their primary objective is not people like you and me who occasionally download some illegal content – however morally corrupt we may be in doing so, and although they will certainly try to educate us – but it is the criminal networks behind the piracy who are often also involved in lots of other technology crimes.

Contrary to popular believe most illegal content is not uploaded to the internet by a bunch of enthusiastic amateurs, who just want to share their (legitimately acquired) music or movie collections with other enthusiasts. And the whiz kids breaking down the security codes of computer programs have come a long way from the old school hackers, who acted out of anarchistic ideals or just for the fun of it. Digital piracy is big business, and it is a business fully controlled by organised crime. And although it mainly takes place in cyberspace, it usually starts with some sort of crime committed in the physical world, for instance a break in to get the master copy of a new movie or music album. The entertainment industry is infiltrated by the pirates, so they can get their hands on content long before the public ever has a chance of buying it. Professional audio and video technicians digitalise and compress the stolen files and upload them to so called topsites. Nearly all illegal content available on the internet originates there. The topsites are located in a place called the darknet, a part of the internet that is hidden from the general public by a thick wall of security measures. If you don't know where to look, you will never find it. As soon as a new file appears on one of the topsites – security professionals estimate there are around thirty of them who distribute half a million files per day – so called couriers will start copying the file to as many other sites as they can, as quickly as they can. In a matter of hours a movie or music album can be duplicated tens of thousands of times, and only then they become traceable by the search engines of the peer-to-peer file sharing sites 'normal' consumers use. These websites earn millions of dollars each year by showing advertisements to the millions of consumers they attract.

The piracy business is a lucrative one. The pirates make money by selling unlicensed hardcover copies of DVDs and CDs directly on the streets or by selling the content to companies that produce them. They can also make money by making content only available for download after paying. At the same time this offers a perfect opportunity to collect user information, including credit card numbers and other bank account details. With this 'business intelligence' the real money can be made and the pirate networks are usually involved in other types of cyber crime as well, like credit card fraud, identity theft and extortion (by threatening to disclose somebody's download behaviour). In fact the spreading of unlicensed software, movies and music has become a tool to infect computers with malware that can take over the control of a computer or copy passwords and other personal data. The Russian mafia for instance produced a few years ago perfect copies of the Windows operating system. They sold them nicely sealed in 'original' packaging and through respected computer stores. But they had a lot more spyware built in than any other Microsoft product. The people who were unfortunate enough to buy them and install the operating systems on their computers, soon found themselves to be in serious trouble, with their computers being hijacked and their bank accounts plundered.

It may seem like a lot of work to go through to get a few passwords and credit card numbers, but the potential rewards are more than worth the effort. Internet security company ISS estimates that in 2005 worldwide a rough 52.6 billion dollars was lost through identity fraud. For example in the same year a Brazilian criminal group managed to steal in only a few months' time 22 million euros. In 2008, in the Netherlands a young man was arrested who had stolen the numbers from several tens of thousands of credit cards. Total damage: around 13 million euros. The criminal networks involved in these types of crime are often the same ones as the pirate organisations. They usually originate in and often operate from Brazil, Russia and China. These are countries that have a long standing tradition in organised crime, that have high poverty and unemployment rates and school systems that guarantee some sort of basic education to a large part of the population. In other words, these countries are the ideal recruiting grounds for cyber crime's frontline soldiers.

The operating areas of these criminal organisations of course are not so restricted. Not only do they target individuals and companies in the Western world, but they also set up European and American branches. Under pressure of the United States and the World Trade Organisation the Chinese and Russian governments come down harder on the factories that produce unlicensed copies of CD's and DVD's. As a consequence, the criminal organisations now more and more set up bootlegging facilities in Europe and the United States, where a lot of the illegal content was shipped to anyway. These factories produce anything from children's movies to child pornography.

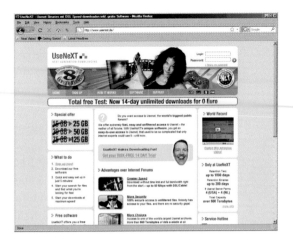

Far more worrying however is the fact that cyber crime networks increasingly try to get control over (parts of) the physical internet infrastructure. After all, if you own the infrastructure, you no longer need to break into it. So criminal networks are setting up their own hosting providers and advertising agencies or they buy themselves into the board rooms of the legitimate internet companies. This forms an enormous threat to the future development of the internet and to the further development of e-commerce and e-government. For instance Dutch police professionals suspect a number of internet providers are already infiltrated by organised crime. This is particularly worrying since the Netherlands are home to one of the biggest internet cross points in the world, the Amsterdam Internet Exchange, which handles a large portion of all the internet traffic around the globe. Imagine this hub falling into the hands of a criminal group. Knowing that from the approximately 50 thousand law enforcement officers in the Netherlands, no more than two hundred are information specialists and only thirty of them are fighting cyber crime on a permanent basis, somehow is not very reassuring. If governments like the one of the Netherlands and some of the other European countries do not start taking cyber crime and digital piracy a lot more seriously, and if people like you and I do not change our content downloading habits, it is safe to suspect that in the coming years cyber criminals will tighten their grip on the legal internet economy, and that some big digital disasters lay ahead of us.

Privatization of security services

The security business includes private personal security, cash transport, event security, security of shopping centres and parking areas, courier services and so on. The privatization of many police functions has created more time for the police to concentrate on the important core jobs. A lot of work can be easily farmed out and, as already noted, the security market is growing.

The demand for crime fighting is increasing in society, primarily from business. Within a few years, security issues will become a standard job for a manager. On the shop floor, management has to take into account matters such as pilfering, fraudulent sick leave and sexual harassment. They will also be confronted by a wide variety of conmen, thieves, vandals, etc. from outside the organization. Insurance and telecom companies have their own risk analysts, and other commercial institutions collaborate with forensic accountants. Business organizations have websites on which they publish pictures of shoplifters. The security industry is expanding further, with security advisers, corporate investigators and private detectives. In short, the corporate world has taken things into its own hands. Private organizations often have a different view of security than the police and other law enforcement bodies, and they develop different methods of handling crime and other safety issues. Bundling the forces and knowledge of private and public institutions will make a lot of future crime manageable.

Conclusion

In tomorrow's world, I foresee a transitional period in which various security enclaves coexist, perhaps separated by physical walls or secured in some other way. Fear management will have increasing sway. Because traditional criminality (the drug trade, counterfeiting) will have links with international terrorism, and because traditional terror organizations such as ETA will join forces with others, security will be a more important issue than ever. We no longer feel safe even in our own homes, and in the long term we will increasingly shut ourselves off from these dangers by turning our houses into forts. Will we ever break free of this spiral while the obsession with security continues? The twenty-first-century will be characterized by living in a world of identification chips, security agents and electronic surveillance. The right to privacy will hardly exist: it is far too dangerous. The security industry can look forward to golden times.

Megatrend 5

Towards a decline of old money and the rise of new money

As she sits on a pink cloud sipping sherry with the Queen Mother, Eva Peron surveys the world below and shares her thoughts: 'I'm I'm amazed at the way Argentina is being reincarnated in your continent. You know, eighty years ago, Argentina was one of the eight richest countries in the world. But we became a bit lazy and spoilt because of all this wealth and a long period of peace. Decline started slowly. If you earn a little less every month, why bother worrying? It happened too slowly to alert people, to inspire them to take action. You only try to turn a trend around when there is a deep feeling of crisis, a real sense of urgency. When Juan and I were elected to the Argentinian presidency, we knew deep down in our hearts that the country needed reforms, harsh measures to stop the decline. We knew the liberal opposition party had the best plans for the country, but we also knew the people did not want to listen, and we loved power so much. So we chose the easy way. Government often offers more glory than opposition, wouldn't you agree?' The Queen Mother answers: 'My child, you can turn a trend and get re-elected, as Maggie Thatcher did in the UK in the 1980s. Britain was on the way down, for a long time by then: nothing left of the glory of the old empire; a role like Africa on the North Sea seemed inevitable for us. Yet she came, decided to change all that, got elected, and re-elected, and re-elected, and really changed the trend. You could have done so too, my dear, you could have been the Thatcher of Argentina.' The ladies sip their sherry and watch what happens in their beloved Europe. The Queen Mother is happy about the way her great-grandson is performing as king. He connects well with prime minister Robbie Williams and even enjoys riding the horse carriage because, since the introduction of the government's new environment laws, the royal family hardly drives cars anymore. The horse-drawn carriage is back; but the king can use internet aboard. The 'coalition of the willing' among European leaders who want to reverse the trend of a declining Europe is working hard to prevent the Argentina model becoming a reality. Queen Maxima of the Netherlands, who is Argentinian by origin, is one of the strongest crusaders against Argentinization of the continent – at least in an economic way. Yet she introduced the tango in every European capital. The tango had only been popular in the past eighty years in the Turkish capital Ankara, since the great Turkish leader Ataturk introduced the Argentinian dance there in the 1920s. Now it's popular in the clubs in Manchester and Paris, Amsterdam and Barcelona. Viva Argentina! □

Old Argentina

Until the Second World War, Argentina was indeed one of the eight richest countries in the world. It exported grain, hides and meat, and used the income from these to develop industry. But things went wrong in the 1950s. Argentina faced competition from cheaper agricultural countries, and its industry had not yet reached a level that would allow it to compete with other industrialized countries. Under the leadership of the presidential couple Juan and Eva Peron, the economy was not modernized. On the contrary, the structural causes of the malaise were allowed to continue: high inflation, low productivity, low exports, share speculation by the elite, and enormous government spending (for example, on the extensive welfare state). The national debt grew and grew because Argentina continued borrowing from other countries. It was only later, under President Alfonsin, that something was done: Argentina received aid from the IMF, the Argentinean currency was coupled to the US dollar, and government spending was curbed. However, the consequence was that the income the population had to spend fell and the economy stagnated. In 2002, the crisis reached a head: we all remember pictures of the long queues in front of Argentinian banks. In 2003, there was some improvement, but Argentina is still not exactly one of the world's most prosperous countries – quite the opposite, in fact.

Old money

Old elites still run the world in many ways. Old American families like the Rockefellers and Kennedys are still pillars of the American society. Likewise, Indian families such as the Tatas and the Mahendras remain pillars of the Indian society. This is also the case in many other countries around the world, except those where former elites have been killed, as in Cambodia and China during the Cultural Revolution. Yet times are changing. Some old families have organized their wealth management well, such as the Heinekens, for example. They educate their offspring wisely, and they are wise merchants – examples of the classical 'mercator sapiens' of the seventeenth century. Others, though, are now falling into decline: the former royal family of Nepal, for example, lost the throne to the new communist government. Others fall into decline for other reasons: bad marriages, alcohol or drug abuse, bad investments or lazy offspring. Sometimes decline is just in the air: after centuries of being rich, people tend to take it for granted and forget that you have to let money work for you. Much of the current old money is concentrated in the West. Many of the families who own old money are part of the bourgeoisie, the merchant class who took over the power from the nobility one or two centuries ago. Some of them are members of the nobility who recognized the tides of change soon enough and switched loyalties in time.

According to the World Wealth Report, produced by Merill Lynch Bank and Capgemini Consulting, old money is on the decline. Old families tend to have fewer children and they tend to let money work less for them than they could have (conservative investments sometimes pay off well, but most of the time they don't). Many old families tend to form coalitions with old politicians and other brokers of power and, when these tend to fall, as happened when the Czar of Russia and the Emperor of China were dethroned, these families lose power and sometimes their wealth as well.

New money

On the other hand, new money is currently being generated by families who used to be from the middle classes or even from the lower classes. The Mittals from India were a middle-class family; now they are one of the richest families in the world. Bill Gates is also one of the new entrants into the ranks of the world's rich. These families can be seen emerging everywhere in the world, but especially in Asia, Russia and the Middle East. Most of the time, these families are happy with their economic

power and leave political power to old money. Yet in most cases, after a certain period of time, these families tend to acquire political power as well. Sometimes they are integrated easily into the current power system and are granted their slice of the power cake by the ruling elites. In other cases, as we currently see happening in Thailand, the ruling elites refuse the new rich their share of the cake. The consequences are social unrest, instability and economic decline for the whole country. The Thailand scenario is definitely one that nobody would want. A soft transfer and inclusion is the best way of monitoring this transition.

New HNWIs in upcoming countries

Globally, the population of high net worth individuals (HNWIs) grew by 6.0% in 2007, to reach a total of 10.1 million, according to the World Wealth Report. HNWI population gains were particularly strong last year in the Middle East, Eastern Europe and Latin America, advancing by 15.6%, 14.3% and 12.2% respectively and outpacing more developed nations. These gains in global wealth continued to consolidate in 2007 — a trend that has been reported for the past twelve years — with the assets of the world's wealthiest individuals accumulating at a faster rate than the growth of the overall HNWI population. Growth in HNWI wealth outpaced growth in HNWI population in all regions.

The 2008 Asia-Pacific Wealth Report is an in-depth look at the changes in the high net worth marketplace in the region. Built on the success of the World Wealth Report, which is now in its twelfth year, the report seeks to understand the behaviour of HNWIs and the responses of wealth management providers in nine markets in the Asia-Pacific region: Australia, China, Hong Kong, India, Indonesia, Japan, Singapore, South Korea and Taiwan.

According to the report, the wealth of Asia-Pacific HNWIs totalled US$9.5 trillion in 2007. The report also reveals India (22.7%), China (20.3%) and South Korea (18.9%) are fastest-growing HNWI populations.

It also examines how both providers and their wealthy clients are looking to Vietnam and Thailand as the next areas of growth. In addition, the 2008 report depicts a region that is enjoying some of the fastest growth rates in the world, with both GDP expansion and stock market performance well above global averages. While growth prospects in the near term may be compromised by the global slowdown, the long-term potential of the Asia-Pacific HNWI marketplace remains strong: the regional economies continue to generate real and sustainable wealth on an unprecedented scale.

Finally, the report shows how competition for high net worth clients has prompted wealth management providers to look more closely at 'emerging HNWIs' and 'ultra-HNWIs', two groups that experienced significant growth both in terms of numbers and their combined wealth in 2007.

Bentley: marketing to old and new money

Bentley is a classic example of a company successfully marketing to both old and new money. On the one hand, old families and nobility like this car brand. On the other hand, new money – pop stars, rappers, movie stars and new entrepeneurs – also like the brand. Yet these two groups do not usually feel at ease with each other. During my lectures for private banks, I always sense the uneasiness between the two. However, Bentley manages to treat the two groups to parties, marketing events and tailor-made cars, each on their own ground, within the confinement of their own cultures. Bentley started this strategy in the early 1990s and has been growing ever since.

A different dream

Wealth and dreams are intricately entwined, and they will be even more so in the future. The 'American Dream' inspires lots of Americans, no matter how poor their start in life, to achieve wealth. 'To get rich is to become glorious,' Chinese leader Deng Xiaoping used to say. Yet these kinds of dreams don't work for

everybody. A European dream would be a wonderful motivator for the European economy: 'Hands together and go for it'. The idea of a European dream was thought up by the American author Jeremy Rifkin in his book *The European Dream*. He is adamant: 'Europe must dare to believe in its own dream.' Europe has a dream, he says, and on many points it is much more suitable for today's world than the American dream: 'Americans are concerned about money; the European dream is about solidarity, sustainability, human rights. The European dream is about involvement of people. That means not leaving everybody at the mercy of the market, respecting diversity (even though you are much too afraid of immigrants), quality of life for society, sustainable development of the planet, social rights and universal human rights, and peace. We shouldn't trade in this dream for a capitalist society such as America.'

Dismantling the welfare state means – to put it simply – a reduction in purchasing power, which leads to a fall in spending and an economy that no longer grows. The problem, according to Rifkin, does not lie in the welfare state. What would we then do? 'Europe has a golden goose that is hardly being fed,' says Rifkin. 'The alternative model for the bankrupt American model that is sighing under a burden of debt is the integration of potentially the richest internal market in the world, from the Irish Sea to the doorstep of Russia: 455 million consumers … . This is what Europe must do. Within fifteen years, there has to be an integrated communication, energy, and transport network for the whole Union. Within ten years, there should be one set of rules for trade and labour. English should, in ten years time, become the lingua franca of the business world. That doesn't solve all the problems. The fear of immigration has to be overcome, because there are many more immigrants and many more children required to prevent Europe from becoming an old-age-pensioners' home. But in this way, you give yourself a few years extra for building a sustainable economy, to think about the role of work and all the other consequences of globalization, and to create a new energy system based on hydrogen.'

'This new mentality can be seen in Eastern Europe,' says former EU Commissioner Frits Bolkestein. 'Eastern Europe is much more market-oriented. Before the ten new member states joined the European Union on 1 May 2004, I visited every one of them. The progress was tangible. The Czech Republic and Croatia are doing very well. They are moving ahead faster than the rest, undoubtedly influenced by the former Austro-Hungarian culture, of which they were formerly a part. Estonia is doing well – people are really committed there. The governments in all these countries enjoy the support of the population. The prime minister of Slovenia said to me: "We have little solidarity here and considerable motivation." That's the way it's working there now. We don't understand that in Western Europe. I was also very impressed by the young people, particularly the young women. They have enormous motivation to perform well. You really can talk about a new Europe and an old Europe. In the new Europe, things are going so well that many East European emigrants are returning from America. There are now indications of a reverse brain-drain in Eastern Europe, and many highly trained people can find work in their home countries.'

New rich and their role in society

Look at the past. Tennis and golf were both sports played by the rich; they are now played by nearly everyone. Owning a second home was once the preserve of the rich but has now come within reach of many more people. Ordinary people like to follow the rich, as long as they behave. With the new rich, new manners are in vogue. Televison soaps and gossip magazines give everyone a view of the real lives of the rich and famous and show us what moneyed people do with their wealth. New money becomes old money as soon as it finds a place that satisfies its economical, cultural and political needs. It then tends to shelter from the public eye. This also happened with the present old money when it still was new money. Until that respectable place is found, new money has a tendency to catch the public eye.

Conclusion

The future will tell how the new money group will take power from the old money group. It is a natural progression that has happened many times in history. It is best when the shift comes gradually and peacefully. I believe that a first step should be taken by old money. After all, old money began life as new money once upon a time. Old money is, therefore, culturally more able to show new money the way to power. This can be done by old money sharing power and coaching new money in dealing with power. If old money resists taking this lead, then new money will take the initiative, and in the past this did not always result in a smooth power transition.

Megatrend 6

Towards an enduring development of technology

Cathy and her friends visit the reunion concert of Swedish pop stars ABBA in Wembley Stadium. In the 1970s, ABBA became famous all over the world with their catchy pop songs such as Dancing Queen. Later generations of musicians used ABBA music in several ways, such as the musical Mamma Mia, which became very popular around the beginning of the twenty-first century.

Cathy does not have to queue for long. Security is tight, yet nobody notices anything of it. The new scanners enable the security officers to see through the clothes of every visitor. There's lots of naked skin on the security monitors. A wet dream to work here on a day like this, she muses as she flirts with the sexy security officer, who does not respond. Probably gay, she shrugs. The air is full of the buzzing sound of wasps, which are flying everywhere, armed with cameras and sensors. Anybody carrying a bomb unnoticed by the bodyscans would be detected by this new generation of wasps that can smell bombs. They are the extra members of the security forces, patrolling every event nowadays.

The ABBA concert is hot; the main event of the year. The world has waited for this reunion since the 1980s when the group split up. Finally it's happening. Cathy is overwhelmingly excited. Her watch shows that her temperature is high, almost feverish, and her pulse rate is also too high. She has to calm down so she pops some designer pills to make her more relaxed. Through her avatar, she connects to her mum who is watching the concert via a camera that projects the images onto the ceiling of the hospital room in which she's lying. She's carrying the child of Cathy and her boyfriend, Lance. Mum, at the age of 68, agreed to carry the child so that Cathy could continue to work and enjoy life without the inconvenience of coping with pregnancy. The baby will be born tomorrow but today she will watch ABBA first. Hurray! Isn't life wonderful? ☐

Drastic changes

Technology will change drastically as we move deeper into the twenty-first century. As a matter of fact, it will totally reshape our lives. Over the past decades, we have become spoiled by relatively peaceful times and an unprecedented prosperity. New times have arrived, however, and technology will play a major role in this new era. The superficial structure of life in this century will change as the technology evolves. However, the underlying structure will remain largely the same. Happiness is, apparently, something that can to a certain degree be manufactured – but people have to make the right choices.

Many traditions will disappear in the new era as new technological inventions cause our lifestyles to change. For example, the time we spend on housekeeping will decrease, although it will not go completely. The new inventions will also introduce new and different work. Education will play a vital part in keeping people up to date and making new innovations possible. The arrival of email has given us a new and time-consuming task – reading and answering messages, and doing it quickly, because people who send the emails expect a prompt answer. We shall need help in managing all this technological paraphernalia, and religion and spirituality will be re-evaluated. Every person feels the need for mythos and logos. Now technology itself will have a mythical function. In industrial and post-industrial societies, technology induces the same mixture of admiration, wariness and awe that people of old felt for natural phenomena such as thunder and lightning, and for the religious implications of these.

Technology has always brought about huge changes to our lives. The introduction of electricity, the lightbulb, radio, television, videos and DVD players, fax machines, computers, aircraft, cars and digital photography all changed our lifestyles and the way we spent our days. This technological revolution is still in full swing. The major technological innovations that will radically change our lives in the first half of the twenty-first century already exist: Sony, Siemens, Nokia, Philips and other technology giants have already applied for patents for various important inventions, as have freelance inventors. Digitalization is now under way in most regions of the world and thanks to the lower wage costs (in comparison with those in richer regions), it can be realized a lot quicker in some lesser developed countries. Technology has given us an enhanced quality of life but at the same time poses questions. Technology should always be judged by its effects on society, such as the gap between rich and poor, or the balance of protection versus invasion of privacy. Here are some examples of what lies in wait for us in the field of technology.

RFID everywhere
Much is expected of the so-called radio-frequency identification (RFID) chip. This is a chip the size of a grain of sand that can couple various processes and place them in a chain. For example, say your car has a malfunction. Its computer becomes aware of this and contacts the garage or the rescue service. It then shows you the way to the garage and orders a taxi to take you home. Our housekeeping will soon be under the spell of domotica (ICT applications in the home) and will soon be managed by home computers. They will track whether we have sufficient food and other household articles; if we're running short of anything, the computer will get in touch with the nearest supermarket to place an order. Outside our homes, we will have a delivery box where the delivery person from the supermarket can leave products, with a cooled section for perishables. Our home computer will know our daily rhythm and adjust various tasks in the house to match it. Do you always wake up at eight o'clock and start your day with a fresh espresso? The home computer will control the espresso machine so that the smell of fresh coffee greets you when you get out of bed. If you are arriving home later than planned, you simply send an sms to the computer and it will heat up your food later. These systems will be user-friendly, with only a few buttons instead of dozens

of complicated functions and thick user manuals. Partly because of the demands of the growing senior market, technology will be applied to ensure that the equipment in the house is much simpler to use.

Smart machines

There are all sorts of innovations that are already technically possible, such as intelligent vacuum-cleaners and the self-controlling lawn mower. These, will gradually enter our homes. The integration of audio, television and computer is nearly complete. The retractable flex-screen already exists. It is a sheet of plastic, the size of a tabloid newspaper, which can be rolled up, folded and viewed anywhere – on the sofa at home, on the train or in the park. You can download anything to it, from newspapers or magazines to books. You either take out a subscription or order a single copy, and there you are: the pages of *The Times*, or the newest issue of *Fortune* or *Time*. If an article particularly interests you, you can mark it and save it. It means less work for the already scarce newspaper delivery kids, and less work for newspaper kiosks and printers, but a very large market for content providers.

In the not too distant future, nuclear energy combined with solar,wind and hydrogen energy will be used as an alternative to oil and gas. Technically this is already possible, but the risks are large and the transition costs are huge. Plus, a terrorist attack on a nuclear power station, for example, would be a humanitarian and environmental disaster. What's more, comparatively speaking, oil is still cheaper. China is demanding more and more oil to fuel its economic growth and, in the future, certainly if the unrest in the Middle East continues, supply could become a problem, meaning that the alternative sources of energy could replace oil sooner than we think. The price of oil will be fluctuating so much that we will be prepared to accept the risks involved in nuclear energy, as the International Energy Agency already says will happen.

DNA and quantum computers

The arrival of DNA computers (computers that, just like living creatures, have their own DNA) has already been announced, and so too have quantum computers, which will achieve what is called 'singularity' by 2020. This means that chips will be capable of doing just as much as the human brain. The consequences of this irreversible process are staggering. Futurologist Ian Pearson thinks that, thanks to the large, collective, autonomous power of the computer chip, human life will come to a standstill by 2085. The use of robots will increase dramatically. In June 2004, the eighth 'Global Football Championship for Robots' was held – the RoboCup 2004 – in Lisbon. More than 1,600 participants from thirty-seven countries participated in the matches, which were held between footballing robots which operated themselves. The first match between football robots and the winners of the European Champions League is expected by 2050.

Food technology

In the food sector, futurist and inventor Ray Kurzweil expects that the production of nano-food will be a fact by 2049. This food, which has the same taste and nutritional content as organic food, is cheap and readily available. By then we shall be familiar with functional food, a method that allows consumers to eat food that better reflects their nutritional needs. Work is also taking place on food delivery systems that allow tastes to be released at the right moment during the meal, and on lab-on-a-chip technology to safeguard food during the production process.

Much is expected of genetically modified (GM) food. There is a battle under way for the legal acceptance of this type of food, but it seems that this is a rearguard action. Consumers are currently critical, because the advantages are not clear to them, and their protests are largely directed at the increasing power of certain manufacturers. If GM foods show clear advantages over non-GM products and there are no major catastrophes, the protests will gradually ebb away. Already 70% of all cotton and soya and 35% of all grain produced in the United States is genetically modified. In Israel, Turkey and the United States, experiments are being held with coloured cotton, which will

allow naturally coloured products to be introduced onto the market. The second green revolution in the agro-industry is about to break out. This is also expected to result in a decrease in the prices of agricultural products rather than an increase.

New medical care concepts

In the medical care sector, a large number of developments attract attention. Important applications in stem-cell technology are expected, including the replacement of heart muscle cells that are no longer functional. Considerable research is also taking place into possibilities for new nerve cells for Parkinson's and Alzheimer's patients and for paraplegics, as well as new skin for burn patients. It obviously appeals to the imagination that human tissue and even organs should be able to be replaced by substitutes grown from stem cells harvested from the body. Discovering this omnipotent stem cell is referred to as finding the Holy Grail of biology. Some expect that this will cause a fundamental change in the field of surgery.

Developments also showing promise include replacing sensory organs such as the light-sensitive tissue in the eye and the cilium in the ear with microelectronic mechanical systems (MEMS). This means integration between the nerve cells in the human body and advanced microelectronics. Here again, applications for paraplegics are being developed. Then there are implanted chips that can automatically dispense the required dosage of medicines (creating so-called smart pills).

Controversial choices for humanity will be how far we want to go with our ability to modify human genes. Related to this will be at what point of 'change' we call a human no longer a human but rather a robot because the artificial part is bigger than the natural part. New innovations should also be accessible for the poor, especially when it concerns solutions for diseases like AIDS. We have to make sure that the rich–poor gap is narrowed by technology and not widened.

Futurologist Wim de Ridder argues that it is certain that communication between people will develop rapidly: 'Our opinions about this are constantly adapting themselves. The chance is great that Big Brother is not the nightmare described by George Orwell, but will be seen as a welcome development. The cameras that are now seen everywhere give us a sense of security that we are members of a collective that – for whatever reason – is interested in us.' Therefore the robot will also find a place in this world. If we want them to, robots can be friendlier than people.

New technology, new lifestyles

During the twentieth century, technology created a new economy: the agricultural economy became an industrial economy. Now Europe is becoming a service economy. The lifestyles connected with the economy also change. Within a century, the lifestyle of a farmer became totally different, and the number of farmers also decreased. New professional groups emerged, with their own new lifestyles. There was, for example, the group of factory workers, with a radically different lifestyle from that of the farmer. Industrialization of the agricultural industry resulted in greater yields: various European nations (France, the Netherlands) became the world's largest agricultural nations, largely as a result of the productivity that was thus achieved.

As I have said, technology changes our lives and our lifestyles. Sixty years ago, my grandmother from India had a full-time job looking after the housekeeping: maintaining the latrine (the predecessor to the water closet) took a lot of time, as did cooking on wood and coal before the arrival of the gas and electric cooker, the provision of fresh meat before the arrival of refrigerator and freezer, cleaning the house before the intro-

duction of the vacuum cleaner, and doing shopping by horse and cart instead of car or scooter.

Technology more than anything else made women's emancipation possible, in my opinion. If men had had to take over the work of women in housekeeping, and it required as much energy now as it did sixty years ago, women's emancipation would never have come about.

Of course, it is possible to add a certain nuance here. Technological and social changes are inextricably intertwined. Before households were electrified, the houses of the averagely well-off had stone or wood floors, with mats that needed to be beaten several times a year. The vacuum cleaner was not particularly well suited to this, and so fitted carpeting was introduced. The new wall-to-wall carpeting, women's magazines announced, had to be vacuumed at least once a week. Beating mats was physically demanding, and men generally helped. But the vacuum cleaner, at least in the first decades of its existence, was used almost exclusively by women. This example illustrates that the career of a new technology can never be seen in isolation. Most changes are not anticipated, and their effects are often contradictory to what their inventors intended, as is shown by Edward Tenner in his hilarious book *Why Things Bite Back* (1996). But that's neither here nor there.

Email and other technical innovations make it easier than ever before to work from home. Now the McOffice is on its way. This is also a service that makes mobile working possible, but then on flex-places for general use. Offices will arise near to residential areas where people can go to work with their laptop and an internet connection. In this way, employees no longer have to contend with the busy traffic and they have a workplace where they are not disturbed by the noise of their children's play. The trend is for large work organizations to grow smaller, so the workers of

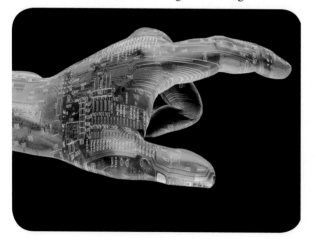

the near future are more likely to work in smaller organizations. Employers will find that it is more manageable and less trouble to work in networked organizations and with 'collective entrepreneurial responsibility' than to work with flocks of salaried people. The first of such collectives will be in the medical care sector: collectives of nursing staff, for example, or of home-care nurses.

Busyness

The way we spend our days is clearly influenced by the technological revolution. We sleep for fewer hours, because there is now a lot to do and experience after sunset. A century ago we slept for twelve hours a night; now we sleep for eight. In a century's time, this is likely to have dropped to six hours a night. Other lifestyles, all sorts of meditation, healthier food, supplemented with vitamin pills and other energy boosters, will give us the energy that we used to derive from sleep. We seem to be heading for the 'end of sleep'.

All those hours that we are awake each day need to be used or filled in ways that make life worth living. We have to be able to use all this increasing amount of human energy somewhere. We have to keep busy, and be entertained. The youth channel MTV maintains that young people are able to do several things at the same time: watch television and at the same time talk on the phone or send an sms, read and answer emails on the computer, and hold a conversation with people in the same room. A spokesperson for MTV commented, 'It is quite possible that research will show that the brains of young people have been changed by this *multiple brain usage*.'

The European research agency Motivaction has published research findings on the way we fill our days. These show a number of changing needs and motives which explain and signal new trends. 'Not wanting to miss anything' has led to 'de-hasting'. People are in search of a good combination of work, care tasks and free time. This arises partly from the phenomenon of being 'threatened by time stress': increasingly, we have the feeling that we are under time pressure. That is why we deal with time more rationally and in a more planned manner than ever before. This is also connected to a 'decreasing identification with work'. Growing prosperity gives us the feeling that work is making too many demands on our private lives. Our striving for economic and material status and the urge to move up the social ladder are decreasing, according to the research. A result of this is the trend of 'nostalgia for domesticity'. People indicate a new desire for the security of the home environment. We prefer to stay at home with friends rather than go out. Staying at home in your spare time is becoming more appealing. The home will once again become an oasis of rest in our hectic and complex society.

Entertaining the cocooned

As mentioned earlier, 'cocooning' is on the increase, largely as a result of our feelings of insecurity. As we stay in for longer, we therefore want more entertainment in the home. That's easy enough, because television, audio and the internet will soon be integrated, and that will allow the home entertainment industry to grow dramatically. We shall soon have various flat screens in the home, in different places, where we can view almost anything.

Space will be put to different uses. We won't need to waste metres of shelf space for CDs; instead, we shall have one small, compact carrier on which we have saved hundreds if not thousands of hours of music. Artists will bring out their new repertoires via the internet and consumers will pay to download them track by track. There will be no more high street music stores.

Equipment will become increasingly invisible, whereas, until now, visibility has been very important. People will no longer boast about their expensive audio equipment from brand X, or their television from brand Y: the technology of the future will wear a burka. At the same time, traditional board games such as Monopoly will regain their popularity, together with digital games both for children and adults. Web-shopping will increase but it won't replace real shopping because that is a form of entertainment that will endure. There will, though, be an increasing integration of Web-shopping and live shopping – for example, with people ordering goods via the internet and collecting them from local shops.

The entertainment industry will, of course, continue to tempt us out of our homes. People enjoy watching films at home, but there are some films they'd prefer to watch in a cinema. The demand for theatre, opera, musicals and the like will grow extensively, just as it will for live concerts. There will be more integration of theatre and dinner, as is found in the Berlin revues, and more tea dances and other forms of dancing at senior-friendly times – the over-forties no longer go out to a disco at one in the morning! All venues will be increasingly wrapped in heavy security because of the fears about terrorism.

Conclusion

The technological revolution is still in full swing and will change our lives, just as it has changed our lives in the past. Technology has a tendency to come closer to our lives. The natural biological technology of mankind meets the artificial communication technology. Technology has provided us with solutions and comfort, but has also created new problems and activities. The internet, for example, offers us the ease of emailing, but these emails take time to write, read and answer. We will have more free time that, in one way or another, will have to be filled. Technology will give us alternatives for fossil fuels and computers will begin to approach the complexity of the human brain. Most importantly, we should use technology to ease our lives and not to lead our lives. Otherwise this phrase becomes reality: 'In his pursuit of perfection, man will make himself redundant'.

Futures beyond the end of industrial history

The future of industrial design in Europe is a topic that firstly generates several questions. What is the future of both European industrial conglomerates and small to medium-size enterprises? What is the future of the creative industry, both globally and continentally? What societal futures are possible for Europe, which is rich in material wealth but shaken in its existential core – as described by the likes of French novelist Michel Houllebecq – as much as in its economic and financial foundations?

It is not the purpose of this short column to analyze the topic in depth. I would simply like to point towards two global macrotrends that have been studied in recent years and some pragmatic case histories that might anticipate how European design practices and communities could evolve. Europeans will increasingly look for those platforms and systems that enable them to adapt to rapid change, starting with newly defined communities of practice and shared interests. An integrated model of industry–design organization that might respond to this trend is one of creative districts. These regional concentrations of know-how developed over time as local clusters blessed by social harmony and high integration of very focused value chains, capable of attaining global success.

Creativity can be one of the engines of an optimistic outlook beyond the current gloomy downturn. Given the urgent need for new ideologies and new policies, the design of new cultural landscapes will be key for Europe. Either managed as enabler of inclusion or engine of tension, politics will rule the agenda of true design: this will be the direction where the greatest achievements or the worst conflicts will continue to unfold in the next decade or more. Here the challenge to European design communities is to become evangelists of social integration, well beyond the line of duty of industrial styling. An example of best practice in this field – which one might want to call 'cultural design'– is the work of Premsela, the Dutch design foundation, which established an extensive programme of exhibitions and events to facilitate discussion about what 'Dutch' design is, and how it can be developed to meet new challenges in society.

The new 'cultural frontiers' are the real opportunity for European creative leaders to make a deep impact on societies. But the future of European design is also deeply connected to the future of industrial Europe. This is where the economy will determine greatly what design will be about. What is the role of the creative industry in a rapidly declining mass-production economy? The destiny of some European brands might be foreseen in the acquisition of MG Rover by a former supplier from China. Successful European brands will become increasingly global by successful growth in emerging markets, which will result as well in a delocalization of competences like marketing and design towards Asia and other emerging areas. But what if Russia, China or even Brazil slow down, as they are in danger of doing at this time? Urban design and social design are the most immediate challenges for creative thinkers. European design will then have to act as the integrator of design and cultures. The public commissions will naturally drive the design industry towards a new ethic, thinking in terms of the aesthetics of infrastructures and other apparently 'humble' domains of our cities and countries: these are the real arenas in which designers need to prove themselves. Its role will be

© Philips Design

to connect people to people, both within companies and within markets – but especially within societies and cultures. Facilitation will be the key, perhaps one day even over creation, in a truly inclusive process of deploying the tools we know and use today towards new futures. Beyond the age of aesthetics, a new vision is required, both for the creative industry and, increasingly urgently, for the way we live. It is time to design not lifestyles, but the very way we live. ☐

Marco Bevolo is a freelance author and conference speaker. He lives in Turin, Italy, and Eindhoven, The Netherlands.

Megatrend 7

Towards a spiritual revolution

Jack and Bill, happily married to each other, are in Rome on holiday. It's a hot summer morning in 2020. They are at the Vatican. Pope Madonna, who was elected head of the Roman Catholic church a year ago, addresses the Catholics in the world this morning through several media simultaneously. She will fly this afternoon to attend the Berlin Council of Spiritual World Leaders, in order to establish a long-lasting peace in the world. In front of St Peter's, thousands of worshippers applaud her fierce speech. Jack and Bill admire her. As always, she is dressed impeccably, yet very sexy. She is adorned in fine satins and linens, and her papal crown is glittering. This afternoon she will meet with Dalai Lama Richard Gere, Rahul Gandhi, leader of the Hindus, calipha Irsjan Manji, leader of the liberal Muslims, and many others in sexy Berlin, spiritual and political capital of the renewed European Union. Jack remembers when the current pope was still a singer, and lived in the UK before her divorce. 'I already adored her then. Now she is able to reach out towards my inner self, my longing for spirituality in this fast-moving, high-tech world. Who am I? Who are we? Where are we going? What is the goal and meaning of life? How can we deal with all the moral aspects of the new world order? She helps me rethink my values, and in this way she is able to lure me back into the Catholic Church after Pope Benedict XVI kicked out all the gays in 2008. A remarkable achievement indeed.' ☐

More spiritual people

According to the most recent statistics, people are becoming more spiritual. The number of adherents to the major religions is increasing relatively faster than the world population, while numbers of non-religious people and atheists are stagnating. The annual growth in the non-religious (0.8%) and atheists (0.2%) is far lower than the growth of the world population (1.2%). Of the major religions, Islam is growing fastest, at a rate of 2.1% per year. The growth in the number of Christians (1.3%) is

only just higher than the growth of the world population. The number of Buddhists decreases annually by 1%. But this is only part of the story.

Although people say that they feel part of a certain religious movement, they experiment more often with spiritual and religious elements of other religions and denominations as well. This is in line with the individualization trend in society. The automatic adoption of the beliefs of our parents has disappeared at the start of the twenty-first century, at least in large parts of the Western world. Religion is increasingly becoming a conscious and personal choice. The young do not only strive for an image and lifestyle, but also choose a suitable moral attitude, a political viewpoint (or in any case an opinion about politics) and a *philosophical* vision. And if the call of the latter is not ear-shattering enough, they simply shop around for bits and pieces of religion. Such reli-shopping can really be an extensive mix-and-match affair. A statue of Mary in one corner of the living room doesn't need to be at odds with a Buddha or totem pole in another corner. Such individualization is also the result of pragmatism. Faith has to fit into the schedule of the busy world citizen. Religious practice has to compete with a busy job and an equally busy social and cultural life.

And although people consider themselves part of a religious movement, this does not necessarily mean that they support every view of that movement or its leadership. Many Catholics, for instance, straight and gay alike, despise the current Pope's opinions about homosexuals, yet they still feel Catholic. Religious leaders should therefore be aware that the overall democratization trend has also reached religious movements. Authoritarian leaders who refuse to acknowledge the freedom that people demand in what to believe in and how they define their own moral and ethical well-being will lose support among their followers. Look for instance to Iran where the young generation despises the current clergy and aspires a totally different kind of Islam than the current Iranian religious and political leaders preach. Next to the trend towards individualization, there is a simultaneous trend in exactly the opposite direction: towards group-forming. We see, for example, a tendency among many Hindu and Islamic young people to form their own identity according to the example given by the faith of their ancestors, often as a consequence of the worldwide tensions between religious groups. The future of God will, for a large part, depend on the tension between individualization and group-forming.

Believing in 'something'

Everywhere in the world, there are many people who no longer believe in God but do believe in 'something'. This is particularly true in northwest Europe and the east and west coasts of the US. In large parts of the world, however, religion has never really gone away. Spirituality in many regions is in fact encapsulated in citizenship. If you trip over, strangers will help you back on your feet. Citizenship is spirituality, and you don't need a God for that. God is in the citizens and in the way we deal with each other.

That has had consequences for formal religious structures and institutions. Many churches in Europe emptied in the past few decades; in the US, people also go to church less often than they used to. In India this is also the case. More and more people only visit their temples, mosques or churches during holidays. Democratization of religion means they can pray at home as well. Yet more people don't pray anymore, but meditate or organize their own rituals in order to become one with the spiritual world.

Increasing Buddhism among Western elites

The personal path and the personal responsibility that are central to Buddhism fit in well with the ideal of self-development that arose in the West during the 1960s. Its subjective spirituality matches our modern individualistic lifestyle. Your own experience is central, and not some divine revelation that is crucial to religions such as Christianity and Islam. The Buddhist tenet that life for the main part consists of suffering and that that suffering is caused by our attachments and desires could have been thought up by a psychotherapist. Self-observation is a central concept in both Buddhism and psychology. An additional advantage of Buddhism for Westerners is that the teaching is not related to a God and thus is not openly contradictory to other religions or to a scientific attitude to life. Thus a number of Brazilian Buddhist schools consciously do not call their teaching a religion but a 'humanistic philosophy'; this makes them appear less threatening and triggers a more positive response from the outside world.

The number of adherents to Buddhism has grown in the West, and that growth was explosive in the 1960s. In America, it was

Beat writers such as Allen Ginsberg, Jack Kerouac and Allan Watts who made Zen Buddhism *bon ton* among American intellectuals. Zen became *Beat Zen*; Zen became hip and didn't only appeal to many Americans of the 'counter culture', but also spread via the youth culture in Europe. In the 1970s and 80s, the Japanese Zen Buddhism was complemented with Tibetan Buddhism when teachers such as Chögyam Trungpa (1939–87) came to the West and founded their own organizations. Initially, it was largely the hippies who sought enlightenment in the East and embraced Buddha for this. As time passed, the contingent of followers grew more diverse and became more of a cross-section of the population, although it is remarkable that it was largely the elite who sought salvation in this teaching, which requires considerable study.

And yet, in the beginning, there were a lot of misunderstandings between the Eastern Buddhist teachers and their Western disciples. The modern Westerner tends to enter into a critical dialogue with the master based on equality, while the traditional Eastern master assumes a hierarchical structure of authority. The Westerner is concerned with universal principles, while the Easterner is more concerned with a personal interpretation of principles. However, the original version of Buddhism was increasingly attuned to the Western situation. Within this Western model, there are very close links with psychotherapeutic concepts. Marriage problems? Conflict with your boss? Difficulties in raising your children? The Buddha will show you the way.

The contact between Buddhism and modernity has not only resulted in Buddhism gaining a firm foothold in the West, but also it has influenced the original Buddhism. In countries where the majority of the population are Buddhists, such as Cambodia, Thailand, Sri Lanka and Myanmar, the teaching has withstood remarkably well the enormous changes that have taken place during the past fifty years, such as the relaxing of the close links between church/Buddhism and the state. Buddhism has also survived the ideological battle fought in the Cold War, a battle that resulted in some countries adopting communism as the new religion. In several countries, the Buddhist monasteries played a leading role in political change and monks turned into political activists. The great socio-economic changes in these countries mean that the monks, more than ever before, are far more concerned with the world around them and involve themselves in community building and education, although this should not suggest that it is the norm. This new, modernized and more or less universal form of Buddhism is also known as 'engaged Buddhism'. Characteristics of this new Buddhism are:

- Democracy, expressed in the dismantling of the strict monastic hierarchy, a greater emphasis on the religious practice of lay people and equality between the sexes (modern Buddhism in Japan is an example of this);
- Pragmatism, that allows a greater emphasis on ritual practices, ethical behaviour and meditation, and less on 'faith';
- Engagement, which means that the spiritual practice is extended with 'service and activism', of an altruistic variety, that is aimed at creating greater prosperity for family, friends and society as a whole, including the environment.

Within the various movements there are different opinions about the extent to which engaged Buddhism should be politically active. Take, for example, two comparable new religious movements from Taiwan: Foguangshan and Buddhist Compassion Relief. Both wish to spread their engaged and humanistic form of Buddhism, but the Foguangshan, which was founded in 1967, pleads for a high level of political activism, while the Buddhist Compassion Relief, founded in 1966, thinks that spirituality and politics should be strictly separated.

Let's look at some figures about the spread of Buddhism in the West. Researchers Wuthnow and Cadge estimated that the number of 'Buddhism affiliates' in the US in 2004 was between 0.7% and 1.9% (which translates into between 1.4 and 4 million Americans). At the same time, they state that the influence of Buddhism in the US is greater than the figures suggest. In their research report they state that '14% of the public claimed to have had a great deal or fair amount of "personal contact" with Buddhists and 30% claimed to be very or somewhat familiar with Buddhist teachings'. That means that between 25 and 30 million Americans are in some way influenced by Buddhism.

In Europe, Buddhism has had the greatest success in France, particularly because the French had many colonies in Buddhist Indo-China and thus had many Buddhist immigrant communities. In addition, the strict separation in France between church and state, the *laïcité*, ensures an open attitude towards non-Christian religions. In the

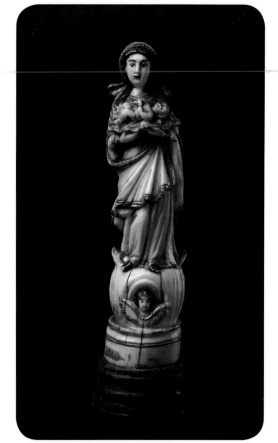

past twenty years, many Roman Catholic monasteries in French rural areas have been transformed into Buddhist temples, study and meditation centres, and in Paris there is a complete Université Bouddhique Européenne.

Nevertheless, the number of Buddhists in 2005 in France is estimated at just 0.8% of the population. Of this percentage, the largest part – around 70% – originally came from countries such as Vietnam, Laos and Cambodia, or they are children and grandchildren of the Indo-Chinese immigrants. The remaining 30% are converted French.

There is something else that is remarkable: Buddhism seems more popular in that part of Europe that was originally protestant. For protestants, modern Buddhism seems a more suitable form of religious expression. This is apparently due to the fact that Protestantism – in common with the modern European Buddhism – has few rituals and involves less worshipping, and because they are less hierarchical in design than Catholicism. In 2005, the number of dedicated Buddhists in Great Britain and the Netherlands was estimated at 0.5% and in Sweden at 0.2% of the population. In Catholic strongholds, such as Poland and Spain, the number was less than one per thousand.

These figures show that Buddhism is not a broad popular religion in the West. This is not surprising when you consider that the Buddhism practised in the West is in fact the form that is practised in the East by full-time monks. The emphasis on text and explanation is too intellectual for large parts of the population; the meditation requires considerable discipline to interest those people for any length of time. In the West, Buddhism is and will remain an elite religion. Nevertheless, the growth of Buddhism will be considerable if the trend of the past thirty years continues. Some more European figures: between 1975 and 1990, the number of Buddhist centres and communities in Germany increased five-fold; in England, the number in the period from 1979 to 1991 increased from 91 to 213. However, by 2020, the Buddhist share of the population in north and west Europe will still be less than 5%; in east and south European countries, it will be even less than 1%.

In the coming years, religion will be more explicitly expressed. We will see the paraphernalia of the various religions more emphatically on our streets. Head scarves and burkas will get competition from crosses, bindi-dots, yarmulkes, magical gem stones, pentagrams, and so on. And the Buddha, too, does well in the lifestyle stakes. We see him appear everywhere, in restaurants, garden centres, interior design shops. The reason that the Buddha is so appealing to the general public is first and foremost because of his appearance. People enjoy looking at his serene head. It brings them inner peace and they forget the ray-race for a moment. Looking at inner peace makes you peaceful. The Buddha is also immensely popular because he has a high tactile quotient. The tea lights and the cheerful colours of Tibetan Buddhism also work well in lifestyle magazines. So too does the sober minimalist design that is associated with the Japanese Zen version of Buddhism.

Buddhism is not only attractive aesthetically but also as a lifestyle for many Westerners suffering from stress. However, there are only a few who can apply the discipline necessary for daily meditation and studying deep texts. Traditional Buddhism has a solution to this: lay people leave the specialist religious work to the monks, who apply themselves to meditation, study, and doing good deeds. With their gifts, the lay people support the monks and thus ensure themselves of a better life the next time round. Lay people restrict themselves to visiting the temple and making offerings and other devotions.

This populist lay version of Buddhism that is now practised especially in Asia and among Asian migrant communities in the West will also serve the broader Western public. Many Westerners who feel attracted to Buddhism but, because of lack of time or discipline, cannot become a part-time monk, will be pleased to make do with a home altar and the occasional visit to a temple where a monk can provide them with guidance in spiritual matters and carry out the rituals that are apparently necessary. A couple of special Buddhist celebrations, such as Magha Puja in January or Vesakha Puja in May, and a few days' retreat once or twice a year will satisfy their deeper religious needs.

Plurality in the religious landscape

With the increasing migration and globalization, we see a worldwide pluralization of the religious landscape. In colonial times, Christianity was spread over the globe by fervent missionaries. Later, the migration of people from the colonies and the economic migrants heading in the direction of Europe and America meant that Buddhism, Hinduism, Sikhism and Islam were no longer exotic. These religions are becoming deeply embedded in Western religious life and are also accessible to people who traditionally did not belong to these religious movements. In practice, globalization doesn't always mean that one religion is completely exchanged for the other.

The contact between various religions ensures mutual influence and adaptation. For example, as mentioned above, the Buddhism practised in the Western world is a decidedly Western form of this teaching.

At the same time, we see that many Buddhist notions have seeped into the religious consciousness of Christians. Finally there is a noticeable tendency apparent in all religious contacts towards religious hybrids, ecumenical movements, and worldwide ethical standards, even though individual contradictions and 'schisms' will initially prevail.

The hybrid form of religion has, incidentally, been common for a long time in countries such as China and Japan. Traditionally, people there have not had an 'either-or' attitude towards religion, but rather an 'and-and' attitude. It has been said of the Japanese that 'they are born a Shinto, marry as a Christian, and are buried as a Buddhist', and that can be taken quite literally. Marriage ceremonies are based on Christian examples and the burial rituals are generally Buddhist. Only 30% of the Japanese population consider themselves belonging to a specific denomination, although the participation in certain Buddhist and Shinto rituals is extremely high. The custom of visiting the graves of ancestors on certain days is honoured by 90% of all Japanese, and three-quarters have a Buddhist or Shinto altar in their houses. The fact that so few Japanese consider themselves members of a specific denomination is based on the experience the Japanese have with these religions. Buddhism is associated with the very lucrative funeral industry, Shinto with the military state, and the new religious movements are suspect since the attack on the Tokyo metro with sarin nerve gas by the Aum Shinrikyo sect in 1995.

Christianity still has the largest number of denominations in the world. About 2 billion people are Christian, but in very many variants or denominations. According to the World Christian Database, there are in Germany, for example, 98 different Christian churches, in Great Britain 253, in Italy 57,

in the US 635, in Egypt 37, in China 141, and in Kenya 128. The other great world religions are also split up into all sorts of sub-movements, although they are generally less numerous than those in Christianity. A teaching such as Buddhism consists of two main movements: Theravada, which is practised principally in Sri Lanka, Myanmar and Indo-China, and Mahayana, which can be divided into Tibetan, Chinese, and Japanese (or Zen) Buddhism. In practice, these traditions are subdivided into sangas, schools and meditation centres, each of which has its own unique characteristics, generally based on the teachings of some great leader or other. Finally, pluralization is carried through to an individual level by the New Age movement, in which everybody follows his or her own spiritual path and paves this with a choice from the gigantic offering of New Age expressions.

'Your will is our command' spirituality

When a religion is totally attuned to the philosophy and models of psychology, we can then talk of 'client cults'. A client cult does not have believers, but clients. Within our present-day society, religion has not only become a private matter, but also a product that can be bought and sold. The client cult fits in perfectly with such a society, as long as it can find a niche where it can attract clients. An example of a client cult is the Scientology church. Client cults offer, for a small fee of course, solutions to actual life problems. Having difficulty finding a new job? Scientology teaches you to be so self-assured that every boss will hire you. Still suffering with a dominant father? Scientology teaches you to lay your past to rest. Even though Scientology, as a result of bad publicity, is in decline, there will always be some bright spark who is able to turn the needs of people into a healthy bank balance by offering quasi-religious solutions. There is always a future for client cults. An example of a club that works in the same vein as Scientology and which, since it blew over from America, has achieved considerable success in Europe is Landmark. This club's seminars are a mixture of scientology, pieces of oriental wisdom, and a lot of basic psychology. Central ideas are 'self-awareness', 'personal growth' and 'positive thinking'. The Landmark seminars are drill-camps, in which those attending are led with a rough hand to the damage to their 'ego'. Landmark hates publicity and in fact does not need the media. One of the reasons for its success is that clients who attend the introduction course are given the assignment to recruit new participants.

Elma Drayer, a journalist with the Dutch weekly *Vrij Nederland*, writes: 'Three days: an intensive course in happiness, full of psycho-chatter, tears and "breakthroughs". Sharing intimacy with hundreds, sometime two hundred at once, and not finding that embarrassing. Only going to the toilet if you are given permission, and drinking nothing but water the whole day long. And after the weekend you are convinced that you have been totally changed. That is Landmark Forum. People "in search of something" are queuing to get in. Landmark is the secret tip for the therapy shopper. Anybody who participates gets in via others: you can only attend if you have an invitation. Landmark Education, the organization behind the seminars, doesn't advertise. Participants who have already 'juice-dieted' or 'rebirthed' in some rebuilt farmhouse claim that Landmark is much more "effective". It goes "deeper", they say. It is certainly true that the missionary-urge among forum participants is

very large. What's more, participants are put under gentle pressure to continue with Landmark themselves. The follow-up course (Landmark Forum in Action) costs around 1,000 euros. "I had to decide," said one of the participants, "before Friday whether I wanted to take part in the second course. If I did, I would get a discount of 120 euros. They force you to make choices. I think that's a good method. Otherwise you continue to doubt." According to less satisfied Landmark clients, participants are pressured in an irresponsible way to register for follow-up courses.'

Erik de Boer, in the magazine *Intermediair*, said: 'I saw one exercise in which those present were split up into groups of three. The task was that two people had to convince the third to register. After a while, they asked: are there still people here who are not going to continue? That appeared to be the case. I raised my hand, together with several others. Then the whole session was repeated. And they constantly stress the same thing: if you don't continue, you haven't got the courage to make a choice.' Landmark, in common with Scientology, loves legal battles. Journalists who dare to call Landmark a 'sect' are hauled up in front of a judge.

2012 and mini-faiths

More people than ever are creating their own mini-faith, often a complex of traditional religious elements, scientific information and mysticism. The fast growing 2012 movement – people who believe in the Maya calender, which ends at 21 December 2012 – already has 290 million hits at Google. The 2012-believers mix the Maya horoscope and religion with Christian, Egyptian and Chinese ancient texts and wisdoms plus some scientific information about climate change, and feel happy and satisfied with their own faith, which already counts more believers than many.

The way in which we regard new technology also has something sacred about it, religious even. The young scientist in Silicon Valley I

mentioned earlier recently said to me: 'I don't believe in God, but I do miss Him because who is going to tell me how far science can go? Within five years, computers will be as smart as human beings. In 2085, the first robot will win the Nobel Prize. Will they still listen to us or will we end up as slaves of our own technology?'

As I have said above, many believe in 'something' between heaven and hell. This something can be a god, but it could also be something else spiritual. In countries such as China, the demise of communism has made way for religion. The way in which Christians react to this can have enormous political implications. Christian missionaries have set their sights on this densely populated area following their successes in South Korea and South Vietnam, where a large part of the population has converted to Christianity in the past few decades. In 2008, the Chinese government announcd that already a majority of the Chinese felt religious again. Yet, what kind of religiousness does the government mean? I think the Chinese are exploring their old spiritual roots, and are going back to the values of Confucius, the spiritual founder of the Chinese nation.

The number of atheists, nihilists and agnostics is decreasing. This group of non-believers can, without losing face, embrace Buddhism or the new multi-religions, such as the Brazilian Candomblé and Umbanda. Christianity is making a comeback among the young in the West and in Africa and Asia, although in different forms and variants. Catholicism is losing ground in South America while Europe increasingly admires evangelicals.

New mythos

Religious symbols (such as a cross on a chain worn around the neck) are reappearing in public, and also in atheist or agnostic circles. Every person has a need for logos (rational matters, such as science, technology and economy) and mythos (inspiration, religion, spirituality). Non-religious people can find mythos in art or nature, sex or other spiritual sources (e.g. the statues of Buddha in many households of rich Westerners flirting with Buddhism). At the same time, it is traditionally true that in times of great technological and scientific progress there is an automatic resurgence of religion. At the very moment that it becomes possible to do things that people thought were ruled or determined by God – flying in a plane or travelling to the moon – they begin wondering if there is more between heaven and earth.

Now that we are becoming more and more successful in tampering with our bodies, our lives and with all sorts of artificial procedures that can improve our health and extend our life expectancy, we start asking ourselves what life is, where it came from and what happens when it is over. This is certainly true now that we can postpone the end. When will the moment come when we do not die any more? Thanks to medical science

and gene technology, we can already replace, renew or give new impulses to parts of our bodies so that we live longer. If we engineer death out of our lives, is there still a god? If women can have children without needing males, what will be the consequences for the balance between the sexes? People try to find answers to questions such as these in religion.

Believing in spirits

We can see the greater belief in spirits as going deeper into such questions. It also satisfies the continuing desire (even among non-believers) for spirituality and a certain contact or communication with 'the other side'. This explains the increasing numbers of mediums, fortune tellers and 'spiritual leaders'. With the growing demand for fortune telling, it is being modernized: you can have your horoscope drawn by computer.

Talking to trees, mice and such like has not found favour with the young, who find it all too airy-fairy, but Eastern healing methods, such as acupuncture, shiatsu, acupressure and herbal remedies have a growing following.

Drugs and spirituality

The use of new mind-changing substances is also increasing, and will become a permanent part of our lifestyle now and in the future. Traditionally, the West has had an alcohol culture. However, migration has taken the West into relationships with people from drug cultures. In the West, you drink a beer or a glass of wine with friends and you do business over meals where the wine flows. Alcohol is the lubricant of bonding. In other cultures, drugs are the lubricant: in Yemen, you chew on qat with your friends and business acquaintances; in Arabic countries you share a water-pipe; and in old China you used opium. The indians of South America used drugs obtained from a variety of plants to contact the spirit world. Brazilian religions, such as Candomblé and Umbanda – a mixture of Catholicism and rituals from Indian and African religions – also make use of drugs, and are now growing in other parts of the world. At the start of the church service, people drink a cup of a bitter, hallucinatory herbal mixture and then the rhythmic mass gets under way.

We live in an age in which alcohol and drug cultures are mingling, and in which the use of new artificial drugs, such as ecstasy, is growing. A comparison with the old Indian cultures – in which drugs were used to induce a trance and thus come into contact with the world of spirits and gods – is not out of place. Perhaps in the new, more spiritual world we shall need a new mind-enhancing drug-mix that suits the current age, its population and these trends. Perhaps it will be a new artificial drug with an alcohol flavour.

Towards a new orthodoxy

At the start of the twenty-first century, we are confronted with a revival of orthodoxy. This revival can be attributed on the one hand to the increasing polarization on the political–religious world stage, and on the other hand it is a reaction to the uncertainty that modern life in a 'risk society' brings with it. That is certainly true of 'secular' Europe. Even though a decreasing number of Europeans are members of a church, the traditional religious forms will not simply disappear as the century progresses. In the United States, Christian fundamentalism has been an important force for much longer and, given the emergence of Islam in Western Europe, this fundamentalism will appear in Europe as well. One trump card that the old churches hold is their extensive management infrastructure, recognizable icons and authentic authority. In this time of story-telling and renewed interest in history, old religious stories can be communicated well, particularly if new media are used for this. The

moderate Christian denominations (such as the liberal Protestants) will become smaller – or even disappear – in the coming years, while the more conservative and orthodox will gain ground. The attractiveness of conservative churches lies in the total dedication, the irrefutable belief and a unique lifestyle, as described by Dean Kelly in his book *Why Conservative Churches are Growing*, which deals with the American situation.

The growth of religious conservatism can be partly explained as a populist revolt against the power of a secular elite (particularly baby-boomers) who still have the reins firmly in their hands in Europe because the members of these elites have studied. This elite is still able to block an ultra-conservative Catholic proposed as an EU commissioner from joining the European Commission (the Italian Catholic Buttiglioni who, in 2004, was rejected by the European Parliament), but it is questionable whether this will still be possible in 2015.

A similar tendency towards orthodoxy can be seen in the Islamic world. Here, it is primarily the confrontation with modernity that drives people towards the certainties of old forms of belief. Brazil also has its orthodox churches, such as the Assembly of God, which proved to have a membership of 8.4 million in the 2000 census (about 4.5% of the total population). The Assembly of God is a response to a less appealing Catholic Church and includes some Afro-Brazilian aspects that people miss in Catholicism.

Converts and new religions

The number of converts will grow, in various directions: Muslims who become Catholics, Protestants who become Catholics, but also Catholics who become Muslims and Christians who become Buddhists. Humanism only has a future if it no longer labels itself – as it does now – as an alternative to religion. It has to coexist with religion, and only then will it have a future market. Eras, such as the current one, with rapid scientific and technological change, are frequently eras that see the emergence of new religions. The religion of the Sikhs in India arose in such a period, and so too did Buddhism. It is quite possible that a new religion will now appear that will attract a large number of followers. That could be a sect (as yet obscure) in California that suddenly breaks through in the West (as previously happened on a limited scale with Bhagwan). It could be a new politician or pop star who suddenly achieves a prophetic or almost divine status, such happened in the Netherlands with Pim Fortuyn.

The future of God

Although religion and spirituality seem not to fit in this high-tech age, they are growing everywhere in the world. People require things such as religion and myths and want to surround themselves with them more and more. Wearing symbols, such as crosses, is once again very popular and people are searching for religion in art and other cultures. Many people do not believe so much in God anymore, but do believe that there is 'something'. An increasing number of believers feel free to join another faith. In addition, new religions are formed and people give certain influential people the status of prophet or even saint. Therefore, we might witness the end of the great religions and the emergence of 6 billion mini-faiths, one for every individual, everybody his own religion. The great religions might fall back on their symbolic values.

Conclusion: for everyone a God
With the increasing pace of life and speed of development of technology, everyone will search for their own way to find a counterbalance in life, whether it means going back to an orthodox religious basis or a building a new mix of everything and in between.

The new feng shui
The Asianization of the world in the twenty-first century will happen in several ways at the same time. One thing is for sure: more Asians will buy or rent real estate elsewhere in the world in the near future. And more Asians will visit other parts of the world. Chinese, Indian and other Asian investors regard property in not only commercial but other terms as well. They inspect the horoscope of a building. Will it bring them good luck or not? The horoscope of a building is called feng shui. It will become more relevant than ever in the new era. Feng shui, which originated in China more than 5,000 years ago, has in the last part of the twentieth century become a part of architecture, building development and home living, both in Asia and the West.

In Asia, naturally, more people are applying it in their homes and offices than elsewhere, but feng shui is not just something for the Asian mind: its overall application is fundamental to all people's well-being. As people everywhere in the world will have more say over their space in the future, with more of them working from their homes, thanks to 'world sourcing', we will see the use of feng shui become more prevalent. Some non-Asian interior designers are already using feng shui with their clients, and the next untapped profession that will start using feng shui in the world will be real estate agents. Real estate is ideal for this, especially for 'hard-to-sell' properties, and there are quite a lot of them in several parts of the world.

Feng shui is developing more into a mathematical science nowadays. Traditional feng shui is based on four aspects: building, environment, people and time. Just as the earth is constantly moving and changing, so are the energies of feng shui. Modern science has shown that geomagnetics are in a state of constant flux. Feng shui calculations show changing results based on the variables of building, people, time and environment. In the twenty-first century, a new feng shui is developing. It mixes traditional feng shui with modern science, globalization and the new energy circuits that are developing in the new economic world orders, as described in this book. In a sleeping country, there are different energy circuits than in a tiger country, for example. Feng shui is developing into a lifestyle, a system of analyzing people's energy.

Feng shui's methodologies will be more like Western scientific inquiry in the twenty-first century. Feng shui practitioners will observe and record, formulate mathematical models of structures, and report findings in both technical and lay people's language. As more Asians live part time or full time outside of Asia, and more Asians visit other parts of the world during holiday or business trips, international trade and business relations intensify. Consequently, you will see more about feng shui being written in non-Asian magazines and newspapers, and more exposure will be given to it on television and radio. As feng shui awareness grows in the world, property investors will realize that it's easier to sell a building that is built according to feng shui, because it makes the target market larger (i.e. they can include potential Asian buyers in their range). This might be new, but it's also necessary in an age of globalization. ☐

Gita Kapoor is based in the Indian capital, Delhi. She is a feng shui master and works for the World Bank, Citibank, Intercontinental Hotels and several other major international companies. Her columns and articles appear in leading Indian newspapers like the Times of India and the Hindustan Times. She is the author of the book 'Feng shui for Indian homes'.

Megatrend 8

Towards climate change, food shortage and growing importance of nature and fresh water

It's early Monday morning. Jim and Clark log in for the virtual meeting with the other members of their team, who are up and about in several places around the world. Everybody logs in through the virtual meeting system. You just stay at home, sitting at your dining table, and suddenly, through three-dimensional projection, you see the 3D images of your colleagues appearing around your own table. Anybody who is still a bit sleepy (because of the time differences) is automatically dressed up in a suit and tie by the computer. Everybody can look each other in the eyes, as if they were physically sitting around the same table, yet everybody is in his or her own home.

There is no longer any need to travel to meet other people on business. Virtual meetings arose as one of the solutions for using less energy, decreasing pollution and countering global warming – a trend that emerged in the early 2000s.

Jim and his colleagues exchange views and ideas for about an hour and make decisions for their company for the coming week. After the meeting, everybody says goodbye, logs off and starts to do his or her part of the job. Jim remembers that there was a time and age when you actually physically met all your colleagues. People voluntarily travelled for hours, suffering traffic jams, delayed planes, crammed trains and other in-conveniences, in order to attend meetings or get to work. Now everything has changed. The low-energy economy of the 2020s encourages people to travel less. If they do travel, they mainly use cars, which are no longer fueled by oil or gas, and they enjoy it.

Solar energy and nuclear energy in particular enable the peoples and companies in their areas in Europe to live more secure and peaceful lives than ever before. They are not really preventing global warming, but they feel good about their new lifestyle and also feel good about the fact that they do not sponsor terrorism anymore. Through their VirtualMe avatar, they are recommended to book a holiday trip to the Emirates, where a wonderful new art exhibition will be launched and the beaches are delightful. Why not? They've earned enough CO_2 emission bonus points to deserve this trip, so why not? Go east my friends; go east! ☐

Introduction

The climate will change in the near future and there is no consensus about the reasons for this. The only thing we know is that it has happened before – and that it will happen again. So, what is going on at the moment? Some claim that the pole shift is the major trigger for climate change. Others say that climate change is caused by the greenhouse effect. And others claim that it is happening because of changes taking place in the sun itself, changes that take place naturally from time to time and which insignificant human beings can do nothing about, either positively or negatively.

Climate changes will give the world in the twenty-first century a new face. Rivers will regularly breach their banks and there will need to be flood areas created to accommodate the water that suddenly rises in the main rivers. The sea level will rise, while some land areas will sink, as is currently happening in Venice. A new form of water management will be essential. Only 1% of all the water in the world is fresh. Fresh water will become scarcer, the sea will be used more intensively (e.g. more food can be harvested from the sea, such as seaweed) and there will also be new ways of generating energy.

It will certainly become warmer in some regions, and at the same time wetter. Conversely, deserts will spread in areas that used to have good soil and grassland. In other regions it might become colder and dryer. Whatever the changes, we'll have to prepare ourselves for them and adapt.

It is encouraging to see that some people have already started to study the behaviour of the earth as a whole with the discipline of 'earth system science'. This discipline treats the earth's geosphere and biosphere as an integrated entity. James Lovelock, father of earth system science, calls the earth's control system Gaia. With a holistic approach to studying the earth, it might be better in the future to see the interdependencies which rule the working of the planet. The challenge for us all is to live within the planet's means. As far as we know, earth is the only planet supporting life so we better take good care of it.

In my opinion, the following three scenarios are conceivable for the coming decades with regard to how to deal with climate change:

1. *The Easter Island scenario* – This is a doom scenario that assumes this will be humankind's final century. In this scenario, there is no solution for the climate problems allied to our use of energy: the earth will continue to revolve, but the human race will disappear in the ensuing ecological disasters. The earth itself is quite capable of coping with any climate change and has done so many times before. Just as earlier, on a smaller scale, when the inhabitants of Easter Island destroyed their civilization and ultimately themselves by chopping down all the trees on the island, we are doing likewise, except on a worldwide scale.

2. *The Luther scenario* – 'Even if I knew that the world were to end tomorrow, I would still plant a tree today,' said the Protestant reformer Martin Luther. This also seems to be the motto of the people who support this scenario. In the Luther scenario, a new energy era will emerge in the short to medium term, in which people succeed in switching to sustainable forms of energy, even though it will prove impossible to rectify much of the damage that has already been done to the planet and we will be faced with serious forms of climate change that could harm many and cost lives. There is an increasing number of supporters for this scenario, mainly among the baby-boomers (born between 1945 and 1964) and among the youth. It means that the West will have to moderate its energy consumption even further and that the energy consumption in new super-powers such as China and India must grow less explosively than is now expected. All sorts of innovative forms of energy consumption and new energy forms will, in this

scenario, quickly reach maturity. This will take place under the pressure of public opinion and from the resulting governmental measures.

3. *The Ostrich scenario* – This scenario is largely supported by those who wish to retain their short-term interests, under the banner 'eat, drink and be merry – and let tomorrow look after itself', and by those who deny that climate change is a result of human activity. At the end of the 1990s, there were many who doubted climate change; now it is clear not only to the meteorologists but also to the majority of people in the street. During the past decade, one climate record after another was set: the winter of 2006–7 was, in western Europe, the warmest since meteorological records began. The British summer of 2007 appears to have been the wettest since rainfall records began in 1914, according to provisional data from the UK Meteorological Office. Britain had 358.5mm of rain, just beating the 1956 record of 358.4mm. Central and southern England were hit with serious flooding. There clearly seems to be something the matter with our climate. Very soon,

Brighton on the south coast will boast temperatures like Saint Tropez, while Saint Tropez will likely have turned into a desert marina. Not that it makes a bit of difference to the supporters of the Ostrich scenario . . .

The supporters of scenarios 1 and 3 are strongly ideological and politically motivated, and even sometimes religiously inspired. In the public debate they are on opposing sides. The supporters of the second scenario are much more pragmatic; they don't do doom, they're fully conscious of the urgency of the energy problems and they realise, to a greater or lesser degree, that everybody – mother or grandfather, citizen or entrepreneur, politician or volunteer – must accept the responsibility for making a new style of energy management possible. Not everybody realises that this scenario, too, will radically cull mankind. We will be confronted with ecological refugees who flee from flooding and drought. Famine and conflicts about food and water are unavoidable, and migration as a result of this will be considerable (including from Africa to Europe) and this will result in tension and armed conflicts, creating winners and losers. In this scenario, an significant portion of the human race will survive the transition to a new energy era in an innovative, creative way, but many will not live to see it.

One thing applies to all scenarios: an ever-increasing world population doesn't exactly make it easy to reduce carbon dioxide (CO_2) emissions and energy consumption.

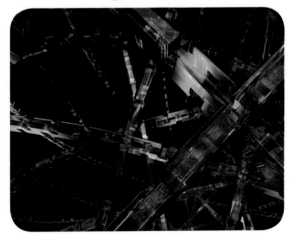

During a recent climate conference, a Chinese representative said that the world should be grateful to China for the one-child policy that applies there; otherwise there would have been at least three hundred million more Chinese than is the case at present. If African and other Asian countries had also introduced this one-child policy, there would

now be one billion fewer people on earth, which would be a blessing for the environment. The good man was, of course, absolutely right. The birth figures in some regions are amazing. Yet, population reduction is barely an issue among environmental warriors, even though this is actually the one measure that really would make a difference. Population reduction is therefore an important environmental measure.

According to demographic studies from the UN, this will eventually happen, even if we are not faced with ecological disasters. There are currently 6.7 billion people in the world and the growth will continue until 2050, when there will be a population of around 9 billion people. After that, the demographic models indicate a decline to around 6 billion world citizens in 2100. The crunch will come in the next forty to fifty years, in which time the population worldwide will increase by 50%. The largest growth will take place in Africa and Asia.

We believe that population reduction should be approached faster and more radically. That's because we believe that this is the ultimate environmental problem: there are simply too many people on our planet. This can be illustrated by the term 'ecological footprint', a term first introduced by William Rees and Mathis Wackernagel, which is used to give people an idea of how much they consume of nature's resources. On average, there are 5.3 acres of land for every person in the world. In 2000, the average person used 6.9 acres. A country that uses more acres than are available in its own country is the United States, with a deficit of 11 acres per person. At the opposite end of the spectrum is Brazil, which uses less acres than it has available; it has a surplus of 14 acres.

All scenarios suggest that crisis is our lot. For example, ice caps and glaciers melt and cause a rise in the sea level. Research has shown, however, that it was warmer at the end of the Middle Ages in Europe than it is now, with vineyards in England and green meadows in Greenland (which gave it its name). There are also indications that it was then possible to sail around Greenland, that there was therefore not as much ice, and yet the sea level was no higher than it is now.

The consequences of global warming, whether or not it is caused by human activity, will become more visible as the century progresses. So too will the need for an ever-increasing number of people to become much less dependent for their energy supply on states such as Russia and Saudi Arabia. Whatever the case, we must learn to deal with climate change and we will have to become more economical with, and develop new sources of, energy. In this respect, all countries have to deal with it and joint action is to be favoured above isolation from problems that might harm other countries more than our own.

Growing awareness of the climate issue among the general public

Until recently, the general public knew about the greenhouse effect and climate change, but few people worked themselves up about it and the issue was viewed largely as a technical problem where experts such as meteorologists and climatologists differed in their views. The discussions concerning the Kyoto Protocol at the start of the twenty-first century increased the awareness of CO_2 emissions, but what made a real impression on people was the extreme change in the weather. In many places on earth, weather record after weather record was broken. And this happened in western Europe as well. We had only just had the mildest winter ever when the most severe January storm of all times and the warmest month of April came along. Something like this makes a deeper impression and, because everybody experiences it first-hand, it has a much greater influence than any climate report, no matter how well thought-out it may be.

The awareness that the extreme nature of the current weather may be connected to human influence broke through in the autumn of 2006 when two publications about climate change made headline news in newspapers and TV programmes. Sir Nicholas Stern, economist and former vice president of the World Bank, presented his report *The Stern Review on the Economics of Climate Change*, in which he calculated how much climate change would cost us. And ex-vice president of the US, Al Gore,

published the book and film *An Inconvenient Truth*, which describes in images accessible for the general public the disastrous effects that greenhouse gases could have in the long term for humanity.

The strength of Stern's message is that he translated the abstract debate on climate into the clear language of money – a language that everybody understands. Stern calculated that, if mankind continues at the current level of CO_2 emissions, it would cost the world community around €5.5 trillion – in other words, 20% of the total economic world production. That would mean a deep economic crisis, a crisis comparable to or even worse than that of the 1930s of the previous century. Climate change is, according to Stern, 'the greatest and most comprehensive market disruption ever'.

Both the left- and right-wing press described the seriousness of Stern's message, even though some had reservations about his calculation methods. Nor could the business community ignore his report. His language is stripped of every emotion or moral, but restricts itself to a clear profit and loss analysis, the language of entrepreneurs.

More Al Gore: Sustainability

With his film *An Inconvenient Truth*, Al Gore has shaken the world, although he is far from the only person responsible for the worldwide awareness of climate change. In America, for a long time the most stubborn polluter of the world, eyes have been opened to climate change and environmental problems by Gore's film, as well as by threatened oil shortages and Hurricane Katrina.

Thirty years ago, sustainability issues were already awakened in Europe with the energy crisis of 1973, but they did not persist when the crisis ended. Nowadays, environment and climate are not only important issues, but specifically working on them is also commercially attractive and sexy. Many large companies advertise using their environmental-awareness credentials and choose to do business in new market niches in the area of environmental sustainability and energy. Less harmful fossil fuels that were previously too expensive for production (such as liquid natural gas) are now being shipped in bulk. Cars are becoming hybrid and will, in the not too distant future, run on hydrogen. Because celebri-

ties drive hybrids, many car owners no longer feel stupid in their small, light, slow but environmentally friendly cars. Companies proudly claim that they work in a 'climate neutral' way. Their CO_2 emissions are compensated for by using energy-saving lamps, by purchasing green energy or by planting trees. In several years, conventional electric light bulbs will be forbidden in several countries.

New ways of producing food

Climate change and natural shortage triggers innovation. People are constantly looking for new answers to cope with the negative effects of climate change.

According to James Martin, only 10% of edible fish remain in the oceans, and this percentage is rapidly declining. In response to this, fish farming is growing rapidly. China leads the way with a production of two-thirds of world's pond fish. A whole new aquaculture has emerged. On millions of acres of rice land, China breeds fish in the rice paddies.

Another example is hydroponics, a technology that allows food to be grown without the need of soil. Plants are rooted in water and are getting liquid nutrients to give them all the necessary minerals. Little water is needed and the right mix of liquid nutrient can be measured by sensors. A big advantage is that hydroponic farms can be close to consumer markets, such as on the sunny sides of glass skyscrapers or under sloping glass roofs in urban areas.

The much criticized genetically modified food also delivers food in a new way but careful scientific study is still needed to see whether it is completely safe.

What the UN tells us on climate change

The International Panel on Climate Change, the climate organization of the United Nations, has four future scenarios for CO_2 emissions. The IPPC makes considerable use of scientific research. Unfortunately, the conclusions and recommendations of the IPCC are rather politicized, much to the irritation of the scientists who cooperated on IPCC reports. Despite this, the IPCC scenarios will be used by governments and other parties involved in the coming era for the development of climate and energy policies, so no matter what one may think of the reports, it is advisable to know them and to take them into account. The IPCC's scenarios are:

- *Scenario A1* – In this scenario, the world enjoys fast economic growth, the world population increases until 2050, after which it declines, and new environmentally efficient techniques are quickly introduced.
- *Scenario A2* – In this scenario, large differences arise throughout the world, the world population continues to grow and there is fragmented and lower economic growth.
- *Scenario B1* – This scenario takes scenario A1 as its starting point, but predicts an economy that increasingly directs itself at services and information and becomes less dependent on the consumption and production of materials.
- *Scenario B2* – This scenario is based on finding local solutions in the area of sustainability, a continuously increasing world population and an average economic development.

The B1 scenario is the best for the climate. This is the only one in which the CO_2 emissions can be reduced in the long term to a level comparable to that of 1990. It is a scenario based on economic growth, coupled to a development in the direction of the service and information sector. Further conditions are a decrease of the world population from around 2050 and fast innovation through new sustainable techniques. The most disastrous scenario for the climate is the A2 scenario, in which there is a fragmented world economy and an ongoing increase in the population. The CO_2 emissions will increase drastically and in 2100 will be three to six times greater than in 1990.

And what about the way the IPCC scenarios reflect our own, as given in the introduction above? Our Easter Island scenario, which assumes hell and damnation, most closely matches the IPCC scenario A2. Our Luther scenario best fits the IPPC scenario B1, because it mentions both sacrifices and opportunities. It is hardly surprising that our third scenario, the Ostrich scenario, which foresees only problems to fire-fight, finds no place at the somewhat alarmist and politicized IPCC.

Turning climate change into a religion

At the moment, a certain polarization can be discerned in the positions concerning the malignant influence of humans on the climate. On the one hand, there are those who preach hell and damnation, with stories of climatic calamity. On the other, you have the 'there's-nothing-to-worry-about' people, who dismiss all stories about climate change as nonsense. Both positions have something of an expression of faith, and are expounded with a fervour that approaches religious. It is almost like two religious sects arguing with each other, each trying to have the other burned at the stake. This is due in part to the complexity of the issue and the flood of 'scientific', yet nevertheless conflicting, data. As a lay-person, there is little choice but to believe one or the other. But there is more.

The climate sceptics accuse the prophets of doom of following a belief rather than any scientific theory. They maintain that humankind needs to find a common enemy (the devil in the shape of a CO_2 producing population) to fight against, to blame for our unequal prosperity (why are they rich while we are poor?) and to embrace the message of salvation. The former British Chancellor, Lord Nigel Lawson, spoke about this in the British topical magazine *Spectator*: 'It has to be said that the sceptical position is not an easy message to get across, not least because climate change is so often discussed in terms of belief rather than reason. It is, I suspect, no accident that it is in Europe that climate change absolutism has found the most fertile soil. For it is Europe that has become the most secular society in the world, where the traditional religions have the weakest popular hold. Yet people still feel the need for the comfort and higher values that religion can provide; and it is the quasi-religion of green alarmism and what has been termed global salvationism — of which the climate change issue is the most striking example, but by no means the only one — which has filled the vacuum, with reasoned questioning of its mantras regarded as a form of blasphemy. But that can be no basis for rational policy-making.'

The German climatologist Hans von Storch also draws a parallel between climate doom scenarios and religion. In *Der Spiegel* he says: 'Unfortunately, many scientists consider themselves far too much as priests who wish to preach their moralising sermons to the people. It is one of the legacies of the 1968 generation, to which I also belong.' According to Storch, nothing may be said about the positive consequences of a climate change because 'playing with God's creation is forbidden'. Climate change is, in fact, viewed as God's punishment for our sinful, hedonistic behaviour.

The fact that environmental groups and disquieted scientists profess their positions concerning the climate with a religious fervour can also be explained in another way. The climate is intrinsically something of a higher order: weather happens to us and literally comes 'from above'. Nature – with a capital N – is traditionally something that gives a meaningful framework in a religious sense: the first religions were based on the worship of Nature, and we are still inclined to regard Nature, including the weather, with an almost religious passion.

The image conjured up by Gore & Co is not far removed from an apocalypse. In its most recent report, the IPCC literally calls the irrevocable change in the climate 'apocalyptic'. Biblical language and imagery abound in the climate debate. The imagery is understandable given that, in the Bible, God regularly calls down natural catastrophes to punish mankind for its sins. Psychologists explain our susceptibility to this kind of doom scenario as follows: it is a way of suppressing inner insecurity and creating the illusion of control. The climatologists of the IPCC remonstrate with us like Old Testament prophets, demanding that we shake off our sins so that we may escape the flood of rising oceans, the extinction of species, famine and manifold other disasters. In this way, they create the illusion that climate change can be halted, as long as we make sufficient sacrifices. It is not that there is no truth in their observations about the climate but, rather, that it seems unnecessary to turn it into a matter of faith and is, in fact, counterproductive because it causes a polarization that prevents parties from joining forces in the search for solutions.

A comparison with religion is also possible on another front: in normal issues of faith, there have always been narrow-minded atheists and fanatical sceptics who constantly challenge the beliefs of others, and similarly, in the CO_2 debate, there are also the 'non-believers' who do not miss any opportunity to pillory the belief of the others. In fact, such climate sceptics are just as much believers as those they attack.

Considering the current polarization in climate positions, the religious endeavour back and forth will only increase. Turning the climate debate into a religion seems almost as irrevocable as the warming of the earth.

Environmental revolution and Latinizing the culture/climate

The climate will change. The environmental revolution will not hit all countries. The UN's Millennium Assessment published in 2005 is relatively level-headed about it all. In certain areas, we are making too heavy demands of the environment. The authors of the Millennium Assessment are correct in saying that environmental problems are a side-effect of poverty. But economic growth is ultimately the solution, as we are now seeing in Asia: richer countries are better able to tackle environmental problems. In poor countries, survival is all that matters. What do you think they prefer to do in Asia, eat or admire butterflies?

A Chinese writer recently summarized it very succinctly: 'When it suited you in Europe to overtax the environment in order to fuel your

economic progress, that was fine. But now we are doing the same, it is suddenly bad for the environment. Is your environmental mafia not involved in maintaining the world's economic status quo by using pious texts?'

Despite the West's love of pointing the accusatory finger at developing countries, it too is not fully committed to the environment. Environmental issues are included in several treaties, but national interests appear to be more important. All member states want their economies to grow, so the environment remains an undernourished child. What's more, there is also still the question of whether global warming is due to the carbon dioxide emissions. As mentioned earlier, many remain convinced that changes in climate are perfectly normal. In the Middle Ages, Europe was on average warmer than it is today, and in the twentieth century there were differences in temperature that could not be explained by extra emissions of carbon dioxide. An interesting book about this problem is *State of Fear* by the late Michael Crichton, in which scientists and environmentalists fight each other for the truth about the rising sea level.

Nature and water management

The warming of the earth is expected to lead to a rise in levels of the sea and the rivers. That will demand a different type of water management. It seems not unlikely that certain coastal areas will have to be evacuated because of the rising water, so counter-measures are essential (e.g. in the form of dykes to hold back the sea). A Pentagon study is rather sombre about this: within a few decades, it suggests, new dykes will be essential in several areas of Europe. Other environmental studies suggest that it will be at least 150 years before this is necessary. It all depends on what you believe.

In northwest Europe, the milder winters and longer summers are already having an effect on flora and fauna. Species that previously did not appear in these areas are now moving up from the south. Dolphins are now seen more frequently in the North Sea. In Amsterdam, there are large colonies of rose-ringed parakeets.

During 2004 in the Netherlands, more than fifty species of plants were added to the standard list, plus forty-eight new species of slugs. According to the book *Warmed up Holland* by Jan van Arkel, the climate border shifts by eleven metres each day. Because of this, species that prefer cold climates are moving farther north (to Denmark, Sweden, Norway and the north of Great Britain) and the Netherlands and Belgium now welcome several species from the south. Should we be concerned about this? Yes and no. Yes, because these countries will also entertain less welcome visitors such as blue algae and new diseases. No, because climate change has always been with us: in the Middle Ages northwest Europe was a lot warmer and the sea frequently washed over the coastal areas of the Low Countries.

In southern Europe, there will be shortages of fresh water and more areas will turn into desert. A lot of course can be done about this. Freshwater streams can be moved along newly dug canals, fresh water can be distilled from sea water (as already takes place in Israel and Dubai), and it is also possible to recycle water. Modern cruise ships already do this: used water from toilets, washbasins and bathrooms is purified and reused. These techniques will soon be used on shore. There will soon be a large market for recycling water in the home if the price for fresh water rises far enough. What's more, 'freshwater pockets' in the sea have been discovered in various places throughout the world, such as along the coast of Saudi Arabia. Often hundreds of metres below the surface level, these pockets contain fresh water within the salt water. They are, of course, not actual pockets, but they are nevertheless water reserves that remain separate from the salt water. At the moment, it is too expensive to exploit these reserves, but if fresh water becomes expensive enough, the exploitation will become profitable.

The Saudis are already looking into this, much to the dismay of Uruguay, which has one of the largest freshwater reserves in the world and thought that this 'new gold' would bring prosperous times in the twenty-first century. But, still, shipping fresh water from Uruguay to southern Europe remains an option. Uruguay was founded by the Spaniards, so why shouldn't they drench the old homeland in the twenty-first century? Everybody in Spain could drink from the Uruguay water trough!

It isn't just southern Europe that is concerned about water supplies. Areas in England and Wales are looking at ways to reduce their population's water use because the supply is getting more restricted every year.

Towards more buildings on water

The ongoing growth of the world's population coupled with the loss of land due to global warming and rising sea levels means that we will need to begin living and working on water in the near future. In water rich countries such as Canada and The Netherlands inspiring examples are currently being developed that might become feasible in the UK and other regions as well. The Ooms Avenhorn Group (OAG) in The Netherlands has created a successful new building system, called simply

'Building on Water', that enables the construction of buildings on bodies of water, from rivers such as the Thames to ponds in parks. This allows municipal authorities, architects, project developers and city planners to make more effective use of existing or newly created water surfaces by taking them into account as new building grounds. The design possibilities provided by 'Building on Water' are virtually limitless – including floating villas, student accommodation, theatres, parking spaces, squares and hospitals. Within a number of preconditions, architects can work in an unrestricted way.

The discovery of water as a building site

The Netherlands is truly a water country. For centuries, the Dutch have been working and living at the water's edge. It is only logical, therefore, that it was here that the innovative idea of building on water was born. Being Dutch, the Ooms Avenhorn Group has long recognised the value of water as a building location. Thorough research within The Netherlands and throughout the rest of the world led to the design of a Canadian building system that the Group took out a licence for, International Marine Floatation Systems Inc. (IMF). In addition to the extensive experience that the Canadians acquired with the system of unsinkable, floating foundations – entire residential areas that are completely afloat have been built in Vancouver and Seattle – the Group has also amassed considerable experience in the area of floating development and construction. Their designs vary from floating villas and villa neighbourhoods to, for example, a Cannes-like marina featuring floating villas, restaurants and shops, and floating residential boathouses; a tremendous victory over – and indeed on – water.

The benefits of 'Building on Water'

Building land is scarce nowadays, especially in inner-city areas so building on existing waterways (rivers, canals) is well and truly gaining ground. Floating buildings are less vulnerable to the rising sea levels caused by climate change. Incorporating water in project plans not only has practical value for future new development and utilisation opportunities but also has aesthetic value. The world over, living on and at the edge of water has a strong appeal – there is just something special about it. Water offers grand views, reflections, ripples, colours, and serenity; and recreational extras – a swimming pool and boat just a few steps away.

Mobility, quality, flexibility and sustainability

'Building on Water' is about mobility and quality, but also about a high degree of flexibility in the design and building process. The floating foundations are made of reinforced concrete that contain polystyrene blocks that in turn contain the necessary pipes and cables to service the buildings they carry. They require minimal maintenance and can remain in the water for numerous years without any form of decay, deterioration or nasty emissions. The system is unsinkable and extremely stable. The floating foundations can be manufactured in any size and shape for building volumes up to a certain height (dependent upon the depth of the available water). The building activity can be completed on location or 'in dry dock', which provides a high degree of flexibility with regard to the logistics and planning of complex building projects, for example in terms of preventing building-related inconvenience at busy building sites.

The floating buildings are sustainable in the broadest sense of the word. An extremely light, environmentally friendly construction method is used, starting with a 'forest friendly' timber structure. Through the development of a special climate-controlled system, the buildings can be exceptionally energy-efficient. The water plays a significant role in this, as it is responsible for heating and cooling the structures.

One of the great advantages of the floating buildings is that they are very easy to tow. No demolition or new development is required; these buildings can quite simply be re-used at a different location. This is sustainability at its very best.

Let the 2012 Olympic Games in London begin… on water!

During an event like the Olympic Games the organizing city gets an enormous temporary influx of visitors who need temporary accommodation. Extra facilities like hotels, restaurants, accommodation for athletes and more are needed.

An Olympic village is created to provide these facilities. Most of the time the village is located outside the city centre as there is no space in the centre. This means that the village is at some distance from the major attractions of the host city. This limits the opportunities for the Games and the city to profit from each others' existence.

But imagine that building a village in the city centre could be realized and in a way that would astonish most visitors.

In 2012, London will organise the Olympic Games. OAG has come up with an inspiring idea to build the facilities in the city centre without having to destroy existing buildings. OAG suggests that the stretch of the Thames between Big Ben and Tower Bridge, in the heart of London, would be the perfect location for a floating Olympic Village. There are three major advantages to this idea:

1. The construction process can be undertaken off-site, which reduces impact on the centre of London. After completion the water buildings could be towed to the desired location.
2. There are numerous facilities in the centre of London that already cater for visitors. The village would become an integral part of the centre and the two would strengthen each other in an unprecedented way.
3. This type of building is more sustainable and has a potential longer term use. After the Games the floating buildings could be sold for other events and towed to different locations. Compare this with previous Olympic villages that are often used inefficiently after the games or have even been demolished.

Participating countries could build their own floating promotional pavilions that could sail together into the heart of London in a grand parade at the start of the games. This would look terrific. After the parade each country's floating pavilion would get its own mooring on the Thames and visitors could visit them by boat or by a system of temporary bridges.

London has a unique opportunity to embrace this brilliant idea. A floating village could be iconic. Visitors and London residents alike would be attracted by the floating village, adding a new element to the Olympic experience.

Message for Boris Johnson: call OAG now!

What exactly is the greenhouse effect?

The atmosphere around our planet works like a blanket. The sun warms the earth and its atmosphere, which in turn reflect back that warmth. Some of this energy is lost into space but some remains trapped in the atmosphere and is reflected back to earth by clouds and greenhouse gases. The more greenhouse gases we produce, the more warmth is trapped in and around the earth. In fact we are confronted with a self-perpetuating effect. Because of heating, more water vapour, for example, is found in the atmosphere, and this, in turn, traps more heat.

Water vapour does not, by itself, have a very strong greenhouse effect, but because of the enormous quantity of it borne in the atmosphere, the total effect is considerable. Research shows that the amount of atmospheric water vapour is increasing by 1% every decade. The most important greenhouse gases caused by man are carbon dioxide (CO_2), methane (CH_4) and chlorofluorocarbons (CFCs). The concentrations of the various greenhouse gases are generally expressed in ppm – parts per million.

Carbon dioxide is naturally present in the atmosphere, and that's good because we would otherwise freeze. Without greenhouse gases, the average temperature on earth would be minus 18°C instead of the current average of plus 12°C. However, too much greenhouse gas is not good either, because that causes too much warming, and that's what we are confronted with now.

The atmosphere of the planet Venus consists almost entirely of carbon dioxide (97%), which makes the temperature on the planet far too high for human habitation. The simplest way of making carbon dioxide is by burning carbon and fossil fuels. It is also, however, released in large quantities naturally, such as by volcanoes. Carbon dioxide, in addition to acting as a protective blanket around the earth, has a number of other useful functions. Plants, for example, need carbon dioxide for the process of photosynthesis. During the process, the plant absorbs the carbon (C) and releases the oxygen (O_2) into the air. In greenhouses, carbon dioxide is therefore used a fertilizer for the plants: the more carbon dioxide in the air, the faster the plants grow.

Carbon dioxide also has a number of very practical applications. For instance, when it is dissolved in liquid it is known as carbonic acid gas,

which we all know as the 'fizz' in our soft drinks. Because CO_2 is heavier than air, it sinks when it is released. This property is used to good theatrical effect in the form of 'smoke machines' that are used on stage and in television shows.

In 1958, the American Charles Keeling started measuring the concentrations of CO_2 in the atmosphere on Hawaii; in that year, he recorded 315 ppm, a figure that had increased by 2007 to more than 380 ppm. The CO_2 concentrations for the years prior to 1958 can be discovered by analysing ice samples. This shows that in the past 150 years, the amount of CO_2 in the atmosphere has risen by 35%. This increase is particularly the result of the use of fossil fuels to keep our factories operating, for the heating of our homes and to keep our cars running.

Of all the greenhouses gases produced by man, carbon dioxide is responsible for around 53% of the greenhouse effect. Other greenhouse gases are present in the atmosphere in much smaller concentrations, but have a relatively stronger greenhouse effect: methane concentrations are, for example, less than 2 ppm and CFCs only 1 ppm, but these gases are responsible for 17% and 5% respectively of the greenhouse effect caused by man.

Carbon dioxide not only makes the largest contribution to the greenhouse effect, but also ensures that the problem will continue for a lengthier time: CO_2 molecules remain in the atmosphere for up to a century whereas methane molecules, on the other hand, are degraded after around a decade. The persistence of CO_2 means that the accumulation of the gas will grow arithmetically if we continue discharging the amounts we do today.

The amount of CO_2 in the atmosphere is currently more than 3 trillion tons, and each year another 14 billion tons are added. The current 'human' discharge of CO_2 is actually twice that amount, but half of this is absorbed, mainly by the oceans and the plant world.

The CO_2 graphs of Charles Keeling show a zigzag line upwards, and the zigzag effect is caused by the cycle of plant growth in the northern hemisphere (the hemisphere with by far the largest area of vegetation): the plants grow quickly in spring and absorb much more CO_2, while in the autumn and winter the plants do not absorb much carbon dioxide at all.

The IPCC has produced an estimate of the most important sources of human CO_2 emissions. The greatest share of the emissions worldwide is still produced by industry, namely more than 40%. In rich nations, though, industry is becoming increasingly energy efficient, which means that in some countries emissions have been decreasing by several percent since 1990. On the other hand, an increase in emissions can be seen in countries that are quickly becoming industrialized, such as China and India. In total, the industrial emission of CO_2 is currently increasing by just under 1% per year. The second largest source of CO_2 comes from our buildings: heating, cooling and electricity are responsible for around 31% of emissions, and those are increasing by just under 2% per year, mainly because we are living in ever-larger houses and making use of more and more electrical appliances. The third sector in the list of the largest CO_2 polluters is transport, with a share of 22%. As far as the increase in total emissions is concerned, the transport sector is the most problematic, with a growth of more than 2% per year. This increase is, in the rich countries, due to the increased ownership of larger cars, in particular the sport utility vehicles (SUVs), and the large increase in air traffic. Since

1990, for example, the amount of fuel used for international flights from Great Britain has doubled. In 2005, the CO_2 emissions from this international air traffic was estimated at 9 million tons, half of the emissions in Great Britain produced by buildings. An additional disadvantage of air traffic is that the carbon dioxide is released at greater heights and is therefore more damaging because it is hardly absorbed there at all. Finally, an enormous increase in the number of cars in China and India is expected now that their economic success makes that more and more possible. If we wish to decrease the greenhouses gases, we will certainly have to pay attention to alternatives in the field of transport.

Who are the largest CO_2 polluters in the world? Obviously, the industrialized countries release much more CO_2 than developing countries. The United States headed the list of CO_2 producers for many, many years, but in 2007 China took over the top spot. The US produces 20% of the annual CO_2 emissions, yet it only has 5% of the world population. Every American therefore produces four times as much CO_2 as the average world citizen. In comparison, the British produce 2% of the worldwide

World Megatrends - The Future of a World in Transition

discharge, yet they make up just 1% of the world population. This amounts to half of that produced by the average American, but it is still twice as much as their 'rightful share'.

Causes of the high CO_2 emissions in the US are its focus on economic growth and lack of attention to energy efficiency. Furthermore, the Americans have, over the years, developed habits that guzzle energy simply because they could afford them. A city such as Las Vegas, where the air-cons buzz day and night, the neon signs flash and the water cascades even though the city is located in an inhospitable desert, is a symbol of the wasteful American way of life. For a long time, the US enjoyed a surplus of oil produced domestically, which kept petrol prices low. Americans like big cars and drive large distances each year. The typically American phenomenon of suburbia – living in places that are relatively distant from their places of work – will certainly be a contributory factor in the enormous mobility of the average American.

As mentioned above, China has now stolen America's crown where absolute CO_2 emissions are concerned. In 2000, China was already responsible for 15% of the world's emissions and that percentage in the following years could only rise. The US Energy Information Administration had calculated that China would overtake the United States as largest CO_2 producer by 2025; it actually happened in 2007.

We must, however, point out that these figures are the total emissions of countries and they say little about the rankings by CO_2 emissions per head of population. If we look at the discharge per person per year, then we arrive at the following top five CO_2 producers: (1) Qatar, (2) the United Arab Emirates, (3) Kuwait, (4) Bahrain and (5) Australia.

In the Arabian oil states that head the list, most of the emissions are caused by the oil industry and by air-conditioning. In countries such as the US, Australia, Canada and New Zealand, buildings (heating and cooling) and distances travelled make the greatest contribution, while in Europe, emissions are mainly produced by industry and transport.

Whereas it is the industrial world that is by far the largest CO_2 producer, research shows that it is the poorer countries which suffer most from the greenhouse effect. This is partly a question of geography: most rich countries are in areas with a temperate climate where several degrees of

warming is not disastrous, and in some areas actually welcome. Most developing countries are in tropical, desert or steppe climates that are ecologically much more vulnerable. The most important cause of developing countries suffering more from the greenhouse effect is, however, economic. The poverty in these countries means that much less money is available to combat the negative effects of climate change. Moreover, these countries are often very dependent on farming, the economic sector that is most sensitive to climate change. The notion that we are all in the same boat so that we can make a concerted effort to combat CO_2 emissions does not seem completely correct.

Temporary building

As a result of climate change, different building and living styles will emerge. Temporary buildings will also appear, because history teaches us that climate change such as we are now undergoing is always followed by a period of cooling down. Decades of increasing temperatures are followed by decades of colder temperatures. Some suggest that the Gulf Stream, which regulates the western European climate, will slow and then stop in the future. This will result in the average temperature in parts of Europe dropping considerably. Temporary building, rather than building for posterity, is therefore more sensible. For the moment this means wooden prefabricated buildings, conventional wooden buildings, and buildings of impregnated cardboard. The 'sustainable building' now in fashion is actually out of date, no longer suited to the current conditions, and not as sustainable as the name suggests.

Building for the future will have a new dimension in the twenty-first century. I recently saw the concrete of the future in a cement factory. Concrete floors and walls will have hollow pipes within them, and on the roofs of the buildings constructed from this new type of concrete there are water pumping installations. Water is pumped out of the ground, through the pipes in the house, and provides natural air-conditioning, which is very practical and should be suitable for housing in the near future. In India and Iran, buildings used to make use of water as a means of cooling and it is interesting that this concept is now returning in a new guise.

Houses will also be built in a different orientation, no longer tending to be north–south with glass patio doors on the south, because it will become impractical to keep south-facing rooms cool. Living rooms would turn into saunas, and combining a sauna with a living room is taking things a little too far in the experience economy.

Market for bold ideas grows

Climate change is being felt the world over and if global warming continues at its current pace, the effects could be catastrophic. Some scientists and engineers are proposing radical, large-scale ideas that could save us from disaster. The BBC produced a documentary, *Five Ways to Save the World*, on this topic in 2007.

The first three proposals featured in the film looked at reducing the power of the sun, thereby cooling the planet. Professor Roger Angel from Arizona – the designer of the world's largest telescope – is proposing to put a giant glass sunshade in space. Professor Angel's sunshade will deflect a small percentage of the sun's rays back into space. Dutch professor Paul Crutzen won the Nobel Prize for chemistry when he discovered the causes of the hole in the ozone layer. His plan is to fire hundreds of rockets loaded with tons of sulphur into the stratosphere, creating a vast but very thin sunscreen of sulphur around the earth. Professor John Latham, a British atmospheric physicist, and engineer Stephen Salter have designed a fleet of remote-controlled yachts. These will pump fine particles of sea water into the atmosphere, increasing the thickness of the clouds and reflecting the sun's rays.

The other two men in the programme want to tackle the problem of excess carbon dioxide – the main cause of global warming. The first one, Sydney engineer Professor Ian Jones, proposes that we feed plankton with massive quantities of fertilizer. This will make the plankton grow and absorb CO_2 from the air. New York-based professor Klaus Lackner has designed a carbon dioxide capturing machine and his plan is to locate many of them across the globe. They would suck in carbon dioxide and turn it into a powder, which he suggests could be buried deep under the ocean in disused oil or gas fields.

Most of the scientists are reluctant advocates of these ideas, and all believe we should be cutting down on our use of fossil fuels to heat our homes and drive our cars. But is time running out for planet earth? Although these ideas might have unknown side effects, some scientists believe we may soon have no choice but to put these radical and controversial plans into action.

Conclusion: Living without oxygen
The changing climate already has considerable influence on our daily lives. And this will only increase. Rises in temperature will allow people in parts of Europe that now have a moderate climate to spend more time outdoors. This has consequences for the way they spend their free time, for clothing and also, for example, for security. Other parts of the world will be confronted with more severe consequences as rising sea levels will directly threaten the lives of people who live near the coast. Western countries have a longer history of dealing with climate change and also have the money to act where possible. For the other countries it is a relatively new issue on their political agendas. It is important for the Western countries to share knowledge and money on climate-change mitigation campaigns. Also, patience is required, and an understanding that developing countries need time to adapt. After all, on top of climate change, they also face an increasing population; the pressures of both problems calls for economic growth and this can't happen overnight. Most of the time, the two issues conflict with each other. People are trying to act with greater awareness of environment, climate and nature. An inspiring example is the idea of president Jagdeo of Guyana, who wants to lease the tropical rainforest of his country to a multinational who deals in greenhouse emission rights. It therefore becomes more in the country's interests to save the rainforest instead of cutting it down. Sustainability in business and life will become the norm because living without oxygen is simply not an option.

Megatrend 9

Towards the people's century and new definitions of happiness,
ideals and ethics

Paul is happy. He's just got a new job in Newcastle. However, he has to inform the virtual thirty-first EU state, which takes care of the portable social security for all citizens of the EU, of this career move. For the past three years Paul has been working in France, and the four years before that he spent in Bulgaria. Since 2010, every European citizen has been entitled to portable social security. It does not matter where you live or work anymore; the contributions made by you and your employer for your social security are deposited in the bank account of this virtual social security state. Paul is happy about this. In the old days, working in several countries was a disaster for your social security, but because portable citizenship and part-time living and circular migrations almost bankrupted the old social security systems, a new system was needed. In more ways than this one, it is a people's century.

This morning Paul ordered his new coffee machine. Through the internet he download-ed his personal code, which enables him to use the machine for his twenty-five favourite tastes of coffee. Whenever he runs out of coffee, the machine warns the supermarket, and he gets his renewals in time – he's never without any of his twenty-five flavours. His colleague Jim bought the same coffee machine, yet with a different code, since he is used to five favourite coffee brands. Nowadays the consumer is in the lead; no manufacturer of coffee machines can make one uniform machine anymore, and thus dictate to the consumer how to use it. This is the age of tailor-made everything and the portable-ization of everything. □

Towards the economy of happiness
Abraham Maslow changed psychology for ever in 1943 by elevating its application to a new and far deeper understanding of what it means to be

human. Instead of trying to make sense of the insanity of broken minds, he explored the sanity that made people exemplary. One of the results from Maslow's studies was that there were layers of needs. If basic needs are not met, then there is a tendency to ignore higher needs. Maslow's 'hierarchy of needs' is often portrayed as a five-layer pyramid.

1. Self-actualization needs (fulfil creative potential, spirituality).
2. Esteem needs (self-respect, personal worth, autonomy).
3. Love and belongingness needs (love, friendship, comradeship).
4. Safety needs (security; protection from harm).
5. Physiological needs (food, sleep, stimulation, activity).

In terms of Maslow's hierarchy, the unmet needs of people in most of the richer regions in the world, and certainly those among the affluent elite, are now almost all in the top level: self-actualization. Since, according to the World Wealth Report, more people than ever belong to these groups, it is fair to assume that self-actualization will become more important to larger groups of people in the next few years. This can already be seen. People like Bill Gates are investing a lot of time, money and energy in self-actualization. In European countries, self-actualization is the major issue for most people. How self-actualization will be realized in the next few years will be related to the principles of 'Spiral Dynamics'. The risk of boredom arises when rich people have too little to do or worry about. The present economic crisis might come as a blessing for those in danger of being bored.

Welfare systems

Many countries have some kind of welfare system. This meant that, until the 1990s, many governments, in particular those in Northern Europe, increasingly trans-ferred activities from the private sector to the public sector. The welfare state enjoyed a golden era. Child care, something that was traditionally undertaken by parents,

became a responsibility of the government. The same was true of care of the elderly: grandmother was put into a state-run elderly people's or nursing home and no longer cared for by her family. However, state involvement is now increasingly becoming a thing of the past. Governments are withdrawing from these areas – largely for financial reasons – and the scope of the welfare state is being reduced.

A trend can be discerned that is moving away from governmental involvement and towards collective opinion-forming and the end of the welfare state. Today we see governments returning on the economic stage and investing massively in banks to save the economic system. In the meantime, there is also a noticeable individualization taking place. Young people in particular clearly show that they want to go their own way, no longer allowing themselves to be influenced by the spirit of the times, but instead making their own choices. Young people think it more important to be an individual than to belong to a group. They prefer to maintain family relationships. Young people are a good measure of how individualization is proceeding.

New citizenship

Family will play an increasingly important role, and government will move further into the background (arguably, it will be forced to do this). This will give society a totally different look. A new sort of collectivism will arise, partly fuelled by successive technological developments. Thanks to interactive media, we should collectively stay abreast of what is happening in the world and form our own opinions about this. For society, this means that power is now shared among many different organizations. This is not a pleasant prospect for the social elite. As self-organization becomes more important, the power of the elite will diminish.

This new society is characterized by Harlan Cleveland, the American political scientist and public executive, as the 'nobody-in-charge' society; the internet and the international monetary market are examples of this. With the introduction of each new generation of information technology (and that will happen every two to three years), our society will become less centrally managed. The reason for this is that the products that people buy and exchange will become increasingly more 'virtual'. When a physical product is purchased, there is a change of ownership. If an idea, a vision, an opinion is sold, both the old and new owner possess it. Cleveland says: 'If it's a thing, it's exchanged; if it's information, it's shared.' The transformation that we are currently experiencing is due to the fact that the most important source of assistance, the internet, is shared by billions of people.

Ideal image is no longer realistic

The ideal image of an independent person with a protected private life and unique thoughts, knowledge and opinions is thus no longer realistic. George Orwell saw that as a threat to the individual. Susan Greenfield, an English professor with particular interest in the workings of the mind, says that the human mind is the personification of a person's experiences. She maintains that the more experience a person gains and gives personal meaning to, the higher the status achieved and the more important somebody becomes. She adds that information technology has an unprecedented influence on our experiences, and enables people to shape their minds in the way they see fit. This leads to a collective ego.

Terror caused by the Nazis or by al-Qaeda is the terror not of people who do not know what they are doing, but of people with a strong group mentality and a clear set of values. The cause of the Second World War is often attributed to the fact that, after the First World War, the German people were unable to exist as private individuals. This was cleverly exploited. The communists, too, believe in the supreme power of the collective. In the twentieth century, the private ego defeated the collective ego; in the twenty-first century the reverse will be true.

In his essay 'Globalization: blessing or curse?' Wim Smit, a Dutch publicist, couples this phenomenon with globalization. This is something that initially was only associated with multinationals, such as Coca-Cola and McDonald's, but now also refers to the way we define citizenship. Ultimately, the latter is a consequence of the former. Smit comments: 'People witnessed a government that was constantly retreating, that handed over many tasks and responsibilities to private enterprise, and thus ultimately became employed by private business. The citizens, on the other hand, had elected that government in a democratic manner and now saw their position as citizen transformed into one of consumer and became, through a non-democratic position in corporate life, the producer of the products and services of private enterprise. In addition, the necessary steps were taken to transfer healthcare and pensions to the private sector, which resulted in a further depreciation of the role of government, and the citizens were given greater responsibility for their health and pension provisions.'

Citizens: investors in themselves

Thus citizens become, in the long run, investors in themselves, and the awareness is and was created that citizens are producers and consumers and investors. Citizenship has therefore changed, and we need not be surprised that there are hardly any organizations that are able to represent this new citizenship in an effective way. Citizens are, according to Smit, eagerly searching for a way in which they can mount effective opposition to the private sector and government, since they no longer have any faith in these thanks to pay-rise restrictions and the 'grab everything you can' culture. There is also a growing lack of interest in politics. Who should we vote for? Who can be trusted and who will stand up for the rights of the citizen? Smit believes that citizens will have to join forces to combat the effects of globalization.

If I connect this opinion to the ones mentioned earlier, I can conclude that technology will play an important role in this. Smit quotes the Italian philosopher Gianni Vattimo, who says: 'The new popular culture of the mass media has not led to increased transparency, either in the political or economic sense; it has led largely to greater chaos and disorder. ... It is precisely chaos that offers the best chances for renewal and change.' That citizens collectively can achieve a lot is something that few would dispute. And that this process has been taking place for some time is demonstrated by the impotency of politics, as we shall discuss later: citizens have lost their faith in old politicians. These old politicians are being replaced by 'political pop stars'. The citizen is gradually taking the lead.

Soft power

Thanks to these developments, we see the appearance of the term 'soft power'. Soft power is the power that is exercised by gaining respect for the aims and the means that are used so that voluntary participation replaces force. The term is attributed to the American political analyst Joseph Nye, who defines it as 'the ability of a country to persuade other nations to participate in its aims without applying any force'. Soft power is not limited to nation-states. Many non-governmental organizations (NGOs) are based on this power. It is stimulated by the rapid growth of the internet, resulting in the emergence of political platforms.

People thus use the internet for social aims, and the Web becomes a political platform. The networks that arise have a common cultural identity, religious, political or corporate ethics, or social value. Many are small and will remain so; others grow to large organizations with much economic and political power. These networks will become more important than geographical networks.

The power of the bloggers is interesting in this connection. Increasingly the internet is becoming a part of the regular world, and provides access to information. Opinion formers will be influenced more often than before by bloggers, people who provide commentary on their weblog about national and global events. Because they have no media behind them and often do not even come out of journalism, they can operate freely and independently. The opinion of the bloggers counts and is accessible for everybody, and thus they become a flea on the hide of the existing authoritative media.

The phenomenon of soft power will be strengthened by the way work is organized. The traditional office, now 150 years old, has had its best time. It is expected that very soon one-third of the workforce will work from home. An increasing number of people work as freelancers – as independent entrepreneurs – and will not be dependent for their identity and career on those that a company places in charge of them. The number of managers will decrease by 90% in the coming ten years. This development is partly caused by the fact that many employees are extensions of computer-managed production.

Robots and other machines change the nature of work. Already 35% of telephone contacts with call centres are handled automatically. Many existing jobs will disappear. New work will emerge. Machines have to be installed and programmed, until this 'second order' of jobs is also automated. This will result in a 'black box' economy, in which a considerable amount of work is automated, and in which people will have to adapt if they wish to continue working. The most stable sector is the care industry. After the industrial and information economies, we are now entering the 'care' economy. People are prepared to pay for interpersonal care. Medical care, education and personal service will be the most important job generators.

Back to the shareholder democracy

The old left–right divide in politics will be replaced by a conflict between 'old' and 'new' politics. Those in power who remain distant and infused with corporate thinking will be replaced by icons of the citizens themselves. And this will result in the corporate democracy becoming a shareholder democracy.

Politics as a recording industry

Many European voters no longer recognize themselves in traditional party politics. Citizens recognize problems and expect politicians to provide a solution, since they believe that they are not capable of doing this themselves. Until now they have frequently been disappointed. The German government has for years been unable to solve the unemployment problem. After each election, promises are made, but employment scarcely increases. In Germany, right-wing extremists are noticeably more successful than in other European countries.

Because citizens appear to believe that traditional parties are incapable of addressing important issues, there is in many European countries a healthy market for 'one-issue parties'. These are new political parties that focus on a single issue, have a charismatic leader in charge and profile themselves extensively in the media. Think of the murdered Pim Fortuyn in the Netherlands, Silvio Berlusconi in Italy, and Jorg Haider in Austria. Feelings of alienation result in an increasing demand for new heroes, new gods, idols, and these are created ever more frequently and creatively, but with an increasingly short shelf-life. They are people who have become folk heroes in ways different from those of traditional politicians, and now take the plunge into politics. For example Pim Fortuyn, who at the start of the twenty-first century became something of a political pop star in the Netherlands, used to be a prophet, and later turned to politics. The one-issue politicians of the future will position themselves with a strong personal profile. People who are already well known on television will enter politics, and the personality cult around tomorrow's politicians will be more important than it is at the moment.

If this trend continues, European countries will see more and more coalitions between one or more 'old' parties and one or more 'new' parties. The new political pop stars combine 'left' and 'right' issues, and this is extremely successful. A left–right discussion within traditional parties has become completely meaningless: voters can be better attracted by a combination of right and left issues and by using political pop stars whom, in the elections, can appeal to both 'left' and 'right'. This is already evident in various European countries. The cabinet of Anders Fogh Rasmussen came to power in Denmark in 2001, thanks purely to his anti-immigration plans. His centre-right coalition was so successful that, in the general elections of 2005, the coalition parties gained 95 of the 179 parliamentary seats. The government is stable, forward-thinking and progressive, and the population politics it applies are light years ahead of those of other countries. The regulations that restrict immigration work well and are an example for the whole of Europe. In Italy, Silvio Berlusconi did much the same. It is a trend that can also be seen in Turkey

(Prime Minister Erdogan came from nowhere to win two-thirds of the parliamentary seats), in Venezuela (where the previously unknown capricious President Chavez gained power democratically), and in the United States (where actor Arnold Schwarzenegger became Governor of California, the sixth largest economy in the world).

'The personal in politics' will be the motto of the politics of the future. The private lives of politicians used to be unimportant. Journalists knew that John Kennedy played around but did not write about it; they thought that improper. The private lives of politicians will become more important than ever as part of their appeal to voters. Politicians who go off the tracks and admit their failings will become popular, just like the former US president Bill Clinton, who was threatened with impeachment but held on to his position thanks to his popularity with the people.

Social debate

Social debate about important matters will take on new forms under the new political pop stars. The gulf between politics and the citizen is narrowed. New networks of people and organizations that wish to reach agreement about the opinion they have in mind arise in various places and in different forms. An example of such a new form is 'The twenty-first

Century Town Meeting', developed by AmericaSpeaks, an institution that organizes various debates in the United States. This model became well known during the discussions about the redevelopment of Lower Manhattan after the 9/11 attack on the World Trade Centre. The climax of the debate was held in a conference centre in New York, and 4,500 people participated. During the meeting, the Manhattan Development Corporation and the Port Authority presented six plans for the redevelopment of the area. The meeting ended with a declaration rejecting all six proposals. At the same time, the developer was given accurate indications concerning the demands that the new buildings must meet. This made it possible for the first stone to be laid in July 2004, and thus the rebuilding of the Twin Towers got under way.

Another example took place in Germany. In recent times, attempts have been made to involve the public at large in the debate about biotechnology. The initiative was led by the lotto organization Action Mensch. An extensive website, billboards in the major cities, and presentations by well-known personalities from, among other things, German television, highlighted and provided information about various aspects of biotechnology. But there was a lack of debate about the content and there was no commitment from the government or big business.

An attractive option is to combine public actions as described here with the suggestion made by Jean François Rischard of the World Bank, to create global issues networks (GINs). A network made up of governments, companies, private organizations and action groups, should be formed for every major world problem. These groups lay down standards and norms – for example, for a responsible attitude towards the environment. Those that do not comply with these standards are publicly humiliated in the media. Reaching agreements and ratifying international treaties often costs many years, if not decades, but such networks can operate much more quickly, suggests Rischard. What's more, citizens can identify much more easily with such a network that is concerned with a concrete problem than with a world government or some other abstract bureaucratic institution. It is an idealistic and somewhat haphazard plan, Rischard admits, but the time is ripe for it. 'Deep down, people feel that the way in which the world is developing has enormously positive sides, but also terribly negative ones.'

Knowledge about how to organize such debates is growing. Larry Susskind, professor at the Massachusetts Institute of Technology (MIT) and frequent author, emphasizes that such participatory processes do not necessarily need to result in any unanimity about the outcome. As an authority in the field of 'consensus building', he emphasizes that consensus should be seen as agreement over a proposal that may not offer the best option for everybody, but can be supported by as many people as possible. This allows people from different backgrounds and with different motives to participate in the debate. Collective opinion-forming has a future. Wim Smit also couples this with globalization. 'Thanks to globalization, almost everything is open to borderless debate.'

The end of the welfare state: back to family life
In the twenty-first century, the citizen is in the lead: citizens are taking control of the organization and management of their lives. Because of this, family life will take on a new guise. An important change is the introduction of the 'rush-hour family', also known as the children and their elderly parents. This also includes taking care of childless aunts or elderly uncles whose children have emigrated abroad.

The rush-hour family will become the cornerstone of society. Their life-style and the way they organize their days will be different from those of 'normal' families. What will change? During the week, life will be organized as efficiently as possible. Much use will be made of technology, and all sorts of convenience products will be used, so that the many activities – the rush hour – can be managed. That means, for example, that during the week there will seldom be time to cook elaborate meals. Ready-prepared meals from the supermarket, easily prepared food, or take-aways (which are rapidly proliferating in large cities) will be used a lot.

Take-aways will change. There will be kilo restaurants, a sort of take-away where the food is prepared in large dishes. Customers fill a plastic dish and pay per kilo. Whether they take a kilo of potatoes or a kilo of pasta or rice mixed with sauce, it doesn't make much difference. The kilo price is the same. Such shops already exist in Brazil and New York, but now, thanks to ethnic entrepreneurship in large cities, they are also making their appearance in Europe. They are a godsend for rush-hour families: fast, cheap and healthy. The wok restaurant also satisfies this need.

Another possibility is that food pills will replace meals during the week. Already a lot of people use food supplements; in the near future, they will be able to use meal substitutes during the week. Since the world population will grow during the coming forty-five years, and regular agriculture, livestock farming and the like will not be able – at least without biotechnological assistance – to satisfy the growing demand, a chemically produced food pill will be a good alternative.

In contrast, the weekend will become an oasis of peace and hospitality. Then, elaborate meals will be on the menu, for the rush-hour family and its friends. Slow cooking will be the norm. People will cocoon, garden, spend time in the open air, but also take part in the nightlife of the cities: weekends will become a mini-holiday. In this way, the 'holiday feeling' becomes an integrated part of our daily lives. The strict division between work and holiday will become more vague. Because an increasing number of people from the higher social classes have two houses, which allow them to experience two lifestyles simultaneously in the new experience economy, they will be able to spend their cocoon weekends either in their place in the country, or in their house in the busy city. This will mean that people take holidays less frequently: the energy and impulses that people get from the holiday feeling will be integrated into their daily lives.

A call to ethics

In this new era, when there are not only global possibilities but also threats coming from everywhere, German sociologist Ulrich Beck talks about the 'risk society' and we hear a worldwide call for more ethics.

With increasing globalization, there is a danger that people with evil intentions can relocate to places in the world where laws or their enforcement are lacking. Think, for example, of the dumping of toxic waste, the expired medications in Africa, the child labour in South Asia. The development of new technologies brings new and different ethical issues: for example, stem cell research. If we don't solve these questions, we will wind up with an immoral kind of Wild West – hurting everyone in the end. But which authority can, or wants to, take on such a heavy moral task?

New world values

Values and standards will become more important in the future. Nout Wellink, president of the Dutch Central Bank, asks us to consider the changing values and standards in these times of economic and political power shifts. He points out that: 'In China, the government has a much more prominent position than it does here. The government reaches into the private life of the average Chinese – something we would not accept in the West. To the contrary: we want to reduce the role of government even more. China also has a completely different idea about democracy and the notion of human rights.'

The fact that Wellink is right is confirmed by this quote from *The China Daily*, defending against criticism of their human rights and Olympics: 'We (the Chinese) have implemented the biggest human right there is: we are able to feed 1.3 billion citizens.'

To some extent we must agree. The World Bank estimates that between 1990 and 2004, at least 400 million Chinese have been lifted from poverty. Since Deng Xiaoping's economic reforms began thirty years ago, extreme poverty has all but disappeared, and the average Chinese has reached an acceptable living standard. With that comes a certain level of security and peace – no small thing!

In the past century, the Western world has indulged in the arrogance of thinking that we are ahead of the rest of the world. This would lead us down the path of rationality, freedom, equality, and secular democracy. But with the increasing power of countries like China, we may need to compromise somewhat on our seemingly obvious values and standards. China is a giant – one that in the foreseeable future will most likely own one-third of the world economy – and this giant is not prepared simply to trade in its values and standards for ours. We Westerners will need to ask ourselves to what extent we're willing to adapt to the values and standards of this new giant.

And anything in this respect that goes for China also goes for countries like Russia, and the oil-rich countries in the Middle East. A major acceleration in the transfer of wealth has, in the past five years alone, shifted trillions of petrodollars from oil consumers to producers. This has altered the world balance of power, and Western ideas about civil society, the environment and women's rights may well be replaced by new sets of values.

We also see this in the business world of today. In the sale of luxury car-maker Aston Martin by Ford, Sharia-compliant structures were followed. Kuwaiti Investors had demanded this.

A reevaluation of democracy

Democracy is the political system at the heart of Western culture. But fewer and fewer people in the West are prepared to fight for the values of democracy. And in countries that are new to democracy, there are doubts about the blessings of this political system.

In Russia, many people value stability more than democracy. With today's global competitiveness, many companies are all too willing to kowtow to authoritarian regimes to gain new business. Paying lip service to values such as human rights is considered bothersome and counterproductive.

The Indian Minister of Commerce and Industry – normally proud to be living in 'the world's biggest democracy' – recently groaned that he sometimes wished for the kind of fast, uncomplicated decision-making processes the Chinese have.

In a democracy like the Philippines, rising food prices (dictated by global markets), incompetent governments, and rampant corruption have made a farce of the institutions that allegedly work for the people. On the other hand, great progress has been made using the Chinese model. Its increasingly open economic system and closed political system seem attractive to many Third World countries. Personal happiness is not defined in terms of free elections, a free press, or freedom of assembly; 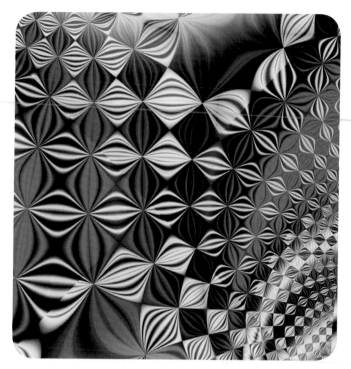 it is defined in terms of opportunities for economic advancement and stability.

According to recent polls taken by social scientists at the World Values Survey, people in Moldova, a poor but democratic country, are among the least happy in the world, while the inhabitants of the People's Republic of China, a one-party state, are among the most optimistic. Maybe we in the West should get used to the idea that not everybody in the world thinks democracy is the best political system. The question for the West in coming years will not be which countries will open up to or adopt our Western model of parliamentary government. There is no question that many things can be done more easily in an authoritarian system. 'Who wouldn't prefer to do business in a country that doesn't have free labour unions? Who would pass up the chance to reconstruct entire cities, without the public getting to have its say?' asks prominent author, Ian Buruma, who advises against preaching purism in matters of democracy.

Conclusion: ME

With rising private wealth, I foresee more public poverty. The internet makes us all free citizens in a 'nobody-in-charge society'. Through the internet, everyone can participate in policy making. This will diminish the power of the elite as they are no longer then ones who 'know it all'. One-issue parties and the personal lives of politicians become more important. Western countries have to share their values increasingly with upcoming countries like China, Brazil, India, Russia and the Middle East region. Western ideas about civil society, the environment and women's rights may well be replaced by new sets of values. Even the idea of democracy as the best form of government will face discussion.

Interior design and architecture of tomorrow

Europe, design and architecture: they have been intertwined for centuries. In several European countries and regions, distinct architectural and interior styles have been created in the past. These architectural styles have become typical for regions, such as the 'vakwerkhause' for Germany, the fortifications of Malta, the white houses of Greece and the wooden architecture of Scandinavia. All of these styles had their own distinctive interior designs and furniture, thriving in their own national or regional environments.

Globalization and migration changed things, naturally. In recent times, German migrants in Brazil built the vakwerkhause in the regions of Rio de Janeiro and Southern Brazil, Dutch migrants in the United States built replicas of Dutch traditional houses and, of course, traditional Spanish and Portuguese architecture and interior design dominates many parts of South America. So, European architecture and European architects were active in globalization, even in colonial times. Sometimes this led to fusion architecture, such as in Indonesia where Dutch architecture mixed with local Indonesian styles and new, interesting mixed forms of architecture developed. All of this was reflected in the interiors.

European interior designs, styles of furniture, lamps, carpets, curtains and other interior items found their way all over the world. The chandelier, for example, was created in Europe but has spread worldwide. In the twenty-first century, Europe will welcome more tourists than ever. They will visit our palaces, castles, mansions (some of them turned into museums, others into hotels) and other distinctive buildings, looking for the charm and romance of old Europe, yet enjoying modern comforts. Design will be one of the pillars of the future Europe. Interior design, traditionally one of Europe's unique selling points, will be an intrinsic part of the design industry of the future.

However, Europe's design industry can only survive and thrive if it is different from design in the rest of the world. Quality of materials should be high, designs should be regionally distinctive, and there should be no room for low-quality products in the European interior of the future. Stylish quality should be our motto. Only then will the Asian and American tourists acknowledge us as 'special'. If Europe wants to become an attractive tourist destination in the future, European designers should realize that more and more tourists from outside the continent want to see the real Europe. We should design accordingly. Yet there is room enough for new architectural styles and redevelopment of old buildings. For instance, in the German city of Leipzig, Die Baumwollspinnerei, an old cotton factory, has been turned into the headquarters of a successful new art movement, the Neue Leipziger Schule. Artists live and work there and its galleries and museums are booming. The old complex has been modernized and has started a vibrant new life. In general, the demolition of old buildings, just because they are too expensive to maintain, should be bound by strict rules. The fronts of old buildings should be kept in good condition, while behind them very modern and spectacular new buildings can be built. No cheap buildings: that happens too often in Europe. Let's change the face of Europe by building beautifully. ☐

The Portuguese interior architect Gonçalo Nuno Pyrrait Marques da Silva works in several European countries. He specializes in the renovation, modernization and upgrading of mansions, palaces and other remarkable antique European buildings.

Megatrend 10

Towards living without oil and the new energy economy

Yao Ming and his family are making a trip to the sea in his new electric car. He loves the car because it does not make any noise while driving and can be recharged in three hours. He bought the car last month and is very proud that he is the first in his neigbour-hood with a car that no longer needs petrol. His neighbours all have a hybrid cars, which still run partly on petrol. Yao Ming found his car on the internet while looking for the latest technology in car making. Chinese car maker Wong Electric Industries promoted the car as the latest in car technology, which outsmarted present hybrid cars. Being sensitive to the latest technology and having a green heart made Yao Ming decide to buy the car. As professor in renewable energy at the Shanghai Green Project University, Yao Ming feels an obligation to set a green example to his students and neighbours. The car was not cheap – in fact it was rather expensive and meant that he and his family had to skip this year's planned summer trip to Europe. They were to have flown with Sunair China, the first airline in China to fly aircraft powered by solar cells alone. His children did not like this but Yao Ming explained that he had to make a choice and this was the most green. He promised they would make several trips to the sea in summer with the new car instead. ☐

Introduction

'The stone age did not come to an end because the stones ran out. It ended because first small and then large groups of people chose to use materials other than stone,' said Sheik Ahmed Yamani, the former Saudi Arabian minister of Oil, in the 1970s. The minister spoke these words as a warning to oil-producing countries that were constantly driving the price of oil upwards. He thought the exorbitant oil prices would stimulate oil users throughout the world to develop alternative sources of energy.

During the last century, the world economy became highly dependent on oil. Oil does not only form the basis of industry, but also of transport and logistics. The world population, which was 2 billion people in 1927, rose to 6.7 billion in 2007 and all these people can be fed, clothed and transported thanks to oil. Large-scale famines, such as those witnessed in the past, have come to an end in large parts of the world, thanks to oil. Food production (indeed, all production processes) have been improved thanks to oil. A blessing, indeed. Or so it would seem.

CO$_2$ emission and political power

There are enormous disadvantages to our thirst for oil, disadvantages that are becoming increasingly evident. The use of fossil fuels such as oil, coal and natural gas leads to larger emissions of greenhouse gases, including CO$_2$. Each year the emission of CO$_2$ in the industrialized world increases and in some regions, in Asia for example, it increases dramatically.

The increased concentration of CO$_2$ in the atmosphere causes global warming and climate changes, which go hand in hand with floods in some areas and droughts and desertification in others. Another factor is that

anti-Western terrorist organizations such as al-Qaeda and anti-Western regimes such as that of President Mahmoud Ahmedinejad in Iran are financed with oil money. And oil makes the Wahabists, until a century ago an insignificant Islamic clan in the Saudi desert, one of the most powerful groups in the world. Russia, too, increasingly uses its energy dominance (oil and gas) for foreign political aims and thus wins influence, particularly in Europe. European countries find themselves in a position of dependency and are faced with three energy problems: one of an *environmental* nature, one of a *security* nature and one of an *economic* nature.

'Oil is ten per cent economy and ninety per cent politics,' wrote Daniel Yergin, director of Cambridge Energy Research Associates. That's right. Oil prices are constantly fluctuating. They rise during political crises, and then drop again. In the times ahead, decisions will have to be taken by both politicians and the business community worldwide about energy management. The question of how to reduce our use of fossil fuels will be constantly raised everywhere – by citizens, by governments and by entrepreneurs.

A moment will come when oil reserves are depleted. But when? And can we, as human beings, really allow ourselves to wait until there is no more oil before changing over to new energy sources? Are we not in a situation in which 'the grass is growing, but the horse is dying'?

OPEC and Peakoil

The media serves us up with both alarming and comforting stories about the dwindling oil reserves. Organizations such as OPEC, the organization of oil-producing countries, and various oil companies would prefer to let sleeping consumers lie, and so they try to reassure us with reports that there are still enough undiscovered oil reserves, or that, thanks to technological innovations, those fields that are inaccessible or unprofitable will be able to be exploited as years pass by. They report that there is sufficient oil for the foreseeable future. The discovery of large new oil fields – for example, under the Gulf of Mexico in 2006 or off the coast of Brazil in 2007 – seems to support this. The higher oil price is also gradually making it commercially worth while to exploit oil-impregnated sand found in countries such as Canada. So, why invest so much time and effort now in new sources of energy?

Then there are the contradictory messages we hear from environmental organizations, such as the influential blogger Peakoil, which state that, in the very near future, a dramatic end will come to the relative balance between supply and demand on the oil market. They point to the emergence of economies such as those of India and China, which will, within a few years, cause a gigantic rise in the demand for oil. Just imagine that in a few years a billion Chinese and an equally large number of Indians all want to drive their own cars. The constant rise in the world's population also causes increasing pressure on the oil market. Peakoil estimates that within ten years, the divergence of supply and demand will have caused a worldwide economic crisis, wars for raw materials and even an end to our civilization.

Who should the consumer believe? Who has got hold of the right end of the stick? As usual, the truth will here again be somewhere in the middle.

The cause of a possible oil shortage should not just be sought 'underground', in the exhaustion of oil wells. Dangers above ground are frequently more threatening. Even if we are able to satisfy the worldwide need for oil in the coming fifty to a hundred years, there are still countless factors that could endanger our energy provision: the political instability in oil-exporting countries such as Nigeria, Venezuela and Iran; the possibility of terrorist attacks on major refineries and pipelines; and the use of oil for geopolitical ends (e.g. Russia and Venezuela pose real threats). On the other hand, the mutual dependency between oil-producing and oil-consuming countries generally prevents any of those involved from succumbing to acts of complete madness.

Mobility
Energy consumption has a direct relationship with our mobility. For instance, more than half of our use of oil is for transport. If we really want to do something to curb our hunger for energy, it would seem obvious to direct our attention to finding alternative sources of energy for our mobility – in particular, our 'automobility'. In the rich countries, considerable experimentation is taking place into sustainable alternatives for petrol, such as mixing it with bio-fuels, using hybrid motors, plug-in hybrids, electric motors and hydrogen technology. More about these technologies can be found in chapter 6.

It is worth noting here that, in the coming twenty-five years, two-thirds of the demand for energy will not be made by rich countries, but by developing countries. At the moment, there are around 800 million cars worldwide. Every day, these cars guzzle 10 million tons of oil products,

more than half of world production. The rapid growth in the emerging economic powers such as Brazil, Russia, India and China (the so-called BRIC countries) will, according to prognoses from the car industry, cause a growth in car sales between 2007 and 2012 – just five years – of 27%. In thirty years, the number of cars in China alone is estimated to reach 190 million. So, even if we in the rich world put serious efforts into alternative sources of energy, the problem of climate change as a result of CO_2 emissions will not be solved that easily.

In addition, a strong growth in air transport is expected. Tourism and leisure travel are increasing and, thanks to globalization, there is also an increase in business travel by air. The relocation of factories to other countries is also responsible for a considerable growth in cargo shipping and this, too, will cause an additional hike in energy consumption and CO_2 emissions in the coming years.

What exactly is oil?

Oil provides around 40% of humankind's energy needs. What better reason to take a closer look at this 'liquid gold'?

Since antiquity, people have made use of the oil that has risen naturally to the surface for various purposes. The ancient Chinese and Egyptians, for instance, used it in oil lamps. In the middle of the nineteenth century, people in the United States began processing oil in such a way that kerosene was discovered, which the Americans used to light their houses, shops and saloons. In addition, natural oil was recommended as a disinfectant, an insect repellent, as hair oil, shoe polish and even as a remedy for kidney stones.

The demand for kerosene increased as the whale oil used previously became more and more scarce. A group of American businessmen then decided to get Edwin Drake to drill for oil in Titusville, Pennsylvania. After a lot of hard work, Drake struck oil in 1859, and from then production of kerosene could take place on a much larger scale. Initially, all the by-products that were released during production, such as petrol, were simply disregarded. However, at the end of the nineteenth century, the 'horseless carriage', which ran on petrol, appeared on the scene. By 1920, around nine million cars were driving around in the US, of which more than half were Model T Fords, and every day a new petrol station appeared. It meant trade.

Oil interests

Slowly but surely, the true importance of oil was realized by entrepreneurs and governments. Around 1930, oil production had started in Texas and in 1933 the Americans started drilling for oil in Saudi Arabia and the British in Persia (what is now Iran).

After the Second World War it soon became clear that the world would be needing a whole lot of oil. Prices rose and the oil-producing countries, particularly those in the Middle East, wanted their share of the profits. This resulted, in 1960, in the formation of the oil cartel OPEC, the Organization of Petroleum Exporting Countries. Since that time, OPEC has become a significant power factor in the world; it is a cartel that can influence the price of oil by increasing or decreasing the supply.

When will oil production peak?

More recently, the vital importance of the energy issue has again been recognized, particularly because of the expected peak in the world production of oil, generally referred to as *peak oil*. The threat of reaching the production peak (followed by a decrease in production), combined with political tension in oil-producing countries meant that the price of a barrel of crude in July 2006 had risen to $77. Since then, in January 2008, the 100 dollars per barrel threshhold was broken and then in summer 2008 came an all-time high of $140. However, this peak didn't last long, and with the onset of the credit crisis the price fell back to $40.

A production decrease does not mean that the oil has suddenly all been used up, but it does mean that the world has passed the peak of production and will be simultaneously confronted with an ever-increasing demand, which means the prices will rise further. Experts do not agree on when this peak will occur worldwide. People in the oil industry and within oil-exporting countries estimate higher worldwide reserves than those people in the environmental movement. It is unclear which of the two sides is right, and that is not really relevant for this book.

For the moment, oil production is still increasing throughout the world. The unexploited oil reserves are divided into three categories, namely, proven, probable and possible reserves, also referred to as P90, P50 and P5. The figures after the P stand for 90%, 50% and 5% chance

of recovering the indicated reserve. The really large oil fields were found decades ago, mainly between 1959 and 1970. The fields that are discovered now are small (50 million barrels) to medium (500 million barrels), which means that they can supply the world with oil for less than a day up to around a week.

The total quantity of recoverable oil is, according to oil corporate BP in 2006, around 1,200 billion barrels, which is equivalent to forty times the current annual consumption. Of the total oil reserves, 62% are in the Middle East, 12% in Europe and Eurasia, 1% in Africa, 9% in Latin America (excluding Mexico), 5% in North America, and 3% in other parts of Asia. Saudi Arabia has the largest reserve, followed by Iran, Iraq, Kuwait and the United Arab Emirates. Countries such as Russia, Venezuela and Nigeria also have considerable reserves of oil.

Because of the rising price and in order to cushion the approaching scarcity in conventional oil, production of unconventional oil will play an increasingly important role. Unconventional oil can be produced, for example, from heavy oil or from oil shale, a sedimentary rock that contains a substantial quantity (10–50%) of fossil organic material (kerogen) and some heavy bitumen, or from tar sand. It is often stated that the advantage of unconventional oil is that it is less polluting than crude oil, but that is not true for the CO_2 emissions. Extracting oil from, for example, tar sand, which already takes place in Canada, requires considerable energy. About 20% of the energy recovered is necessary for the exploitation and separation processes. In Canada, use is currently made of gas, but gas too is becoming increasingly scarce. It is estimated that at least 1 trillion (1,000 billion) barrels of oil can be produced from tar sand, but the recovery remains difficult because the it contains only a very low percentage of kerogen, the actual raw material for oil. The most optimistic estimates for 2020 indicate a production level of 4 million barrels per day from tar sand in Canada and 3 to 5 million from heavy oil in Venezuela (currently, respectively, 1.5 and 0.4 million barrels). However, the latest fall in oil prices is likely to delay this exploitation of this more expensive oil.

The demand for oil

Oil currently caters for around 40% of the energy needs of humankind, gas and coal each around 25% and all other forms of energy collectively around 10%. At present, the demand for oil is rising, and the two most important reasons for this have already been given: on the one hand, the explosive rise in the world population and, on the other, the rapid increase in the welfare level of the BRIC countries. Based on data from the International Energy Agency, one can assume that the demand for oil will continue to increase annually by 2% until 2025 and reach almost 120 million barrels a day. That rise is largely accounted for by countries such as India and China. In comparison, in Western Europe the demand will hardly increase at all through to 2025, while in China the increase threatens to be more than 80%. The demand for other fossil fuels such as coal and natural gas will also rise.

It is clear that energy consumption is not divided equally throughout the world. Energy consumption is coupled to prosperity. The richer people are, the more energy they use. The industrialized countries are therefore the greatest energy guzzlers. That said, the upward trend in oil use in Japan and Europe has actually been reversed in recent years, although consumption in the US and Canada is still increasing and there is an explosive increase in consumption in the BRIC countries. In partic-

ular, though, it is the increase in energy consumption in highly populated countries such as China and India that is causing most concern and
which is leading many people to a growing awareness that we could be
rushing towards a peak oil scenario.

It will, by the way, not only be oil that peaks; other sources of energy
will also be faced with the same phenomenon. Until recently, the peak
for coal was around 2060, but when we consider that many of the coal
reserves in China are of poor quality, we can properly assume that the
peak for coal will take place earlier. The Germany Energy Watch Group,
a group of scientists who decided in 2006 to join forces to research the
actual position of energy reserves, now expects that coal will peak around
2030 and uranium, the fuel for nuclear energy, around 2035.

Energy as power

It is not only the fact that our reserves of fossil fuels on earth are finite
that makes it essential for us to concentrate heavily in the coming years
on alternative sources of energy; there are also plenty of other reasons to
become less dependent on fossil fuels. The countries that import oil and
gas are, because of their dependence on these raw materials, extremely
vulnerable to political pressure from oil-producing countries. We have
already discussed the extent of the power enjoyed by the OPEC cartel,
and individual oil- and gas-producing countries such as Iran, Russia and
Venezuela use their oil wealth for geopolitical ends.

European security services report that Saudi Arabia uses its oil wealth
to finance groups throughout the world who export the Wahabist version
of Islam, not only to countries such as Indonesia, but also to Europe. The
current regimes in Venezuela and Russia also use their reserves of oil
and gas for political ends. In February 2007, Russia and Iran, together
holding more than 40% of the world's gas reserves, announced that they
were considering setting up a cartel of gas-exporting countries. And
Russia punishes countries with which it is in conflict by cutting off their
energy supplies, as has already happened with Georgia and Ukraine. On
a more positive note, the mutual dependence of oil-producing and oil-
consuming countries is too great to lead to truly major conflicts in the
short to medium term.

Looking for energy answers

Let us focus on the possible solutions to our energy problems. There are three groups of stakeholders who will be required to take the initiative in this: namely, governments, the business community and the general public/consumers. The international, national and local governments will define the playing field within which the energy transition must take place; they must provide the aims, the legislative framework and the standards that we will have to satisfy and they will have to enforce adherence to these. Governments should take the lead to break their economies' addiction to oil. The business community will play an important role in meeting the objectives by developing sustainable business as the norm and by investing considerable time and money in new technologies. Finally, the general public, via a change in its energy consumption, will have to implement the changes together with the business community.

When searching for solutions for our oil dependency and the excessive emissions of greenhouse gases, people often think in terms of technology. Of course new technology is important, but it is not the be all and end all; there are other ways of making big improvements. Consultants McKinsey & Co published a report in May 2007 entitled *Curbing Global Energy Demand Growth: The Energy Productivity Opportunity* in which they calculated that with simply efficiency measures we could reduce the projected increase in the demand for energy of 2.2% per year until 2020 to just 1% per year. That is a reduction in demand growth by 64 million barrels of oil per day, one and a half times the daily energy consumption in the US. Such a considerably higher energy efficiency requires decisive action from all the players mentioned above and a considerable change in behaviour. We expect that that will happen.

Contribution by governments

We can already see how governments throughout the world are addressing the theme of climate change on various levels. The reasons why politicians and administrators do this vary. Sometimes it is a sincere attempt to take responsibility for management of the climate, arising from the trend of *nippydom* (new hippydom). Ideals from the hippy era about how to treat nature are expressed in new ways by this generation of politicians. In other cases, the environmental awareness of politicians is only a thin veneer and nothing more than pure opportunism, arising from a cheap desire to score points or a new excuse to raise taxes.

It is a fact, however, that after long periods of reticent government, those same governments are once again demanding a leading position in various fields. Climate change, and the measures that are necessary to learn to live with it, help governments and governmental bodies to create a certain legitimacy about these ambitions. At the start of the twenty-first century, governments and politicians shape their ambitions concerning climate management in various ways.

It seems that there is considerable diversity in the way citizens think about the role they want the government to play in environmental issues. The authoritative research by European Values Studies shows, for example, that when confronted with the proposition 'I am prepared to give part of my income for the environment', the Germans, French and British do not react very enthusiastically, while the Danish and the Dutch state in much larger numbers that they are prepared to make a personal contribution for this. In 1999, only 32% of Germans responded positively to this proposal, together with 46.2% of the French and 48.8% of the

British; on the other hand, 74.6% of the Dutch and 78.8% of the Danes agreed. Another proposition stated 'the government must make efforts to prevent environmental pollution'. To this, 70% of the Germans, 84.1% of the French and 77% of the British responded positively; only 23.3% of the Dutch and 30% of the Danes responded positively. Apparently the Danes and the Dutch see the solution to the environmental problem more as a personal responsibility, while the Germans, English and in particular the French shift the responsibility to the government.

The cause of this remarkable difference should, perhaps, be sought in the religious background of the various nations. The Netherlands and Denmark are the most Protestant nations in the list, and Protestants, in contrast to Catholics, place greater emphasis on personal responsibility and lean less heavily towards hierarchical authority.

The contours of an era of new energy politics are beginning to emerge. In total, six trends regarding government contribution to the energy economy can be spotted, which are dealt with extensively in my book *Leven zonder Olie* ('Living without Oil'). They are:

1. more global and regionally bundled government initiatives;
2. more ambitious and measurable governmental objectives in CO_2 reduction;
3. energy confrontations and energy power politics;
4. end of liberalization in the field of energy;
5. public–private partnerships and unlikely coalitions in the energy market and with regard to CO_2 emissions;
6. more expensive regular energy, more economical use of energy and stimulating alternative forms of energy.

An energy policy is for all times, but in the near and distant future, various classic and new lines in energy policy will converge. How do you keep energy accessible, clean and cheap and how do you organize your dependence on or independence from energy sources? How do you deal with energy as a geopolitical instrument and how do you deal with energy protectionism that rises on the wave of nationalism and regionalism that sweeps across the world and threatens globalization?

These will be tense times for politicians and administrators. However, it will give them a chance, through the issue of energy, to show the general public the importance of good national leadership and the added value offered by politicians and politics. China, for example, is taking firm action to make its energy policy less dependent on oil. By 2010, already 10% of the nation's energy has to come from renewable sources. As with executing the one-child policy in 1979, China will be determined to succeed. This can result in a win–win opportunity, where China's growth comes from saving the planet. (Or, one could argue, saving the planet for a second time after the one-child policy was introduced.) China might understand the need for changing much better than the Western countries that are addicted to oil.

Contribution by corporates

A good entrepreneur has a nose for business. During the coming transition years, a new energy economy will come into being and many entrepreneurs will have a gut feeling that there are chances to be had. The British governmental report on the economic consequences of a climate change, written by the former chief economist of the World Bank, Sir Nicholas Stern, states, for example, that the market for low-carbon technology around 2050 could be worth some €390 billion, and that is only a conservative estimate. At the moment, the energy and transport sector represents 15% of the world economy, amounting to around €32 trillion. When clean, energy-saving technology grows by just under 10% until 2050, we can talk of a market worth €475 billion. And this doesn't take into account environmentally conscious innovations in the manufacturing of consumer products and in many other industries. In America, venture capital investments in the emerging 'clean-tech' sector increased from 2% of the total investment in 1999 to more than 13% in 2006. In Europe, more than €1.7 billion was invested in clean technology between 1 January 2003 and July 2006.

Consumers have become concerned about the environment and look at products and services offered by companies through 'green-coloured spectacles'. Sometimes the critical attitude of consumers is benevolent; at other times it becomes malevolent. But in all cases, companies must, in this time of transparency, in the century of the citizen, take the ever-greener attitude of the consumer into account. In an era in which consumerism must be answered in such a way that the consumer pulls the strings and that companies and brands must, if they wish to survive, follow the consumer, it is logical that corporate life becomes greener. Companies of all shapes and sizes will, in the times ahead, adapt their products and services.

This will happen in several ways. The contribution by corporates follows five trends (again discussed in more detail in *Living Without Oil*):

1. harmonization of green-ness and profitability;
2. making the perception the 'green is cheap' rule;
3. standardizing green labelling;
4. CO_2 neutral financial services;
5. expansion of the voluntary emissions trade.

These five trends together form the megatrend of corporate life turning ever greener. In the years ahead, green will hit all levels in the world of business, from its own efficiencies in the use of energy and mobility policy to products and services that will be positioned as being as green as possible in order to profit from consumers becoming greener. The environment is trade, and one of the world's old laws still holds true: 'money makes the world go around'.

Contribution by citizens

A part of the 'clean' environmental alternatives that will become available in the future can be sought in innovative technology, often stimulated financially by the government, introduced by the business community. However, at the individual level, our own energy management also has a considerable influence on CO_2 reduction and it seems that the general public is also increasingly taking the initiative, a development that reflects the trend of active citizenship. As mentioned earlier, in May 2007, McKinsey published a report in which it stated that of the worldwide growth of 2.2% annually in the demand for energy which is predicted up to 2020, more than half (57%) will be generated by consumers.

This shift towards the consumer sector has a great deal to do with the transition from an industrial economy to a service economy. Much of the gain in energy productivity that can be made in the years ahead is partly in the hands of consumers. This doesn't involve measures that will greatly reduce living comfort, but simply means becoming more environmentally aware at each new purchase. Within this, there is a valid economic law that makes environmentally aware behaviour extra attractive: environmentally friendly products are, in the long run, almost always cheaper than products that harm the environment, certainly now that the government is starting to tax the most polluting products extremely heavily. People don't go greener only for the earth and the next generations; they do so also (and perhaps especially) for the sake of their own wallets.

The contribution by citizens can be seen in eight trends (again described in more detail in *Living Without Oil*):

1. increased valuation of citizenship through environmental measures;
2. more economical housekeeping;
3. polarizing and 'moving to the right' of environmental awareness;
4. ever-greater need for energy information;
5. shift from symbolic to effective environmental measures;
6. the emergence of environmental pressure groups and environmental terrorism;

7. increasing popularity of the environmental theme in advertising agencies;
8. glorious future for green feel-good events and green charities.

These eight trends together form the megatrend of new citizen initiatives in the field of energy. Citizens – or, rather, consumers, will play a key role in the implementation of sustainable energy consumption and in achieving a carbon-neutral world. They have power in numbers and can, with their purchasing behaviour, make or break companies.

It seems that a permanent change of heart had taken place by 2007 in the environmental consciousness of citizens. The greatest concern for climate change is found in the rich countries, but even in emerging economies, such as India and China, people are no longer unaware that prosperity puts a strain on the environment.

Conclusion: New energy

Most developed countries are so addicted to oil that they cannot imagine living without it. Because of this addiction, there is at present still too little support for investing in renewable energy sources. Countries like the United States might be surprised when in the near future they are overtaken by China regarding the succesful use of renewable energy in their economy. When that happens, China will be the saviour of earth while the United States will still be the archetype polluter.

Megatrend 11

Towards bespoke wellness and healthcare

Janice is dozing in her beachchair in Cornwall. She is 54 and leads a busy yet happy life. She is reading a novel while her heart surgery takes place. A minuscule robot has been implanted in her body through her veins, and it's currently walking in and around her heart and repairing the damage that needs attention. An endocardium, a pericardium, the whole cardiac region will be as good as new by the end of the afternoon – without surgery, without any pain. The only thing that bothers her is that while this operation takes place, she is not allowed to use a computer, mobile phone or any other electric equipment, because it may disrupt the mini-robot working on her heart. Hence, she's stuck with old-fashioned magazines and books again: nostalgia meets modernity. She shrugs. Next week she will get a new ear. She had a car accident several weeks ago and since then her left ear has not been functioning well. Repairing it would prove too expensive, the insurance company decided. A new human ear is currently being grown on a mouse in the hospital, tailor made and tailor designed for her. It will be ready next week, and then her old ear will be removed and replaced by the brand new one. After she has recovered, she will get a new kidney, collected from Miss Piggy 77, a sweet pig, who will donate one of her kidneys to Janice. Nowadays pigs' parts fit very well into human bodies, so pigs are used more for medical than culinary reasons. The Party of the Animals in the European Parliament, wants to stop this, but the predominantly Dutch–British party is hardly taken seriously in the continent, so they stick to terrorism. The clinic warned Janice to be discreet about her pig's kidney, in order not to attract too much unwanted attention to the clinic.

Never enough time

In this era, when people never have enough time, where they have to deal with new techniques, worldwide competition and ageing, they place ever-greater value on good health and wellness. The citizen is becoming more vocal and wants more freedom over his or her own body. Healthcare and wellness must therefore be increasingly bespoke. New medical developments and large, integrated relaxation centres offer this possibility.

Wellness

The word 'wellness' is already used in German and other languages. It covers a mixture of welfare, well-being, personal care, relaxation, loss of haste, and is virtually always coupled with water. Wellness centres are virtually always located in spas and other health centres with water, with swimming pools, mud baths, physiotherapy, fitness studios, saunas, solaria, detoxification and other cures. 'Relaxation' is the key thing. Wellness, in its strictest sense, is a way of managing stress. Wellness is one of the main pillars of our lives in the twenty-first century.

Seniors in particular, with a lot of spare time and money, and the need to spend their lives pleasantly with a minimum of stress and a maximum of relaxation, see much in wellness. Spas, thermal baths and other public facilities for wellness have a good future in this market.

People will integrate wellness into their daily lives, in luxury bathrooms with all sorts of extra facilities to help them relax, such as whirlpool baths, bubble baths, massaging shower-heads, mini-sauna and solaria. In addition, they will regularly visit masseurs, physiotherapists (either specialized or general), beauty specialists and tanning studios.

We want to exercise more – something that is essential because we are becoming fatter thanks to our sedentary lifestyle. Children today are heavier than they were in the past, because of the time they spend sitting behind PCs and in front of the television, activities that have replaced running around and playing. More sport and more exercise will therefore become an important factor of the wellness trend, even though plastic surgeons will frequently be consulted for weight reduction. Liposuction, liposculpture, and other forms of fat removal by medical specialists will be used increasingly to take care of excess fat.

At the same time, people will want greater contact with nature. We have lost this because of all the high-tech influences in our lives. They will garden more and visit natural sites. Eco-tourism is in; people will take more walks through forests and along beaches. Nature reserves in the countryside, woods, lakes and beaches will have good times ahead – as long as they are made accessible for the people of the near future.

East European milk and honey

The communist Eastern Bloc was not famous for its refined cuisine. Cabbage soup and dry bread were the staple diet for many East Europeans in the Soviet years. What's more, they had to stand in line for it, too. The cleptocratic dictator of Romania, Nicolae Ceauçescu, gave the international (Western) press photographs of market stalls full of shining peppers and fruit, which were, in reality, plastic lies. That there were few nice things to eat, primarily in the large cities, does not mean that the East Europeans do not have any taste. In fact, countries such as Hungary and Romania will become the new culinary competitors of Italy and France.

The trend has been visible for several years in Western Europe: 'know what you're eating'. The eco-gastronomic Slow Food organization contrasts itself to junk and fast food. The philosophy of Slow Food is that people have the right to enjoy good food and that in doing so that should take into account culture, nature and their own bodies. Anybody wishing to make an impression on his guests will serve the best, unsprayed produce from the area, preferably seasoned with passionate stories. A dinner trip to Hungary or Romania is right at the top of culinary things to do.

The most authentic dishes should be eaten 'from the ground or cattle shed, from tree or fish-hook'. Romanians are hospitable and harvest from a wide variety of surroundings.

It would be extremely difficult to force the most typical snacks and drinks down your throat, but when they are seasoned with memories of scents and nostalgic discussions of the Romanian table, they change into delicacies. In Romania, you can sip away at *Ciorbá de burtá* or *ciorbá de vácuá*, sour soups made from tripe and veal. The dishes, still exclusive for many West Europeans, have strange names such as date bites, trout balls, *plácintá* (pancakes) and *gogoái* (donuts). It goes without saying that, on location, they should be washed down with wines and the widely distilled *palincá* and *rachiu*.

Even before it joined the European Union, Romania was a country that seemed to breathe luxury and passion: the Habsburg palaces and streets, the roaring Danube and a culture of intellect and art largely survived both Nazism and Communism. Chic shops and restaurants give the cities a romantic allure. Traditional cities and areas of luxury and passion lose their value because of the crowds of tourists. Venice, for example, is now more like Disneyland than the floating city of Monteverdi, Guggenheim and Titian.

Leisure time will, in the coming decades, form an increasing part of the European economic base. It may not be such a bad idea to invest speculatively in leisure real estate in countries that still have an abundance of authenticity.

High-tech healthcare

The healthcare of the future is to be characterized as 'high tech, high touch'. The most remarkable general social development at the moment is the incredibly fast growth of computer technology: a spectacular growth in the memory and processing capacity of chips, rapidly diminishing prices, and further miniaturization. Every three years, the memory capacity of chips quadruples and the performance of microprocessors increases by a factor of four to five. It is expected that by 2011, one single chip could contain as much information as more than a thousand volumes of the Encyclopaedia Britannica. The gaming computer that Sega introduced in 1995 contained a chip with more processing power than the Cray supercomputer, which, in 1976, was only accessible to top physicists.

It is not only the capacity aspect of the chip revolution that is amazing; so too is the pricing. Take, for instance, a PC supplied by the shop on the corner. The technology inside such a PC contains about 100 million transistors and myriad minute circuits, yet you can buy it for around €800. And in the coming years, the cost of computing power will drop even further.

Thanks to miniaturization, the chemist will see instruments getting smaller and smaller. Pumps, valves, chromatographs – they all now fit on a single chip that can be used to analyze DNA, air or food. What consequences will these developments have for the medical sector? The computer will not only be used for 'computing' (data processing, calculations, data storage) but also increasingly for communication and coordination. Thanks to speech recognition we will, in ten to fifteen years, have at our disposal computers that understand everything we say and answer us. Such an interface will allow us to operate equipment, send messages, manage entry and recognition, and request information. Within a few years we will have pocket-size equipment that combines the power of the traditional supercomputers with video telephony and wireless modems. Everybody will thus be able to have a 'personal digital assistant' (PDA).

PDA: monitor your health

People will be able to monitor their own health. Their PDAs will allow them to analyze information about their condition at home. A labchip can perform a blood test at home. The anamneses can, if required, be updated interactively every single day, which creates remarkable possibilities for early diagnosis. Preventive measures to avoid further medical complications can be ascertained electronically. Patients can also be referred to a general practitioner or specialist at a much earlier stage. An advantage of all this is that the initial advice is both anonymous and personal. The work of GPs and specialists will change thanks to this 'self-diagnosis'. Patients will be able to request the opinion of their doctor via an electronic consultation. And, if a visit to the GP or specialist is necessary, the doctor will have a large amount of relevant and up-to-date information about the patient before he or she even arrives at the surgery.

Further decentralized diagnosis at the GP's or specialist's premises is also possible. The development of expert systems has greater than ever consequences for professionals in the medical sector. These are systems that use the history of the patient and his or her test results to provide support during the diagnosis and the development of a treatment plan. Thanks to this support, medical specialists and paramedics will be able to concentrate more and more on the communicative aspects of their profession. Their added value will in the long run probably rely less on their medical–technical knowledge and skills, and more on supporting patients in sickness, recovery, and acceptance of a handicap. This means that communication with patients will take a more central place than it does at the moment.

Patient information

Patient information will no longer be spread out among different institutions. There will be no more separate files for the hospital, home care or clinic, but one integrated electronic file which, with the authorization of the patient, can be accessed by various parties. The speed of providing information is also increased thanks to this. If a patient goes home to recover under the care of home care specialists and his or her GP, all relevant information will be available to the home care nurse and GP: prescribed medication, treatment and nursing plan, and appointments for check-ups at the hospital.

Hospitals have considerable planning problems. Fixing waiting times for appointments and the planning of consecutive tests, admission and surgery is enormously complex. The logistics problems in a hospital are – at least superficially – comparable to those of a large manufacturing company. It is all about throughput times, available production capacity, supply of patients, average downtime and so on. In such companies, including highly complex ones in sectors such as the aviation industry, there are planning systems that allow them to do this and the same systems will soon be applied to healthcare institutions.

School and care

The school system will change. Children and young people will attend school or study part-time, as suggested earlier; in the remaining time, they will carry out care responsibilities as a sort of community service. That implies a longer period at school. Primary school will stay as it is now, but once children go to secondary school and on to higher educa-tion, they will have to undertake care tasks in addition to their school work. They will therefore enter the full-time employment market at a later age than now.

At the same time, citizens will invest more in their health and in preven-tion of illness, partly with the use of medical bio and gene technologies and by the introduction of preventive medicines. Since it is no longer the government that makes these investments, but the citizens themselves, this will give rise to a new class system. Part of the population will be excluded, since they will not be able to afford all these novel opportuni-ties. This is the genetic struggle between the haves and the have-nots; the DNA divide. The fight is far from over.

Care tourism

Recuperation from operations and other procedures will take place more frequently at home and in 'care hotels' rather than in expensive hospitals. But care tourism will also come into being: elderly people from northern Europe needing care will allow themselves to be spoiled in in the warmth of southern Europe, where carers speak their language and the costs are cheaper than in clinics back home. What's more, the nursing homes in southern Europe will have accommodation for the patients' families, who can spend quality time with their relatives. In northwest Europe, fami-lies are not (yet) welcome in nursing homes. Care tourism will increase significantly in the coming decades. Having operations performed abroad – for example, having plastic surgery while enjoying a holiday in Thailand – will also be more prevalent in the future. This will drastically change the face of healthcare.

Home carers will have technological aids with which they can report electronically the condition of the patient to headquarters. Freelance home carers will take over part of the work from existing home care institutions, individually or as members of a collective practice. Personal budgets (PBs) will become more common, and relieve the pressure on home care; voluntary aid, whether free or paid, will once again make an appearance. Voluntary work in the care sector will increase.

The LHD plan

Even death will become a personal responsibility. Something like dementia will raise
important medical ethical questions, which
will cause heated public discussion: is euthanasia justified in certain cases? Citizens will
probably come up with their own solutions for
this in practice, such as a personal euthanasia
arrangement. Before they start to suffer from dementia, they will hand
over the management of their estate and other business concerns to an
agency, which will then manage everything for a modest fee, saving them
from having to burden their family and friends. Every citizen will have
his or her own plan for life, health and death: the LHD plan. They will
reach agreement about this with their health insurer and their nearest
and dearest, and everybody should be happy.

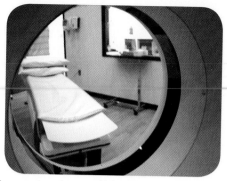

At the moment, invalids already can receive a fully personalised treatment in health resorts, with individual nutrition advice, lifestyle analysis
and an extensive genetic screening. Thanks to the personal treatment, the
guests can, despite all the problems of their limitations, enjoy their lives
to the full.

Research agency Innovaction uses the term 'Personalized Food' as an
indication of our future eating behaviour. To remain in good health, we
will become more active, find a better balance between work and relaxation and eat what is good for us. The stomach will no longer allow itself to
be filled with food from the special offer counter, but with food that feeds
the body and mind.

Conclusion: The future of health

Wellness and healthcare will become increasingly important, and will
also change considerably. The ongoing technological developments will
have an inceasingly influential impact on healthcare and offer solutions to
many health problems. People place high demands on healthcare provision and will get ever-more responsibility over their own lives. Care will
become more made to measure. People will take more responsibility over
decisions about their lives and health, and even their deaths.

Megatrend 12

Towards new power balances, the new boys surplus
and management of anger

Palestinian student Rachid is listening to his father Abderrachid telling a story about the days when he was a young man. He has heard it many times before but he knows his father likes to tell it and he respects him a lot, so he listens with a smile. 'It was 2009, you were just born, and your father fought every day with the Israeli soldiers, my boy. We had only stones to throw at them. It was a hopeless situation. We were frustrated. We saw no improvements in our lives and had no other things to do. But this all changed that same year because our great leader Marwan Barghouti, with the help of president Obama, persuaded the Israelis to help us create new land in the sea next to Gaza. On this artificial land we, the Palestinians, could start our own state. It was clear at that time that such an immense and special project could help the troubled and unstable region find its way back to prosperity and peace for all its peoples. We made the promise to Israel to stop working with Iran and in return Israel helped us to create the new land. For the next ten years we built our country and made it the beautiful place it is now.' Rachid loves his father and the hard work he has done for the state of Palestina. He realizes that without the change of twenty years ago, he and his brother would still be throwing stones at the Israeli soldiers. ☐

Synchronicities

Synchronicity is an explanatory principle, according to its creator, the Swiss psychologist Carl Jung (1875–1961). Synchronicity explains 'meaningful coincidences,' such as a beetle flying into his room while a patient was describing a dream about a scarab. The scarab is an Egyptian symbol of rebirth, he noted. Therefore, the propitious moment of the flying beetle indicated that the transcendental meaning of both the scarab in the dream and the insect in the room was that the patient needed to be liberated from her excessive rationalism. His notion of synchronicity is that there is an acausal principle that links events having a similar meaning by their coincidence in time rather than sequentially. He claimed that there is a synchrony between the mind and the phenomenal world of perception.

Jung coined the word to describe what he called 'temporally coincident occurrences of acausal events.' Jung variously described synchronicity as an 'acausal connecting principle', 'meaningful coincidence' and 'acausal parallelism'. Jung introduced the concept as early as the 1920s but only gave a full statement of it in 1951. It was a principle that Jung felt gave conclusive evidence for his concepts of archetypes and the collective unconscious, in that it was descriptive of a governing dynamic that underlies the whole of human experience and history – social, emotional, psychological, and spiritual. Events that happen which appear at first to be coincidence but are later found to be causally related are termed as 'inco-incident'. Jung believed that many experiences that are coincidences due

to chance in terms of causality suggested the manifestation of parallel events or circumstances in terms of meaning, reflecting this governing dynamic.

At the beginning of the twenty-first century, his theory is more popular than it ever was. Bestselling books such as *The Secret* are rooted in the principle of synchronicity.

Age of Aquarius

One of these days the Age of Aquarius is supposed to start, and the current Age of Pisces is supposed to come to an end. As noted earlier, astrology is more popular than it ever was, and millions of people are currently studying and anticipating the new age. Whether you believe in this or not is not really of any relevance. What is important is that so many people do believe in this, which might make them, in terms of the Synchro-

nicity theory, act in a different way than they used to before. The estimated start date is thought to be sometime around the turn of the millennium, though the exact date is contested among astrologers, astronomers, theologians and others. However, millions of people say that the effects of the Age of Aquarius can already be felt.

I can sense that an era has come to an end. Finance, energy, food, water, overpopulation, climate change – the main issues of today and tomorrow – will need to be addressed in bold new ways, if we as humanity want to make this century the one that really matters: the one in which we can achieve what is necessary, or perish and celebrate this as our last century. As an optimist by nature, I passionately believe that we can tackle all these major issues, and harmonize material and spiritual worlds.

Renewal

As discussed in the first megatrend, the new world order with the twelve pillars of power is definitely in need of new ways of world government, in new ways of creativity. The impotent United Nations urgently needs to be replaced by a true 'World Government'. The transition of power needs to be reflected in international institutions, and the negative aspects of human nature, such as greed, must be managed. If not, we will experience many more crises than the current one in the international financial industry. Although states seem to be more popular now, this is only temporary. In the end, new ways of modern government need to be designed, fitting with people who are smart, who can share know-how and experiences in real life and through the Web. Renewal is not only a matter of economics or politics, it is also a matter of spirituality.

The key phrase for Aquarius is 'I know', but that knowledge is not a righteous, superior or exclusionary knowledge; it's the sort of wisdom that draws people together, for Aquarians are, above all else, social animals. They crave interaction with large groups of people, thriving in humanitarian and social causes and in any situation where collective thought, innovation and cooperation are required. They tend to be eccentric and disdainful of tradition and, while they love magic and believe in the esoteric arts, they prefer to discover knowledge through scientific experimentation and exploration.

Technology is like a hobby for the water bearer. Aquarians stockpile all the new gadgets on the market and are at ease in front of a computer or connected to a cellphone. Sure, they're trendy – they need to be at the forefront, in the midst of the social action, up on the hottest fads – but they also truly love other people and believe strongly in the independent spirit.

Sociable, open-minded, innovative, eschewing tradition, scientifically and technologically driven: if we extract these qualities from the individual and apply them to the world, we can see what the Aquarian Age is all about. We will loosen the ties of tradition and forge ahead in a cooperative effort to improve human relations and also the relations between ourselves and our world. We will be respectful, yet also playfully intelligent and rebellious. We will admire and encourage individuality and embrace differences rather than fear them.

There's no way to know where the Age of Aquarius will lead us all. Who knows what the world will be like in the year 4000? As science proves that we are all one race – that no matter our colour or origin, we are all essentially the same beneath our skin – we will also grow, change and learn to adapt to one another's cultural and individual differences. We have an opportunity to apply the most positive qualities of Aquarius – intellectual openness, humanitarianism and compassion for the environment – to making our world a more considerate, benevolent and accepting place.

Finally solving major political problems

If the new time and age is as predicted by atrologers, this must be the time to finally solve festering political problems in a bold, creative way. If states are eroding and becoming less important, since tribes of individuals form new coalitions and are happy with these societies of their own making, why bother about a state for Tibetans, Kurds, Basques, Palestinians and other tribes who crave their own state, yet don't have it? Maybe we should allow them to experiment with their own states. Later, when they are ready, they can get rid of it, as others are getting rid of conventional state concepts. For example, in the Age of Aquarius, considering the trends mentioned before, what might the scenarios for the troubled Middle East look like? I thought up the following three scenarios, of which the first one is my favourite, the one I think we should pursue passionately.

Before we move on to these scenarios, I'd like to share a story with you. A camel and a scorpion walked along the river Jordan. Both wanted to cross the river. The camel could swim; the scorpion could not. He therefore asked the camel for a ride. The camel refused: 'You are not to be trusted. If I let you climb my back, you'll sting me and kill me.' The scorpion replied: 'Why should I do that? Then we would both drown.' The camel, after a while, decided to believe the scorpion. 'Hop on, we'll cross the river now.' The scorpion hopped on and the camel swam. When they were in the middle of the river the scorpion suddenly stung the camel. As his life ebbed away, the camel asked: 'Why?' The scorpion answered: 'Because we are in the Middle East.'

For a long time, this story typecasted the stalemate in the Middle East. Yet, could this change? Let's explore three likely scenarios if the megatrends described earlier are used.

Aquarius scenario

In this creative scenario, which fits the coming new Age of Aquarius, a solution is found, which aims to create happiness and positive energy in a region currently scarred by wars, hatred and distrust. A major historical lesson is finally learnt and brought into practice: ethnic cleansing works. A large part of southern Israel is merged with the Gaza strip. To the west of this piece of land another large area of land is created, reclaimed from

the sea, financed by Israel and inspired by the Palm Islands constructed in Dubai. The total amount of land thus created amounts to about 20,000 km², roughly the current size of Israel, combined with the occupied territories. Egypt adds part of the Sinai to this. So, a nation of about 30,000 km² is created, larger than the old Palestinian mandate territory ever was, the territory Israelis and Palestinians have so long so bitterly fought over. On this land, using the most modern techniques, and funded by the World Government, an ultramodern Palestinian state is created, with high-tech infrastructure, a solid economy and a positive attitude towards the future. The borders are guarded by peacekeeping troops of the World Government. The country is led by a strong, corruption-free government, probably led by Marwan Barghouti, who could be the Palestinian Nelson Mandela. A one-child policy, inspired by China, is immediately introduced. Palestinians who currently live in Gaza, the West Bank, Jordan, Syria, Lebanon etc. all settle in this newly created land. The redundant boys, who might create a civil war in this new state, are not allowed into the country. They are educated as soldiers and become members of the permanent peacekeeping forces of the World Government. These forces are also deployed to combat drug barons and warlords in several regions of the world, like Colombia and Afghanistan. This way, the example of Bolivia is followed: the redundant Bolivian boys serve in current UN peacekeeping armies, and so can't cause any unrest at home.

To end sexual frustration amongst the boys in the fighting age between fifteen and thirty-five, gay marriage is introduced and sexual liberation both for men and women is introduced. 'Enjoy sex, not war' is the new fashionable mantra. The new Palestinian country is not necessarily a democracy. The members of the small but highly efficient government, modelled on Singapore, are paid well. The country has no army, just like Costa Rica, only a strong police force. In the modern education system there is no place for educating youngsters with hatred and frustrations. Fundamentalists are tried and get the death sentence. At the festivities for the fifth anniversary of this new state, the Al Aqsa Mosque, which was transferred from Jerusalem to the new capital, New Jerusalem, is happily inaugurated.

As with Armenia, created as a homeland for Armenians, and Israel, created as a homeland for Jews, a lot of Palestinians prefer not to live in this newly created homeland for their tribe. However, even if they stay abroad, they keep sending money, which is invested wisely through a state investment fund, modelled on similar funds in the Gulf states and Singapore. After a couple of years both Palestine and Israel and other nations in the Middle East together join forces and create the Middle Eastern Union, modelled on the European Union. It is a Turkish initiative. With their economies thus interdependent, it is no longer in anybody's economic interests to wage war.

The region survives the end of the oil age because the new solar energy plan of Desertec, led by the Jordanian Prince Hassan, has come into effect. Other minorities in the region have gained their own homelands as well – the Kurds, the Christian Arabs and others. After all the migrations, new borders and ethnic cleansing, a whole new map of the Middle East has emerged.

In the region, the group of 80 million redundant boys has come down, since a tsunami took care of this slight problem.

Armageddon scenario

The world becomes independent of oil. This causes much unrest in countries which are dependent on oil revenues, particularly in Iran. Therefore, an endgame strategy is launched. First, the initiators of the new energy economy are murdered, starting with the presidents of the USA and China. Napoleon once said: 'When I saw how many men were willing to die for a medal, I came to realize how much power I could gain.' In the beginning of the twenty-first century we see the same thing happening in the Middle East. So many young men and boys are willing to die for the dream of a 'once-in-a-lifetime-shag with 27 virgins in Heaven'. (Nobody told them you had to read this from right to left: they'll have to 'share one virgin of 72 years old'.) As Gunnar Heinsohn, the great German specialist in genocides, discovered, the current group of 80 million redundant boys in the Middle East can be used by one or more politicians to catapult him or them and a new fascist ideology to power, causing tens of millions of casualties in the process.

In this scenario, one or two of these politicians get their way, maybe Osama bin Laden, maybe the current Iranian president Mahmoud Ahmedinejad, maybe someone else. They mobilize this tribe of 80 million boys. First they take small prizes: the rich Emirates and Kuwait. Then they march towards Russia, Europe and Israel. Europe is overrun, and becomes Eurabia. Many Europeans convert voluntarily to Islam; other Europeans are allowed to keep to their Christian faith, yet are in fact enslaved and have to work for their new masters in the system of Dhimmitude, which existed in previous Islamic empires. Millions are murdered, especially the retired people who are of no use to the new masters.

While Europe is colonized, the war in the Middle East continues. Israel is finally overrun. Only the city-state Tel Aviv is allowed to remain in existence. But Israel does not fold without a 'big bang'. Using nuclear weapons, Masada is reincarnated: tens of millions die. Russia loses part of its country. The invaders form a coalition with the Russian Muslims, who already form the majority of the country in 2034, and they run half of Russia together. The other half stays Christian. This war too costs tens of millions of their lives.

The politicians who started all of this believe that now their Messiah will come back to earth: the Mahdi, as the Shiite Muslims believe. But He does not come. Finally one of the politicians declares himself the Mahdi. The people don't believe him and he is lynched. After years and years, the wardrums stop beating, the streams of blood covering all of the Middle East stop flowing. A new day has begun.

Festering wound scenario
In this scenario, nothing really changes at all in the troubled Middle East. The wounds keep festering; things go on as they've been going on for decades. Frustrations and apathy grow, yet nobody does anything to bring the region forward. Some parts of the region thrive, as the Emirates and Oman. Others are torn apart by civil wars, such as Iraq after the foreign troops have left. The world is not able or willing to find real alternatives for oil and natural gas to quench its unstoppable thirst for energy. The other countries just struggle as they have always done.

Reality check
'Listen now to a further point: no moral thing has a beginning, nor does it end in death and obliteration. There is only a mixing and then a separating of what was mixed, but by mortal men these processes are named *beginnings*.' The Greek philosopher Empedocles wrote these words a long time ago (492–432 BC) in the Age of Pisces. There has always been throughout history a certain tension between East and West. In 500 BC,

when the West (Europe) was not yet Christian and the Middle East was not yet Islamic, there was already tension between the two regions. As time passed, the concept of 'East' changed occasionally for Westerners. During the Cold War (1945–1989), Russia was 'the Evil East' and during that period the West did not really consider the Middle East, which had traditionally been 'the Evil East' as such. But for the majority of history, tension existed between East and West. Can we really change this now? Yes, we can.

Not always tensions between East and West
Such tensions were not always there. There were periods of cooperation and mutual positive influence, periods in which the orient was held in high esteem by the West and during which Western culture, science and societies were considerably influenced by the East. Think of the period between the end of the nineteenth century and the first quarter of the twentieth century: art nouveau and later art deco were strongly inspired by the Middle East, and there have been more of such periods, even in pre-Christian and pre-Islamic times. The Western king Alexander the Great adopted much from the Orient in his time. And in those periods, the East also adopted much from the West. Think, for example, how well the East cherished and preserved the Greek remains, monuments and knowledge (including mathematics) for the world after the decline of the Greek civilization.

I call these the 'mixing periods'. These periods of positive mutual images and mutual influence in history are always interspersed with periods of mutual rejection, which resulted in wars and the demonization of each other. I call these the 'division periods'. Both have their function; both are 'new beginnings' as defined by Empedocles.

Thinking in enemy concepts
In 1959, when the European Union was still in its infancy, Maurice Couve de Murville, the French Foreign Minister during the government of President de Gaulle (1958–1968), said that Europe could only become one if there were a common enemy. And the most probable common enemy of Europe would be, according to the minister, Islam. When he said this,

nobody in Europe was really focused on the Islamic world in the Middle East. The 'Eastern danger' that concerned Europe was Russia. In recent decades, the number of Islamic immigrants into Europe has grown to more than 20 million. So many Muslims had never before lived in Europe in times of peace. At the same time, the number of Christians and Jews in the

Middle East decreased drastically, due to emigration. Founding mosques and owning the Koran was permitted in Europe, while in the Middle East it was still forbidden to build churches and synagogues, and owning and distributing the Bible and the Torah remained problematic. 'First build a cathedral in Saudi Arabia and then we can talk further,' said Margaret Thatcher about this phenomenon during her time as British prime minister. The tensions between Europeans and Islamic immigrants grew particularly in working-class areas in the major Western European cities; it was here that these immigrants settled and here, too, that the streets became more and more Islamic. This induced an alienated feeling among indigenous Europeans, the feeling that they had become guests in their own homelands.

Terrorist acts of Islamists, who hijacked Islam, have not helped to improve the image of Muslims in Europe; nor in India and the Americas. Cartoon riots and conflicts about gay or women's rights in Europe also did not help.

An interesting trend, considering this, is the publication of a series of books in various countries; books which became bestsellers and had Islam as their theme. The Israeli writer Bat Ye'or wrote the book *Eurabia* in which she predicted that Western Europe would become Islamic in the twenty-first century and that the East European countries would leave the EU and form independent Christian principalities. Other bestsellers with an Islamic theme include *The Rage and the Pride* by the late

Oriana Fallacci, which appeared in Italy; *While Europe Slept* by Bruce Bawer, which was published in Norway; *Allah knows better* by the late Theo van Gogh, which appeared in the Netherlands; *Hurrah wir kapitulieren* by Herman Brodyk, which appeared in Germany; and *Islamists and Naivists* by ex-minister Ralk Pittelkow and current minister Karen Jespersen, which was published in Denmark. In America, Mark Steyn wrote *America Alone* in which he argues that Europe will certainly turn to Islam and America will be the only free Western power. What all these bestsellers have in common is that they signal that the Islamic influence in Europe is growing rapidly and that this process might be at the cost of traditional European values and norms, cultural identities and lifestyles. A well-organized minority of around 10% of the European population could, in the theory of these authors, become the masters of Europe and impose its will, religion, and norms and values on all Europe.

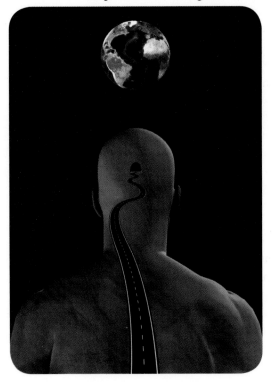

These authors neglect the fact that Islam and Islamic-Fascism are not identical. Various studies show that the large majority of Muslims does not support Islamic-Fascism at all. There are many talented, creative and ambitious people among the liberal Euro-Muslims, such as the French minister Dati.

'Demographic warfare' is addressed by Spengler in the *Asia Times*. According to Spengler, the birth rate in the Middle East will decline rapidly in the coming decades. He says: 'Urbanization, literacy, and openness to the modern world ultimately will suppress the Muslim womb. The sharp fall in the Muslim population growth rate expresses the extreme fragility of traditional society. Translated into the Islamist vocabulary this means that a

Muslim sense of vulnerability and outrage is further exacerbated by the seemingly unstoppable encroachment of American popular culture and modes of consumerism and the transparent hypocrisy of the American rhetoric of universal rights and liberties. It is also stoked by Western ambivalence towards economic disparities in the world.'

Rapid urbanization, to be sure, produced growing pains in every case on record. Britain transported its displaced population to America and then to Australia, including the 'clearing' of entire Scots villages whose inhabitants were forced onto ships bound for Canada. However, Britain's urbanization coincided with rapid economic growth and improving living standards. The Arab world's urbanization has only created a stagnant pool of urban poor. As the London *Economist* summarized in the United Nations Arab Development Report for 2002: One in five Arabs still lives on less than $2 a day. And over the past twenty years, growth in income per head, at an annual rate of 0.5%, was lower than anywhere else in the world except sub-Saharan Africa. At this rate, says the report, it will take the average Arab 140 years to double his income, a target that some regions are set to reach in less than ten years. Stagnant growth, together with a fast-rising population, means vanishing jobs. About 12 million people, or 15% of the labour force, are already unemployed, and on present trends the number could rise to 25 million by 2010. Just as the Muslim population peaks, the one bounty that nature has bestowed upon the Arabs, namely oil, will begin to diminish. According to the US Department of Energy, conventional oil production will peak just before 2050 at the present 2% rate of production growth.

In short, the Muslim world half a century from now can expect the shitty end of the stick from the modern world. It has generated only two great surpluses, namely people and oil. By the middle of the century both of these will have begun to dwindle. But, at the moment, it has 25 million idle young men. No leader can remain in power who does not give them a destination to march to. By no means does that imply that all of these 25 million will become suicide bombers, but a great many of them are likely to emigrate to Europe, including Eastern Europe, where populations are stagnant and about to decline. A Muslim takeover of Western Europe surely is a possible outcome.

Liberal Islam

On 12 June 1755, the faculty of philosophy of the University of Konings-bergen bestowed the title of doctor on Immanuel Kant. On the paper that was presented to Kant on that occasion is written, in Arabic, 'bismallah ar-rahman ar-rahim', which means 'In the name of Allah, the Beneficent, the Merciful'. That a young Prussian university (it was founded in 1544) should mention the first verse of the Koran on its diplomas demonstrates that it wished to be associated with a noble tradition that expressed itself in Arabic. Thus, in a remarkable way, attention was given to a language and a philosophy that was then associated with progressive thought. Islam at the time was inquisitive, tolerant and offered considerable intellectual freedom. Researcher Oussama Cherribi (a lecturer at the Emory University in Atlanta, who calls himself Sam, because the name Oussama is not particularly popular in the United States nowadays) wrote that the sermons given in the mosques of tenth-century Damascus and Baghdad were much more liberal than those preached in the twentieth-century mosques of Berlin, Copenhagen and Paris. Arabic was then the language of science, including in Europe; even Jewish thinkers such as Maimonides wrote in Arabic, and Pope Silvester II learnt Arabic in 999 in order to understand science. Koningsbergen is now called Kaliningrad. It would surprise me if official university documents still included a quote from the Koran.

The Danish Queen Margrethe II, in her authorized biography, calls on Europe to oppose all forms of radical Islam: 'We have in recent years been issued a challenge by Islam, both nationally and internationally. It is a challenge we must take seriously. We have ignored the issue for too long, either because we were too tolerant or too lazy.' According to the Queen, each of us must decide for ourselves whether we are tolerant 'through indolence or conviction'. In her biography, the Queen says she accepts that people abroad will be indignant about her attitude.

Meanwhile in other regions ...

What I've mentioned in the foregoing pages only illustrates how urgently new kinds of leaderhip are needed in order to solve the current crisis in Islam, related to the boys surplus theory. I'm confident that there are enough reasonable people who really want to join forces in order to prevent a catastrophe, as described in the Armageddon scenario.

The Middle East is not the only troubled region on earth. There are many other areas with issues that also need to be addressed in a bold and creative way. Pressing issues include the transition of the energy economy, the future of nature, what to do with the losers in globalization, how to manage anger, and how to manage migration and the unease this creates.

Who are we?

The late Samuel Huntington's book, *Who Are We? The Challenges to America's National Identity*, was published in May 2004. Its subject is the meaning of American national identity and the possible cultural threat posed to it by large-scale Latino immigration, which Huntington warned could 'divide the United States into two peoples, two cultures, and two languages'. Huntington believes that there is a core American identity, shaped by dissenting Anglo-Protestantism. In the past, all immigrants (the first Americans, he points out, were settlers, not immigrants) were willing to subscribe to this identity. But among those arriving today, according to Huntington, are many who refuse to share – and even denounce as criminal – America's cultural identity. He warns that, unless the United States insists that immigrants accept this identity, which is unlikely given the global priorities of business and the multicultural fantasies of liberal elites, 'the United States of America will suffer the fate of Sparta, Rome, and other human communities.'

Immigration poses endless dilemmas, and there is no way of knowing whether the success of past immigrants in adopting the American creed will be replicated by immigrants today. But insisting on creedal rather than cultural assimilation at least gives them a chance, which they certainly need. There is rising opposition to immigration among ordinary Americans and, if Huntington is any indication, among academic observers as well. The cause of creedal assimilation is not well served by a thoughtless and insipid cultural relativism that makes no demands on those who make the United States their home. The one thing required to navigate this difficult terrain is leadership. What does not help is political correctness. The German philosopher Peter Sloterdijk says: 'Of the 12 million immigrants in Middle Europe, only 2 million are economically productive; the rest cost the European tax payers a lot of money because of the benefits and subsidies given to them, and that causes the great resistance to immigration in Europe.' I expect the end of political correctness regarding mass migration.

As said, I expect that the 'digital immigrant' and robotization will slow down and eventually end mass migration. However, I also believe the theory that currently more people are happier in colder countries than in warm countries, as described in megatrend 9. Therefore, in the future, migration to seek freedom and happiness somewhere far from where you originate will go on.

It is not only in the US that opposition towards migration is growing. In South Africa, more and more people tend to resist the mass migration of people from other African countries. In Argentina, there is growing resistance to the mass migration of people from other South American countries. And Indians tend to resist the mass migration of people from Pakistan and Bangladesh. In order to prevent the latter, India is currently even building a wall on the border of Bangladesh, just like the Israeli wall on the border of the West Bank.

Good governance and the future of philanthropy

The new world order won't be free of brutal dictators. History was never fair to all, so why should the future be fair? However, it can be slightly more fair than in the past. Look, for example, at Zimbabwe, once one of Africa's richest countries, now bankrupt thanks to dictator Robert Mugabe. Yet, nobody is kicking him out. Look at Cambodia, ruined in the twentieth century by dictator Pol Pot. For years and years the atrocities went on; everybody knew; nobody kicked him out – until the Vietnamese did, at a hefty price. According to several Cambodian sources, General Chu Huy Man of the Vietnam People's Army, the liberator of Cambodia, still gets all the revenues of the Angkor Wat temple complex, the major tourist destiation and major source of income of the poor country. More than thirty years after the end of the Pol Pot era, nobody has been tried yet. The military junta in Myanmar (former Burma) refused foreign aid for their own population after a tsunami hit the country hard.

Despite all these negative examples, I expect that thanks to the democratization of information, thanks to ordinary people broadcasting what really happens in these places to the world, 'coalitions of the willing' will be formed who will step up pressure to realize classic and new concepts of good government. Regional economic blocs will feel pressured by these coalitions to act more swiftly than they have been doing up till now. But they can only act with military aid. Peacekeeping troops or insurgent troops who remove dictators might therefore have a bright future.

The coalitions will exert pressure on banks or countries with banking systems that function as safe havens for dictators, to freeze their bank accounts. And pressure will build on dictators if they know they might be tried, as happened to Saddam Hussein. Good governance will be rewarded far better in the near future.

We will also see more private citizens taking philanthropic initiatives. Bill Gates, for example, has been doing more for malaria relief in Africa than many professional NGOs specializing in development aid. The foundation created by Sudanese-born British businessman Mo Ibrahim is awarding an annual prize for good governance in Africa. The award is intended to honour exemplary former African rulers and set an example for current leaders to follow. The Mo Ibrahim Award is given to the continent's best governing and most outstanding former leader. The prize, worth $5 million and dispensed over a ten-year period, with an additional $200,000 annual stipend after that, was established by Ibrahim, a British telecommunications magnate, in 2007.

In the near future, more people like Bill Gates and Mo Ibrahim will emerge, taking charge of issues that need to be resolved urgently.

Management of anger

As previously mentioned, not everybody can be a winner in the future. The technological revolution will rob many people of their jobs. Recently, I interviewed some postmen who had been sacked. One of them was sixty-two and had spent all his working life as a postman, delivering letters and cards to people's homes. Now he is out of a job because so many people prefer email. He is angry and says: 'Because of you people and this damned technology I am now out of work.' There are many more like him. How will we deal with the pent up anger of men like this postman? The German philosopher Peter Sloterdijk says that management of anger is one of the major issues of the future. I agree with him and I'd like to add that management of boredom is a major issue as well.

What's to be done, not only with all of these angry people but also those who are simply bored? Sloterdijk expresses his hopes for a 'peaceful utilization of monotheistic energies'. After all, he says: 'The greatest achievement of institutionalized Christianity is, to extend the metaphor, that it has given rise to a highly developed reactor technology. What in naive hearts might easily spark combustive mania can, through ascetic and meditative practice and learnable forms of spiritual inquiry, be contained within a workable format.'

Conclusion: The future is now

The world has always been something of a salad bowl. Thanks to relocations and a continuing flow of migrants, people in more regions than before are now used to the presence of those with other nationalities, religions and ethnicities. It has not always turned out well: several ethnic conflicts have flared up, such as in the Balkans, and in Northern Ireland there are still violent confrontations between Catholics and Protestants.

In the Middle East, the tensions between several tribes are part of life. However, we are entering a new age in history. A new global culture might emerge. Whatever happens, the new world will have winners and losers, just as the old world had.

A mixture of private citizens taking the lead and public institutions will design the new kinds of governace that will be needed in the new world. There is a lot to be positive about, but also a lot to be worried about. Nobody ever got anywhere with pessimism, so the best way to design new ways of good governance and to manage anger is to do so with optimism.

The answer to intimidation is civil courage

At the beginning of 2006, commotion arose concerning a number of satirical cartoons published in the Danish newspaper *Jyllands-Posten*, including several portraying the Prophet Muhammad. Now, there is something remarkable about this Danish Muhammad cartoon crisis. In principle, Muslim law – the Sharia – is only valid in Islamic countries. Two Danish imams confirmed this shortly before the conflict: 'Non-Muslims can do what they wish; I do not get worked up about a non-Muslim drinking, eating pork and having extra-marital sex.'

Ayatollah Khomeini departed from this traditional view when he issued his fatwa against Salman Rushdie, author of several books including *The Satanic Verses*. This writer may have been a Muslim, but he lived in England.

The Islamic ambitions after the cartoon crisis, however, went much further. At a 'dialogue conference' in Copenhagen in March 2006, the Islamic TV-imam from Egypt, Amr Khaled, said: 'Danish school children must learn about Islam in such a way that repetition of such an event is avoided. This is not simply a wish. This is a demand that we make.' He was supported by Tariq al-Suwaidan from Kuwait: 'There should be

Muslims who check what Danish school children learn about the Prophet Muhammad.' This was unprecedented interference in the internal affairs of another country.

The Danish cartoon crisis concerned freedom of expression. This, and everything connected to it, is the subject of *Islamists and Naivists* by the Danish couple Karen Jespersen and Ralf Pittelkow. In a clear and unadorned manner, they describe the cartoon crisis and the motives and means of Islamists in Europe.

The Universal Declaration of Human Rights, which was adopted by the UN in 1948, says in article 19: 'Everyone has the right to freedom of opinion and expression'. But the Universal Islamic Declaration of Human Rights of 1981 states in article 12a that the Sharia determines the degree of that freedom of expression. That is reflected in practice, for the Islamic countries in the Middle East are among the most oppressive in the world as far as freedom of expression is concerned. Nowhere is the Arabian press as free as it is in Israel.

The nineteenth-century philosopher John Stuart Mill forcefully defended freedom of expression in his book *On Liberty*. He also criticized the opinion that that freedom should not 'be used to offend another. If you start by censoring everything that offends or could offend somebody, then you undermine freedom of expression.' Political author Ayaan Hirsi Ali faced much criticism when, at the beginning of 2006 in Berlin, she demanded the right to offend. But freedom of expression includes the right to offend. What is offensive is for a judge to decide. Until he has reached his verdict, expression is free. Didn't Luther once offend the Catholic Church?

Jespersen and Pittelkow correctly make a clear distinction between Islamists and Muslims. Islamists are aiming for a totalitarian dictatorship in which the Sharia applies, ruling people in their most personal lives and thoughts. Their final aim is an Islamic world state, based on a literal version of the Sharia. It is an anti-humanist and anti-democratic ideology that is hostile towards freedom.

In countries where Muslims are in the minority, Islamists aim for a parallel society in which the Sharia rules. Thus, the leading British Muslim Kalim Siddiqui requested a 'non-territorial Muslim state'. For the same reasons, Islamists oppose integration, for that could mean that Muslims disappear 'as salt in water'.

In addition, Islamists want general legislation to leave room for the Sharia. That explains the interference in Denmark. Some in the West accommodate this demand. The government of the province of Ontario in Canada wanted to declare the Sharia applicable to Muslims who desired it. Fortunately, this proposal was rejected, partly because of a protest action by Ayaan Hirsi Ali.

In Germany, a Muslim woman wanted a quick divorce, because her husband beat her. The (female) judge rejected the request, arguing that the Sharia permitted this. Each step towards the Sharia further isolates Muslims wanting reform.

One of the weapons Islamists use is intimidation. Because of this, plays are cancelled, professors and politicians require security guards and writers no longer dare publish under their own name. Sometimes this degenerates into self-censorship.

The subtitle of the Danish book is: *a bill of indictment*. Against whom? Against the 'naivists'. These are the innocents who do not recognize the danger of Islamism that aims at a non-integrated, parallel society and recognition of the Sharia as the basis of justice. The authors have particularly targeted political correctness based on a guilty conscience and a 'cultural self-hate'. They give a number of examples of this.

The most appalling is from the mouth of Mona Sahlin, Swedish minister of Integration, who, in 2002, said in a mosque that many Swedes are jealous of the immigrants, because they have a culture and a history that binds them together. The Swedes only have a mid-summer night 'and other such crazy things'.

Prime minister Erdogan of Turkey, which is a candidate member of the EU, called the Muhammad cartoons 'crimes against humanity'. Undoubtedly encouraged to do so, EU High Commissioner Javier Solana gave the assurance that in Europe people considered the cartoons an 'unfortunate act', which was viewed with 'disapproval and disgust'. During a trip to the Middle East, he repeated: 'Rest assured that we will do our utmost to ensure that nothing like this ever happens again.'

The important book by Jespersen and Pittelkow ends with an epilogue concerning the legal case brought by three Islamic organizations against the French satirical magazine *Charlie Hebdo* that published the cartoons. The magazine was acquitted. The judgement concludes that publication of the drawings is part of a relevant social debate and is thus not an offence. That may be true. But a certain civil courage and perseverance is essential. ☐

Frits Bolkestein is professor of European Studies at the University of Leiden in the Netherlands. From 1999 to 2004 he was EU Commissioner for the Internal Market and Taxation.

part 3

Agenda for the next 5 years:
Prepare yourself for the Megatrends

Much of what is written in this book might seem far-fetched to many people, but the future starts now. Some might think the ideas I have presented are science fiction and that there is little likelihood of many, if any, of the scenarios discussed materializing at all in the near future.

However, there is actually a significant likelihood that many of the issues related to the megatrends I have described will become reality. So, how can you prepare yourself for the megatrends?

If you are a citizen:
- Have only one child, if you decide to have any kids at all. Having none is best; this is a crowded planet.
- Raise your child with a passion for creativity and embrace technology.
- Create your own personal God so you become free of dogmatic religious values and organizations.
- Embrace the knowledge economy and the economy of happiness.
- Be aware of the vulnerability of nature and the earth and behave accordingly.
- Don't donate any money or offer other support to organizations which don't actively promote independence of fossil fuels, a lower birth rate and a more respectful treatment of the environment.
- Be tolerant and educate your children in the values of tolerance and multiculturalism. Yet firmly oppose intolerant people and show your kids how to do so.
- Organize or join groups who lobby against weapons of mass destruction, perverted subsidies and stupid political policies.
- Oppose political correctness at all costs.

If you are a business leader:
- Oppose perverted subsidies in your own industry.
- Aim at becoming sustainable and independent of fossil fuels as soon as possible.
- Contribute to a decreasing world population.
- Invest in ethics and moral standards.
- Invest in future-oriented leadership and creativity.

- Aim at becoming independent from banks.
- Create a coalition of the willing with other companies and with consumers.
- Invest in the diversity of your management: don't forget women, gays and other minorities.

If you are a politician:
- End perverted subsidies.
- Lead your region or country as soon as possible towards independence from fossil fuels.
- Invest in new nuclear energy (pebble stone nuclear plants).
- Design a wise and sustainable population policy; no mass migration.
- Firmly oppose religious fanatics and their dogmas.
- Make your government lean and mean. Use e-government, artificial intelligence etc. to perform better.
- Synchronize the work of several tribes of civil servants.
- Re-colonize lost regions in a coalition with others and be harsh.

If you are a philanthropist:
- Only invest in the first, second and third world. Not in the lost regions; only in re-colonized countries and regions.
- Finance projects related to decreasing population.
- Finance projects that support the establishment of renewable energy.
- Invest in entrepreneurial women throughout the developing world.

If you are a banker:
- Go back to your roots. Finance economic growth, innovation, creativity and entrepreneurship. Stay away from voodoonomics and fancy products which are unethical and which you don't understand.
- Invest micro-loans in poor countries. You will create new markets which can become valuable for you at a later stage.
- Finance projects that work with renewable energy sources.
- Focus on one category in the following list and excel in it: investment banking, retail banking, private banking or asset management.

If you are an entrepreneur:

- An economic crisis is the best time to start your own company, as many wannabe entrepreneurs don't have the courage to make a move.
- Base your company in areas with a boys surplus – a cheap and willing workforce is waiting for you.
- Focus on the fastest growing consumer group in the world, those aged sixty and over.
- Differentiate your marketing between old and new money consumer groups.

reference sources

Part I

Armstrong, Karen, *De strijd om God. Een geschiedenis van het fundamentalisme*, De Bezige Bij, Amsterdam 2005.

Beaud, Michel, *Geschiedenis van het kapitalisme. Van 1500 tot heden*, Spectrum, Utrecht 1994.

Berkhout, Guus and Wim de Ridder, *Vooruitzien is regeren. Leiderschap in innovatie*, Pearson Education, Amsterdam 2008.

Black, Jonathan, *The Secret History of the World*, Quercus, London 2007.

Bodanis, David, *Het elektrisch universum. Een geschiedenis van de elektriciteit*, Ambo/Anthos uitgevers, Amsterdam 2005.

Coolsaet, Rik, *De geschiedenis van de wereld van morgen*, Uitgeverij Van Halewyck, Leuven 2008.

Fernández-Armesto, Felipe, *Hoe de wereld werd ontdekt. Geschiedenis van de ontdekkingstochten*, Spectrum, Utrecht 2007.

Goff, Jacques Le, *De geschiedenis van Europa*, Promotheus, Amsterdam 1997.

Hunt, Lynn, Thomas R. Martin, Barbara H. Rosenwein, R. Po-chia Hsia and Smith, Bonnie G., *The Challenge of the West. Peoples and cultures from the Stone Age to the Global Age*, D.C. Heath and Company, Lexington 1995.

Jones, E. L., *The European Miracle. Environments, economies and geopolitics in the history of Europe and Asia*, Cambridge University Press, Cambridge 1996.

Oudheusden, Jan van, *De wereldgeschiedenis in een notedop*, Prometheus, Amsterdam 2000.

Schobbe, Frans, *Mythen, heldendicht en verhalen uit de geschiedenis. Kleio's gefluister*, Christofoor, Zeist 2004.

Sesam Atlas bij de Wereldgeschiedenis. Deel 1 Van prehistorie tot Franse revolutie, Bosch & Keuning, Baarn 1965.

Sesam Atlas bij de Wereldgeschiedenis. Deel 2 Van Franse revolutie tot heden, Bosch & Keuning, Baarn 1967.

Stam, Anne, *Geschiedenis van prekoloniaal Afrika*, Uitgeverij Voltaire, 's-Hertogenbosch 2002.

Turner, Colin, *De geschiedenis van de moslimwereld*, Deltas, Aartselaar 2002.

Van der Wee, Herman, and Erik Aerts, *De economische ontwikkeling van Europa, 950–1950*, Uitgeverij Acco, Leuven 1997.

Williams, Jessica, *50 facts that should change the world*, Icon Books, Cambridge 2004.

Part II

Armstrong, Karen, *Holy War*, New York City, 2001.

Armstrong, Karen, *The Battle for God*. New York City, 2000.

Bakas, Adjiedj, *Megatrends Nederland*, Schiedam, 2005.

Bakas, Adjiedj & Creemers, Rob, *Leven zonder Olie*, 2007.

Beck, Don, *Spiral Dynamics*, Blackwell, Oxford, 2004.

Bistrup, A., *Margrethe*, Copenhagen, 2005.

Bolkestein, F., *The Limits of Europe*, Tielt, 2004.

Cleveland, H., *Nobody in Charge: Essays on the future of leadership*, 2002.

Creveld, M. van, *The Transformation of War*, Jerusalem, 1991.

Crichton, M., *State of Fear*, HarperCollins, New York City, 2004.

D'Souza, D., *The End of Racism*, New York City, 1995.

Das, R. en R., *Future Flashes*, Baarn, 2004.

Djavann, C., *Bas les voiles* (*Take off the veil*), Paris, 2004.

Fallaci, O., *Anger and Pride*, Rome, 2002.

Ferguson, R., *Colossus*, New York, 2004.

Ferraresi, P. M. et al., *Unequal Welfare States: distributive consequences of population ageing in six European countries*, Rome, 2005.

Friedman, T., *The World is Flat*, New York, 2005.

Fukuyama, F., *The End of History and the Last Man*, Washington, 2003.

Gogh, Th. Van, *Allah weet het beter*, Amsterdam, 2004.

Gray, J., *Al Qaeda and What it Means to be Modern*, London, 2003.

Greenfield, S., *Tomorrow's People: How twenty-first-century technology is changing the way we think and feel*, 2003.

Haass, R. N., *The Opportunity: America's moment to alter history's cause*, Washington, 2005.

Heinsohn, G. *Söhne und Weltmacht. Terror im Aufstieg und Fall der Nationen*, 2003.

Huntington, S., *The Clash of Civilizations and the Remaking of World Order*, Riverside, 1998.

Huntington, S., *Who are We?* Riverside, 2004.

Imber, C., *The Ottoman Empire*, New York, 2002.

Jespersen, K., and R. Pittelkow, *Islamists and Naïvists*, Copenhagen, 2007.

Jordan, M., *Nostradamus and the New Millennium*, London, 1998.

Lachmann, G., *Tödliche Toleranz*, Die Muslime und unsere offene Gesellschaft. Munich, 2005.

Leonard, M., *Why Europe Will Run the Twenty-first Century*, London, 2004.

Lewis, Bernard, *What Went Wrong? The clash between Islam and modernity in the Middle East*, London, 2002.

Lewis, Bernard, *The Crisis of Islam: Holy war and unholy terror*, London, 2003.

Lutz, P. and E. Obersteiner, *Megatrends Osteuropa*, Vienna, 2004.

Manji, I., *The Islam Dilemma*, Toronto, 2004.

Martin, J., *The Meaning of the Twenty-first Century*, 2006.

Meadows, D., *The Limits to Growth*, Club of Rome, 1972.

Mehta, S., *Maximum City*, Mumbai, 2005.

Menzies, G., *1421: The year China discovered the world*. New York, 2004.

Naisbitt, J., *Megatrends 2000*, New York City, 2000.

Napoleoni, L., *Modern Jihad: Tracing the dollars behind the terror networks*, London, 2004.

Nye, Joseph, *The Paradox of American Power: Why the world's only superpower can't do it alone*, 2002.

Pilny, K., *Das Asiatische Jahrhundert: China und Japan auf dem Weg zur neuen Weltmacht*, Frankfurt, 2005.

Rashid, A., *Taliban: Militant Islam, oil, and fundamentalism in Central Asia*, London, 2000.

Rees, M., *Our Final Century*, London, 2003.

Rees, W., Wackernagel, M., *Our ecological footprint*, Gabriola Islands, BC, 1996.

Ridder, W. de, *De strijd om de toekomst*, The Hague, 2003.

Ridder, W. de, *Koers 2020: Een gouden decennium in het verschiet*, The Hague, 2004.

Stasi, B., *Commission de Reflexion sur l'application du principe de laïcité dans la Republique*, Paris, 2004.

Steyn, M., *America Alone*, Washington DC, 2006.

Tenner, E., *Why Things Bite Back: Technology and the revenge of unintended consequences*, New York City, 1996.

United Nations, *Millennium Ecosystem Assessment*, New York City, 2005.

Wheatcroft, A., *Infidels: A history of the conflict between Christendom and Islam*, London, 2005.

Wilson, D. and R. Purushothaman, *Dreaming with BRIC's: The path to 2050*, Goldman Sachs, 2003.

Websites

www.chinanet.be
www.cia.gov
www.ebrd.com
www.economist.com
www.esa.un
www.europa.eu
www.ipcc.ch
www.migrationinformation.org
www.spiraldynamics.info
www.worldbank.org
www.world-tourism.org
www.wto.org

Photos

Trend Office Bakas thanks all photographers who contributed to the book. Special thanks to Avi Goodall for backcover photo and Kuiper-Compagnons Rotterdam The Netherlands for photos on pages 247 and 249.

index

Iran, 68, 211, 280, 288

Islam and Muslims, 40–43, 49–51, 94–95, 110–111, 123, 128, 151, 169, 209, 211, 226, 288, 316–319, 320, 325–327

Israel, 154, 311–314

Italy, 107, 108, 113, 114, 120, 268

Japan, 38–39, 43, 59, 63, 64, 66, 83, 87, 88, 107, 108, 134–135, 218

Judaism and Jews, 42, 46, 62, 95, 128

Jung, Carl, 307–308

Kennedy, John F., 269

Khomeini, Ayatollah, 68, 325

Kissinger, Henry A., 90

Kondratieff Wave Pattern, 97

Kremlin+ economic bloc, 86

Landmark, 219–221

Lawson, Lord Nigel, 242

League of Nations, 66

Lenin, Vladimir Ilyich, 60, 61, 110

letterpress printing, 47

LHD plans, 305

lost regions, 93–95

Lovelock, James, 232

Luther, Martin, 50, 233, 326

Luther scenario, 233–234, 241

luxury apartments, 133

Mao Zedong, 64, 65, 110

Maritime Asia, 86–87

Marx, Karl, 52, 55, 60, 69

Maslow's hierarchy of needs, 261–262

media and terrorism, 150

medical advances, 55, 118, 200–201, 202, 297–305

Mercosur, 85–86

Mexico, 175

Middle Ages scenario, 77

migration patterns, 56, 65, 95, 113, 114, 123, 128–129, 132–133, 135–137, 145–146, 215, 217, 235, 317, 321–322

military force and ambitions, 88–89, 149

mini-faiths, 221, 227

mixed power regions, 92–93

mobile phones, 173

modernist architecture, 146

Mogul Empire, 49, 50

Mongolians, 38, 44, 49

monotheism, 40, 42

moral groups, 97

Mormons, 95

Mossad, 150

Muhammad, 41, 95, 151, 325–326, 327

multinational corporations, 66, 89, 92

Mussolini, Benito, 63

mustard gas, 165

Mutsuhito, Emperor, 59

Myanmar, 323

myths, 34, 52

nano-food, 199

Napoleon Bonaparte, 52, 84, 314

nationalism, 131

nature, 33, 75, 114, 122, 243, 245–246, 299

nazism, 110